# THE SECRET TO EVOLVING
## FROM MANAGER TO LEADER

**ANN TARDY**
*Founder of LifeMoxie*

# Moxie For Managers
## The Secret to Evolving From Manager to Leader
By Ann Tardy

oolboxCreative.com

*The person who is a master*
*in the art of living*
*makes little distinction*
*between their work and their play,*
*their labour and their leisure,*
*their mind and their body,*
*their education and their recreation,*
*their love and their religion.*

*They hardly know which is which.*
*They simply pursue their vision of excellence*
*and grace in whatever they do,*
*Leaving others to decide whether*
*They are working or playing.*

*To them, they are always doing both.*

**Taken from the Zen Buddhist Text**

*"The things we fear most in organizations*
*– fluctuations, disturbances, imbalances –*
*are the primary sources of creativity."*

**Margaret J. Wheatley**

*"The most unrealistic person in the world*
*is the cynic, not the dreamer."*

**Paul Hawken**

*"Life is about not knowing,*
*having to change,*
*taking the moment and making the best of it,*
*without knowing what's going to happen next.*
*Delicious ambiguity."*

**Gilda Radner**

# Dedication

To the leaders who make us all want to follow you into battle.
To the managers who strive daily to become those leaders.
To the people who make leading and managing such a rewarding
experience.

# Contents

# Introduction

Debbie is a real estate agent who works for my mom. She had just undergone heart surgery when my mom visited her at the hospital. As my mom walked into Debbie's hospital room, she noticed the doctor in the room with Debbie. My mom excused herself and said she'd wait outside. But Debbie interjected, exclaiming, "No, No! Come in!" Then she turned to the doctor and said, "This is my manager. She has complete privilege to see whatever is in my medical files. You can tell her everything."

In 1986 my mother promoted herself from stay-at-home mom to real estate agent and eventually to Vice President and Manager of the Fox Valley office of Baird & Warner, the oldest and most respected real estate firm in the Chicagoland area. With my mom at the helm, the 100-agent Fox Valley office has consistently been ranked among the top 10 offices for 12 of the past 13 years, two of which it was ranked No. 1, with annual revenues of approximately $10 million. Twice she has been named Realtor of the Year by the Fox Valley Real Estate Association. In addition, she teaches real estate license preparation classes to escort aspiring realtors into the business while allowing her to recruit the best ones from each class to join her office.

Unquestionably, my mom is a successful manager. But the issue that had me curious was how she created a team of people who go to war for her every day, when other "successful" managers struggle to create such enviable loyalty and enthusiasm. What I discovered is that my mom (1) models the moxie that we'll explore throughout this book, (2) focuses on being an effective leader, not just an important and busy manager, and (3) influences people to be 100 percent responsible for their own successes and failures.

In so doing, she hasn't created Baird & Warner loyalty; she has created Cathie Tardy loyalty – as evidenced by Debbie, the heart surgery patient. That's the impact of moxie.

## How I Discovered the Moxie Factor

I grew up under the influence of my mom, who managed and led our family with the same moxie she uses to manage and lead her office. But I was not convinced the rest of the world operated this way. I had to discover for myself the magic of her approach to managing and leading people.

I chose to look for it in California because of the lure of San Francisco, and ended up discovering it in Silicon Valley. While growing up professionally in this land of entrepreneurs, I discovered the moxie factor as a result of the managers with whom I had the great fortune to work. The Valley is a mecca for the enthusiastic, passionate, determined spirit that is required in a moxie mindset.

From my first job to my last, I have had the privilege of serving with managers who not only led with a moxie mindset but continually fanned it in me. First there was Glen Rossman, managing partner at Coopers & Lybrand, and my first boss following law school. As you'll read in Chapter 12, Glen encouraged my brazen interoffice memos (the standard mode of communication prior to e-mail) chocked with observations and ideas for addressing the neglected morale and borderline apathy that hung in the office air like San Francisco fog. As a result of Glen's moxie leadership, I was urged to think bigger, contribute outside of my job description, and execute.

Following Coopers, I joined the corporate and securities practice at California's oldest law firm, Pillsbury Madison & Sutro, LLP, to assist entrepreneurs secure venture-backed financing to launch or grow their start-up companies. It was the beginning of the dot-com bubble, and there was a frenzy in the air. Within my first month at the firm, I was handed a $30 million deal to manage on my own. "Let us know if you need any help," a partner said. The feeling of ownership they granted me was energizing! On a daily basis, I was reminded that without a doubt I was contributing to the success of both the firm and my entrepreneurial clients.

After Pillsbury, I joined Fenwick & West, LLP, another innovative law firm that takes an interesting approach to its associates, as you will read in Chapter 4. At Fenwick, I became the associate assigned to work with Weave Innovations, an innovative and promising start-up led by another moxie leader, Robert Siegel. Soon thereafter I left Fenwick to join Robert's growing company as Corporate Counsel and again was allowed and even expected to impact the success of the company. When Weave fell victim to the dot-com bust, I joined Riverstone Networks, founded by a take-no-prisoners moxie leader, Piyush Patel. I was granted the opportunity to launch the company's legal department on the eve of the company's public offering. Finally, my last foray in the legal profession gave me an opportunity to lead with my moxie when I launched my own law firm, representing start-ups of all sizes. I danced with growing entrepreneurs for five years before merging my firm with De La Housaye & Associates, another firm led by a moxie mindset, Angela De La Housaye.

For 14 years I was a corporate attorney, reputed to be a dry, boring, stale profession. Yet, being an attorney allowed me to generate amazing career experiences as a result of my moxie role models. Because of the moxie leadership and influencing I received from my mom, Glen, Robert, Piyush, and partners at Pillsbury and Fenwick, I learned to be 100 percent responsible for my experience at work. I learned to own my own successes and failures. I learned that if I loved my job it was because of me and if I no longer loved my job, it was also because of me. I always had a choice to stay or to leave. Each of these leaders modeled a moxie mindset, paving the way for my own to flourish. Then each of them stepped out of the way and allowed me to use my moxie to not only succeed, but to prosper.

## It's All About You

Everything you're about to read – all of the strategies to employ when working with people – must first be applied to you. Before you can encourage a moxie mindset in others, you need to cultivate it in yourself. Your people are not morons (in spite of what you may sometimes think). They know when you show up in body only, when you pontificate but don't walk your talk, and when you espouse behaviors that you don't emulate. Your own disenchantment and estrangement – even in fleeting moments – are transparent. You cannot hide a smoldering fire – there's too much smoke. Your actions will always speak louder than your words. Your disappointment, disillusionment, and disconnection are contagious, infecting everyone you interact with.

You are about to learn a different talk. Be prepared to walk it. Be prepared to apply everything you are about to read first to yourself and then to the people you work with.

In spite of what your parents and various bosses may have told you, it really is *all about you.*

Because it's all about you, you must work first on your own moxie. Like flight attendants instruct at the beginning of each flight, put on your own oxygen mask first before helping others with theirs. You are no help to people if you are gasping for air. Likewise, you can expect a moxie mindset in others only after you've adopted one yourself. Let's call it the *moxygen mask*. It's time to raise your expectations for yourself before raising them for others.

## It's Not About You at All

While it's all about you, it's not about you at all. This is the continental divide that separates the moxie from the mediocre. Most managers forget that it's actually not about them at all. Mediocre managers operate as if people have jobs only to serve managers. Moxie leaders, on the other hand, operate as if their job is to serve other people.

As we will see in the coming chapters, every person on the planet believes the world revolves around them. And the surprising truth you are about to discover is that people actually thrive under this belief. Your secret to becoming a moxie leader is to make it about other people every single day. To be clear, your world does indeed revolve around you, but your success rests in your power to make people feel as if the world revolves around them. Not *your* world, just *their* world. Rest assured – I'll show you how.

If you want to be a moxie manager, your objective must be to make people as successful as possible; not to make yourself, your company, or your shareholders as successful as possible. Just people. When you serve people's success first, your success will be guaranteed and exponential. This is the key to moxie leadership. It is incredibly challenging, but unbelievably fulfilling.

## There's Nothing to Develop

Dr. Jeri Quirk walked into a room brimming with parents anxiously awaiting her arrival to provide them with answers to their sleepless nights. They came to discover how to fix their child's waning self-confidence. She walked to the front of the room where someone had written on the chalkboard the name of her workshop: "Developing Self-Esteem in Children." She carefully erased the word "Developing," turned to face the already-apprehensive parents, and smiled warmly. She said calmly, "I know you all came to hear about how to develop self-esteem in your children, but I'm here to tell you that there is nothing to develop. They already have self-esteem, we just need to get out of the way and let it flourish." For the next two hours we didn't talk about our children's self-esteem; we talked about how adults squash self esteem with strict rules, incomprehensible policies, and seemingly harsh consequences.

This concept applies to moxie. There's nothing to develop. People already have moxie. They already have passion. They already have potential. We just need to get out of the practice of squashing all of that. Similarly, there is already a leader in you. There's nothing to develop. There are just a few layers to uncover. In the chapters ahead we're going to look at your power to influence people which will peel back those layers and uncover your brilliance and theirs.

## What's in Store for Us

Throughout this book, we will look at the concept of moxie and how you too can influence the moxie mindset through your day-to-day interactions with people. We'll explore the behavioral influences that are at work on you and every person you deal with each day. We'll look at strategies for heralding an approach to work that echoes every fabulous manager I – and I would venture to say you – have had the pleasure to work with. And you'll learn how to influence people to be 100 percent responsible for their experience at work. Get ready to discover the art and science behind people successes and failures (including your own) that will catapult you into moxie leader status and leave mediocre managing behind forever.

## Are You Ready to Manage Differently?

If you are somewhere between the CEO and the receptionist, you are in the middle of your organization. You may have even been called a "middle manager" at some point. While that tells me where you are on the ladder and it tells me that you are responsible for someone or something, it doesn't tell me anything about your commitment.

Since you are reading this book, however, that tells me you are committed to not just managing, but to managing people differently. To showing them the way to be great and successful, to helping them to become bigger and bolder than they ever thought possible. Your commitment is to lead people, and to lead them differently. Not just be the boss, or the person in charge.

But to do all of that you need to evolve into someone who doesn't just think outside the box, but *acts* outside the box, someone who creates new boxes (maybe even some triangles and circles), and someone who enables and encourages others to do the same.

So let's start referring to you as a leader in the middle, "a middle leader."

Even if you manage only one other person, you have the opportunity to impact that person, influence their behavior, and change, compel, enthuse, enrapt, and enthrall them. You also have the opportunity to influence the people next to you and the people above you, to change, compel, enthuse, enrapt, and enthrall them all. So yes, technically, you are the manager, but that title sells your potential unacceptably short.

Instead start thinking of yourself as the maverick, the rebel, the iconoclast, the revolutionary, and the exception. Only with that kind of mindset and approach to your role will you have a shot at creating the environment at work that you want and need in order to make a difference in the company and in the world. And frankly, anything short of that is not worth showing up for. There are too many ways to make money in this world to waste your time (and your life) with mediocrity, complacency, and "business as usual."

It's time for "business as *unusual.*" It's time for "*business as extraordinary.*" It's time we all stop selling ourselves and our people unacceptably short.

Here's what you're about to discover:

1. It's all about you ...

2. ... but it's really not about you at all.

3. You are 100 percent responsible for your own successes (and failures)

4. ... and so is everyone else.

5. Understanding what influences people will give you the knowledge you need to be the superhero who helps them own that responsibility

6. ... but, influencing and igniting a moxie mindset in others requires first that you model it for them.

7. A moxie mindset is one in which people are enthusiastic, passionate, determined, perseverant, gutsy, resilient, resourceful, audacious, accountable and 100 percent responsible.

8. A moxie mindset is essential to make the kind of difference that you are starving to make with people, with your organization, in the community, and on the planet.

9. As a leader in the middle, you have the power to strike the match that will start it all.

There are 10 central strategies for igniting the moxie mindset in the people around you and fanning the moxie flames. We will explore each one in depth in the forthcoming chapters.

1. Give Them a Battle Cry – people need to go into battle for a heroic reason

2. Fuel Their Self-Delusion – help people feel like it's all about them

3. Pause for the Applause – recognize and appreciate regularly

4. Lift the Fog – communicate, communicate, communicate

5. Crush the Patterns – use actions to create new thoughts to then create more actions

6. Label Intentionally – eliminate toxicity and tap the power of labels instead

7. Deliberately Spoil Sabotage – foster a failure-free approach and address fear of rejection

8. Advocate for Discovery over Proficiency – make it about learning, not about already knowing

9. Teach the Art of Bouncing – shift the focus from excuses to solutions

10. Make Waves, Not Ripples – change, shake things up, innovate

# Chapter 1

## The Moxie Mindset

. . . . . . . . . . . . . . . . . .

Breast pumps. The partners at the Big Four accounting firm boasted with pride as they described to me their new employee initiative focused on engaging the women at the firm. Breast pumps. Wasn't it brilliant, they beamed. Presenting breast pumps would undoubtedly evidence the company's commitment to the women's success and to their support of life choices. So the partners ceremoniously distributed breast pumps to every woman at the firm, even those who did not have children. They then took it one step further, setting up a lactation room outfitted with a phone, fax, and Internet connection.

Let's set aside for a moment the fact that the entire initiative is insulting to the women at the firm—lactating or not. It remains questionable whether a woman was even in on the decision, so we'll cut the partners some slack for not recognizing the insult. Let's forget that for all of the time, energy, and money expended to implement this attempt at goodwill, it really only pertained to a small segment of the population at this firm. And let's even forgive them for creating a program that would outlive its necessity (women only breast feed on average six months, three of which they are on maternity leave). The question is, when their self-congratulatory pats end, will these partners realize the lunacy in assuming that breast pumps will foster the moxie mindset, the work ownership, the resiliency, enthusiasm, resourcefulness, and innovation this firm needs from its people in order for the business to survive and thrive in turbulent economies?

## The Moxie Mindset

Moxie occurs when three elements are present. Someone (1) uses guts, irreverence, spirit, and determination to succeed in spite of circumstances, (2) applies that attitude and approach to a commitment – a battle cry, (3) and leverages the 10 Influencing Tenets (described below) to influence others to support the success of that battle cry.

Moxie combines attitude, approach, and action. First there is an attitude of eagerness, guts, and determination. Then there is an approach that is perseverant, committed, and innovative. And finally, this attitude and approach in concert with relentless and accountable action. In short, moxie is an enthusiastic, uncompromising movement toward a goal in the face of obstacles, with ruthless integrity. You may have heard a sports announcer say, "That guy has court moxie!" We want people to say about you, "That guy has leader moxie!" or "That woman has leader moxie!"

With a moxie mindset, people operate unabashedly, with grit and guts, audacity and determination, resilience and staying power. It's the zest and the fortitude to be the victor, not the victim, at work and in life. With a moxie mindset, people are cognizant that they are 100 percent responsible for their own successes and their own failures, without question. With moxie, there is no room for entitlement, whining, backstabbing, or sabotage. With moxie, people go to war for their leaders, for their purpose, and for themselves. With moxie, people answer to their commitment, not to their feelings or their fears.

In 2009 while shopping on The Bike Rack's website for her dad's birthday gift, 10-year-old Riley Christiansen discovered a video about Project Mobility. The video reveals the joy that kids with disabilities experience when they ride a bike for the first time in their lives thanks to customized, specially engineered bicycles. (www.thebikerack.com) Riley was so moved by what she witnessed that she resolved to surprise a kid with one of these bikes for Christmas. When she learned that each bike costs about $3,500, she was not deterred. She just picked up a pencil. Through an avid letter-writing campaign, Riley raised $12,000 – enough money to surprise three kids with adaptive bikes on Christmas Eve. That's moxie.

Everyone has it, but not everyone uses it. Mediocre managers are uncomfortable with people who use their moxie, so they attempt to squash it. And when those people allow those mediocre managers to suffocate their moxie, we get an office – and a society – of complacent, mediocre victims.

On the other hand, a manager who operates with a moxie mindset stands out from the crowd by constantly confronting the status quo, challenging others to do the same, and accomplishing extraordinary feats. A manager who operates with a moxie mindset is the kind of leader who people *want* to follow, instead of have to follow. Are people following you because they *have* to, or because they *want* to?

Throughout this book we will explore the strategies that will give you – the manager, the leader in the middle – the tools you need to leverage your own moxie and ignite the same mindset in the people you interact with every day.

## Moxie at Work

The benefits of moxie at work are endless. With a moxie mindset people are responsible for their own experience at work. It is never your fault if they hate their job, but then, it is never your glory either if they love their job. People with this mindset are enthused, resourceful, innovative, and resilient. But it's not something that the company does for them. It's not something that they are entitled to. It's not something that results from a company-sponsored employee engagement program. It's something that they create, they earn, they generate and re-generate, and they sustain. Ultimately, success never happens at work or in life without someone operating with a moxie mindset.

It is easy to spot people who do not operate with a moxie mindset. They complain and blame you, the company, their colleagues, the corporate policies, the bureaucracy, and even the customers for everything bad about their job. One manager regularly quips, "Work would be great if it wasn't for the customers and the co-workers." We also see people operating without a moxie mindset when they derail efforts for policies, when they naysay and self-sabotage, when they justify "business as usual," when they gossip and promote secrets, when they procrastinate with process, meetings, and to-do lists, and when they forget why they were at one time excited about their job.

There is no end to the business books that examine the extraordinary success of companies such as Southwest, Google, and Walmart. But without the *people* who lead these companies with a moxie mindset, these businesses would not know such success. It's the *people* who decide to be extraordinary, outrageous, committed, and unusual that allows these companies to be the same. It's the *people* who decide to question the status quo in favor of doing it differently that create companies that do it differently.

## Influencing the Moxie Mindset

You have the power to fuel, fan, or fight the moxie mindset in others. Everyday, you have an opportunity to either support their "business as *unusual*" approach or to challenge it. You are not responsible for their moxie, but you have the power to influence it.

The moxie mindset is grounded in the concept of intrinsic motivation. Without motivation, our moxie dies, but a moxie mindset is more than just being motivated to show up and do a job. A moxie mindset takes motivation to a whole new level. It's being uncompromising in our commitments and our integrity. It's being relentless and adamant, enthusiastic and accountable, resourceful and clever, courageous and determined.

Thus, it is critical that as managers who want to lead you first understand the concept of what influences people's intrinsic motivation so you never have to believe in or rely on extrinsic motivation to get people to do their jobs.

Just like we cannot motivate people, we cannot make them act with moxie. But we can *influence* someone's intrinsic motivation, and similarly we can *influence* them to use their moxie and operate with a moxie mindset.

The moxie mindset is critical to your success as a leader. Without it you are just a manager babysitting people to ensure they do their job. We have all worked for people like that. They have a title that signifies that they are the boss, but they are clueless about leading people. When you use your moxie mindset to ignite this mindset in others, you become a leader of people.

As a leader in the middle of your organization, you are in a unique and powerful position. You have an untapped ability to influence behavior and effect change in others above you, below you, and next to you. While everyone is responsible for their own experience at work – successes and failures – you can influence the mindset that is responsible for owning this responsibility. The moxie mindset is like a flame – it needs oxygen to continue burning or it will die. You can suffocate the flame or you can fan it. The choice is up to you.

You cannot motivate people. People must motivate themselves. External factors only influence people's intrinsic motivation. As middle leaders, however, your job is to influence that intrinsic motivation. Why? Because if you don't, someone or something else will. Your people are already being influenced everyday. You cannot afford *not* to use your power to influence.

## The Influencing Tenets

There are 10 Influencing Tenets that are at the foundation of your power to influence the motivation and behavior in others. These influences are working on people every day. And, believe it or not, these influences are simultaneously working on *you*.

1. We all think the world revolves around us.

2. We each desperately need meaning in our lives and our work.

3. We each are dying to make a difference.

4. We all just want to be winners, not losers.

5. We each crave control.

6. We each urgently want to feel as though we are important.

7. We each have an insatiable appetite to be respected, appreciated, valued, and heard.

8. We all are at risk of succumbing to the herd.

9. We each allow our beliefs and thoughts to dictate our ambitions and perseverance.

10. We each dreadfully fear rejection.

When Richard was recently promoted to manage a new team, he navigated the situation vigilantly, intentionally leveraging these influencing principles. Richard's new position was one for which many people at the company had interviewed, including four guys on Richard's new team. Richard knew he would invariably face some resistance from each of them.

Understandably Richard's four guys would be reluctant to embrace Richard as their new boss. They just got turned down for the job he got. This creates cognitive dissonance. If they support the selection of Richard as the boss, it would mean they agree with being rejected for the job. And the only thing worse than being rejected is agreeing with the person who rejected you! If they didn't reject Richard, they would be rejecting themselves.

Immediately after taking on his new role, Richard met with these men individually to address the obvious. He said to each of them, "I know you interviewed for my job. The reason you were not chosen has nothing to do with your skills and everything to do with your lack of exposure to senior management. So here's what I'm committed to doing this year as your new boss. I want to help you get that exposure so that senior management gets to know you. I want you to be in a position to take my job when I move on."

Stunned, they were forced to suspend the story they had made up about Richard. Instead they accepted his observations, thanked him, and agreed to be mentored by Richard to gain that exposure and prepare themselves for a future leadership opportunity at the company.

In the process, Richard made the world revolve around these four individuals. He taught them what it means to bounce from a perceived failure. He gave them a goal to work on, and committed to working on it with them. He made them feel important, while helping them create meaning in their work. In one conversation he gave them permission to drop the notion that they lost. Instead he showed them that they have the power to win next time. He expressed his appreciation and respect for them, not allowing their beliefs to dictate their ambitions and perseverance. In doing so, he saved them from succumbing to the herd while at the same time mitigating their fear of rejection.

That's what moxie in leadership looks like. That's what we're going to explore throughout this book.

## But the Fear of Rejection Lingers

People fear rejection more than they fear anything else in the entire world. That single fear dictates their actions and inactions. If people argue otherwise, they are just doing the rejecting to prevent getting rejected. Tough and gruff people are known to say,

"I don't care what they think." In other words, I've already rejected them so they don't have any power to reject me. But at the root, we all fear being rejected.

In a survey of 3,000 people, 41 percent ranked "speaking before a group" as their number one greatest fear, whereas death was ranked number five. People fear public speaking more than dying. It makes sense. When people speak in public, they risk getting rejected by others, but when they die, there is no risk of getting rejected. In fact, they perceive that the community will love and appreciate them even more dead than they do now, predicated by the outpouring of emotion we all witness at funerals.

## ...And Mediocrity Harbors

As you will discover throughout this book, people are hardwired to hold themselves back. They welcome the status quo because it feels familiar. It's comfortable. They know what to expect. And they know what we expect of them. In the status quo, the fear of rejection is greatly mitigated. People know how to win with the status quo. Becoming creatures of habit, they soon crave predictable, safe routines.

Mediocrity is born.

When we work for managers who sing the "that's just how things are done" song, complacency sets in and that *mediocrity grows.*

And when we work for managers who refuse to make a decision without 17 committee meetings and 28 reports to back up a decision and then tolerate rabbit holes and nonsense in the process of getting to that decision, *complacency sets in and mediocrity grows.*

And when we work for managers who squash passion, forget about purpose, and denounce enthusiasm, *complacency sets in and mediocrity grows.*

And when we work for managers who make sure we know that it's not all about us, *complacency sets in and mediocrity grows.*

And when we work for managers who go out of their way to point out our weaknesses and flaws, who berate, belittle, disparage, criticize, deprecate, condemn, accuse, and scold us as if we were children, *complacency sets in and mediocrity grows.*

And when we work for managers who fail to communicate their expectations, recognize our efforts, or appreciate our contributions, *complacency sets in and mediocrity grows.*

And when we work for managers who deplore failure, but refuse to educate, train, or develop us, *complacency sets in and mediocrity grows.*

And when we then *become* those managers, *mediocrity flourishes.*

### Why the Moxie Mindset Matters to You

You can advocate for others and influence their moxie mindset by using the Influencing Tenets in four ways: (1) Understand how people operate – what influences their behaviors, (2) Understand what causes them to self-sabotage (or worse yet, flat line), (3) Understand how pivotal your own moxie mindset is to theirs, and (4) Influence the people around you to use their moxie to be bigger, bolder, and smarter. Only when we understand how to influence the intrinsic motivation in others, can we affect real change. And only when we can affect real change can we make a difference. Transformations, reorganizations, culture change. All of these are impossible without individuals changing their behavior.

So while it starts out to be all about you, soon you discover that it's really not about you at all, and then you learn that it really is all about you in the end. Your world never stops revolving around you. You are the hero of your own story.

People will run to – not be freed from – corporate America when we as middle leaders learn to instigate, influence, incite, and ignite the mindset required for a new approach to work. Are you ready to become the middle leader who "gets it"?

When there are plenty of places to work and new companies starting every hour, when capitalism allows and the law supports people leaving one company to work for a competitor across the street, when there is a plethora of opportunities to quit and become an entrepreneur, people refuse to stay very long in jobs that don't acknowledge these influences and leverage them positively. And if they do stay as a result of a wary economy, rest assured that you may have them in body, but you've lost them in mind, spirit, and soul.

Magic will happen when you operate with moxie – when you use guts, courage, determination, and resilience to succeed *no matter what*, when you prioritize people's success, when you influence people to succeed *no matter what*, and when you influence them to own their successes and their failures. It won't take long before your moxie approach raises the bar for all others who follow you, lead you, and walk beside you.

# Chapter 2

## Batteries Not Included

· · · · · · · · · · · · · · · · · ·

In 1989, Rob was the new kid at NYNEX, the phone company
that eventually became Verizon. Because he had to pay his dues,
the team handed him the accounts that no one else wanted – law
firms. Rob soon discovered that selling traditional phone lines to
law firms was fruitless – they already had phone lines. They didn't
want to buy more phone lines. Rob needed a fresh approach. So he
studied everything that NYNEX had to sell – from phone lines to
conference call boxes to cell phones – and then he thought about
the type of people who worked at law firms.

At the time, cell phones were starting to gain some notoriety.
Motorola had just released their sleek and sexy "flip phone," but
at $500 each, they were expensive. What kind of person would
purchase a $500 cell phone just to be reachable at any moment
while looking like Tom Cruise from *Mission Impossible*? Who had
that kind of ego?

Lawyers.

Rob seized the opportunity. Everyone else thought the law
firm accounts were "dogs with fleas." Rob saw them as a potential
gold mine. He started with the most prestigious law firm on Wall
Street in New York City. But none of the partners had a reason
to meet with him – in their minds they didn't need phone lines
or any other NYNEX product or service, so Rob needed to create
a reason – envy of the new cell phone. He began by setting an
appointment with a junior associate to demonstrate the features

of the new flip phone. Rob knew the garden-fresh lawyer would be hungry to prove to his friends and family that he had made it. A sleek and sexy $500 cell phone would do the trick.

While Rob and the junior associate were walking down the hall from the receptionist to the associate's office, Rob pulled out the shiny new phone and put it in the associate's hands, explaining its lustrous features. Rob would get the associate so engrossed that they would stop walking in the middle of the hallway. A few partners would pass by, and with their curiosity piqued, they would ask Rob to swing by their office before leaving.

Back at NYNEX, Rob's colleagues scoffed at his first sale. Did this new punk really think he was going to reach his sales objective by selling one cell phone to an obnoxious New York attorney? Rob ignored them. He continued making appointments with junior attorneys, holding court in the hallways, selling phones to boost their egos, and making his way into partner offices. Soon Rob found himself in the partners' offices of all the major law firms introducing them to *their* new cell phones and conveniently upgrading the phone systems for their entire firm.

In that one year alone, Rob sold $3.2 million, surpassing his sales goal by 120 percent. Rob didn't know he wasn't supposed to be successful. He just knew that if he didn't sell something to these accounts, he would be out of a job – his first job.

What did Rob do that other people didn't? He was relentless. He was clever and resourceful, determined and persevering. He was uncompromising in his commitment. He took action in the face of his circumstances. He leveraged the principles of influence strategically. He used sales moxie.

What do most people in Rob's situation do? They complain that their boss just gave them the short end of the stick. They grouse about their colleagues being losers. They grumble about their clients being jerks. Then they do what everyone would do in this situation – they unnecessarily cold call a partner, asking him to buy a new phone line that he doesn't need. They do the bare minimum to get by. Sometimes they reach their sales goals; more often they don't, and when they don't they have a myriad of excuses. Their lackluster approach produces lackluster results.

## Motivation

How did Rob's manager at NYNEX get Rob's moxie and not just another warm body collecting a paycheck and flinging excuses? Was Rob just more motivated than the others? If so, was Rob's manager just lucky or did his manager do anything to boost that motivation? Let's look.

Motivation can be intrinsic or extrinsic. Extrinsic motivation comes from something outside of us that compels us to take action. When that external motivator disappears, we no longer take action. My favorite T-shirt reads, "The beatings will continue until morale improves." The irony just highlights the lunacy of relying on extrinsic motivation.

Intrinsic motivation, on the other hand, is inherent and natural, not dependent on external factors to exist. The drive to take action exists internally. However, our intrinsic motivation is regularly *influenced* by external factors that attempt to encourage or disrupt that drive to act. To fully understand how we can extrinsically influence the intrinsic motivation in others, we need to explore the factors that influence motivation.

## The Hawthorne Effect

In 1924, Harvard Business School Professor Elton Mayo began his observations of workers at the Western Electric Hawthorne Works factory in Cicero, Illinois (a suburb of Chicago). Over the subsequent eight years, he conducted tests to ascertain what factors influenced people to work harder. He selected a group of workers, put them in a special room and continued to change the working conditions while observing the results. For example, he changed the lighting, the temperature, and the number of breaks, to see if any of the changes improved their productivity. They all did, but not for the reasons he originally predicted.

Professor Mayo discovered that individuals altered their behavior when they knew they were being observed. They worked harder when they knew someone was watching, and this thereby increased their productivity. Hawthorne Factory workers were motivated when they were singled out and involved in the experiments. They felt important. Mayo concluded that just by being selected for a part of the experiment, individuals were motivated to work harder. What made the difference? The psychological need we each have to believe that others care about us, and that others are open, concerned, and willing to listen to us. This has come to be known as the "Hawthorne Effect."

## Factors that Influence Motivation

To improve the performance of workers everywhere, Mayo advocated for a more "caring" organization. Mayo identified through his experiments six ageless factors that influence intrinsic motivation, thereby creating a more "caring" organization. As we will see, each of Mayo's ageless factors is grounded in at least one of the 10 Influencing Tenets:

1. Purpose and meaning

2. Making a contribution/difference

3. Control and flexibility

4. Use of our talents and abilities

5. Supportive colleagues

6. Appreciation

*1. Purpose and Meaning: We each desperately need meaning in our lives and our work.* We want to know that what we do every day actually makes a difference. Our yearning to know that our work has some purpose and meaning will overpower even the most golden handcuffs. Without purpose and meaning, we default to focusing on benefits, bonuses, and bribes, and it's never enough to sustain our motivation. We will constantly crave more of it.

The generation born between 1980 and 2000 has been nicknamed the "Millennials" because they are the first generation to enter the workforce at the beginning of the new millennium. This younger generation has being credited with the pursuit of purpose and meaning in their work. But it's an absurd tribute. Innately, every human being wants some purpose and meaning in their work. Ironically, a whole new generation wants what no one else wants? Ridiculous. What really happened is that the parents of Millennials raised their children to seek out meaningful work and to settle for nothing less, like they often had done. The Traditional and Boomer generations, the generations in the middle of the 20th century, hoped for meaningful work. The next generation, Gen X, asked for it. The Millennials are just demanding it.

*2. Making a Contribution/Difference: We each urgently want to feel as though we are important.* We all want our contributions to be significant and important. The exact contribution is subjective and personal, but we want to feel like we are contributing significantly in some way with our day-to-day activities. It could be that we welcome new people to the company and we have the ability to make a difference in that person's experience. It could be that our research moves a big project forward for the team. It could be that we develop relationships for the company that keep the doors open and every person employed.

Quenching the thirst to be important and make a difference is the reason that so many people are drawn to work for non-profits and start-up companies. They not only desire the feeling that their work has a purpose but that their specific job makes a difference in the accomplishment of that purpose. What better place to feel that our work makes a difference every day than in an organization whose sole existence is to make a difference in the world – either by changing business or changing the planet, or both?

But start-ups and non-profits are not the perfect arena either. Non-profits may exist to make a difference in the world, but quite often those who run them don't know how to help people feel like they make a difference in that difference. That is, they too fail at influencing their people's intrinsic motivation and fostering their own people's moxie mindsets.

One of my favorite jobs was working for Weave Innovations, a start-up company in Silicon Valley that employed 25 other sharp, committed individuals. The success of the business relied on each of us showing up and executing. At the time I felt like we were working on something meaningful, and that I could directly contribute to the company's success. And because there was so much to do and only a few of us to do it, I was granted an enormous amount of flexibility to do my job and control over how my job got done. In addition, my role as the Corporate Counsel challenged me professionally. It not only employed my abilities acquired during my law career, it also tapped into my talents for strategic thinking and relationship development. The CEO looked to me for much more than just reviewing contracts. As a result, I felt extremely important. No wonder I woke up every morning excited to go to work. I could not wait to get to a place that needed me.

*3. Control and Flexibility: We each crave control, and we all just want to be winners, not losers.* Another factor that influences motivation and our moxie mindset is knowing how to win. We not only want our work to have meaning and purpose, and want our work to be an important contributor in that meaning and purpose, but we also want to know how to win. On top of that, we want to control how we win.

In general we feel that we are capable of figuring out on our own how to do our jobs. Hence, the ubiquitous loathing of the micromanager who makes each of us feel like we are 10 years old again listening to our parents tell us what to eat, wear, do, and say. It diminishes the contribution we make because someone is telling us how to make it instead of allowing us the freedom to make our own contribution.

Without control and flexibility, people feel inferior, distrusted, and caged; they feel that their integrity, intelligence, and competence are in question. On the flip side, people support that which they help to create, thereby ensuring that they will support the result of their efforts when they are in charge of some aspect of their work. You want buy-in. Handing over some of the control creates the requisite buy-in.

What do the multi-level marketing industry and the real estate industry have in common? They each allow individuals an enormous amount of control and flexibility over their own success. These industries give people the structure and formula with which they can win in business, as well as the power to do just that. These industries do not have much tolerance for excuses such as the dilapidated real estate market or the sinking economy. The people who prosper in these industries do so because of their resourcefulness and resilience. And those traits are never reliant on the market or the economy. How can you give people the formula to win and the power to use it?

*4. Use of Talents and Abilities: We all think the world revolves around us.* We all believe that we have talents and abilities and we don't want them to be ignored. We want our talents and abilities to be to be utilized to make a difference. That makes us feel significant and important. When our work leverages our talents and abilities, we feel we are needed and that the world really does revolve around us. This helps to give our work meaning and purpose.

There is nothing worse than being under-employed. We feel like we are wasting our time and that brain drain is setting in. We are meant for bigger things, we muse. We look at the nincompoops doing jobs three levels up from us and wonder why in the world they are in charge when our talents are perfect for that role. It's frustrating and infuriating.

*5. Supportive Colleagues: We all are at risk of succumbing to the herd, and we each dreadfully fear rejection.* The only thing worse than being under-employed is working for an organization that feels like high school all over again. The biting, naysaying, backstabbing, mistrusting, suspicion, and cynicism. If we can't stand the people we work with, there's no amount of purpose, meaning, contribution, flexibility, control, or use of talent that is going to save us. We want to find the nearest exit as fast as possible.

*6. Appreciation: We each have an insatiable appetite to be respected, appreciated, valued, and heard.* Finally, we want someone to notice. We are driving the company's purpose, we are applying our talents and abilities to contribute and make a difference, we are making decisions, we are playing nicely with others – and we just want someone to recognize and appreciate all that we do, day in and day out. The less we feel recognized and appreciated for our work, the less we want to use our talents to contribute, the less we take the initiative to make decisions, the less we work on being supportive of colleagues, the less we appreciate others, and the more we become complacent, mediocre, and sometimes sabotaging. It's a vicious cycle.

## What about Intrinsic Motivation?

The 10 Influencing Tenets are busy influencing people's intrinsic motivation. When you leverage these Tenets, you can actually help people to be responsible for their own experience at work. And when people get that they are 100 percent responsible for their own successes and their own failures, there are no limits on their ability to succeed. When you do not heed these tenets and as a result the factors that Professor Mayo identified are not present, people must rely solely on their intrinsic motivation. It is possible, but it becomes difficult for anyone to sustain over time. Not using the Tenets may actually result in influencing intrinsic motivation *negatively,* which results in people doing just enough to get by, if that.

Let's look at the influence that Rob's manager had on Rob, our ambitious NYNEX salesman. While Rob was intrinsically motivated, his manager's use of the Influencing Tenets positively influenced Rob's intrinsic motivation to persevere. Rob's manager allowed him to control how he succeeded on the job. He encouraged Rob to use his intelligence, resourcefulness, sales skills and talents, and his relationship abilities to surpass his sales objectives. And then he recognized and appreciated Rob's client accomplishments. He regularly acknowledged the difference Rob made in the success of the team. And while Rob's colleagues were not initially supportive of Rob, Rob's manager was louder than them and he made Rob listen to him instead of them. Soon they too came around with their support.

Like Rob, my grandmother was ambitious. She was a telephone operator in Chicago for Ma Bell, the moniker used at that time to refer to all AT&T companies. Ma Bell offered my grandmother self-respect, dignity, a paycheck, and a sense of independence. In return she gave Ma Bell 25 years of her enthusiastic, above-and-beyond effort. Regularly my grandmother set the record for the number of calls answered in a month, raising the bar for the required minimum number of monthly calls for all other telephone operators (much to their dismay).

Also like Rob, my grandmother had managers who influenced her intrinsic motivation. My grandmother's efforts did not go unnoticed nor did they get squashed. Her managers acknowledged, appreciated, and applauded. They did not deprecate, deflate, and denounce. Upon her retirement Ma Bell gifted my grandmother with a Ma Bell-inscribed ruby ring, which she proudly wore until the day she died. More importantly, her managers allowed her to contribute and make a difference.

It wasn't money that made my grandmother an enthusiastic and effective contributor at Ma Bell. She certainly didn't make a lot of money. She and my grandfather raised their children paycheck to paycheck. As a Ma Bell operator, though, she found a purpose separate and apart from her purpose as a mother and a wife. Her managers underscored how meaningful her work was and helped her to identify the difference she made in people's experience with the phone company, thereby contributing to the success of Ma Bell. In addition, my grandmother was allowed to control how she contributed. She was able to make decisions about how to help people on the phone using her own intelligence, resourcefulness, and savvy. Every operator-assisted phone call did not require some script or some supervisor's approval to take action in service of customers. Her managers helped her to see that while it wasn't an easy job it definitely made great use of her talent for thinking quickly and helping others resourcefully. In addition, she enjoyed the camaraderie of her colleagues immensely in spite of raising the productivity bar on them. Finally, Ma Bell managers regularly recognized my grandmother's efforts and appreciated her. Not just after 25 years but throughout her career.

With these factors influencing my grandmother's intrinsic motivation, she showed up every day ready to execute, contribute, and succeed. Was Ma Bell responsible for motivating my grandmother? No. Were her managers responsible for her successes? Not any more than they were responsible for her failures. But her managers were responsible (1) for not de-motivating her, (2) for influencing her intrinsic motivation, and (3) for allowing her to realize that she was 100 percent responsible for her own experience at work. And they did all of that.

## What about Employee Engagement?

When the Gallup Organization released its findings on employee engagement in 2004, their research revealed what many leaders feared: only 29 percent of employees are truly engaged, 54 percent are not engaged, and 17 percent of employees are actively disengaged. The collective leadership nodded in recognition of those figures. People pretended to be shocked, but really, who was surprised? Nobody, except of course, those disconnected, embittered managers and leaders who couldn't find their way to the cubicles or the front lines if their stock options depended on it.

As defined by the Gallup Organization, employees are engaged when they work with passion and feel connected to their company. "Not-engaged" employees are showing up to work but are checking their passion and energy at the door. Whereas "actively disengaged" employees are not just checked out; they are actively sabotaging the work and accomplishments of their colleagues. It is estimated that together, the detached 54 percent and the undermining 17 percent are costing companies millions of dollars in low productivity and high attrition.

But really, what good does this information do for us middle leaders? How does this help us to influence the actions in others, to influence them to own their own work experience, to invite them to use their moxie? A focus on employee engagement is a waste of your time. There is nothing in the employee engagement definition that will help you lead better, change behavior, innovate, or make waves.

Employee engagement is like the war on terror. We're not sure exactly what it means, we can't exactly describe it, we don't know what to do about it, we never really know if we are making any progress, and we will never know if we have won.

There are five major problems with a focus on employee engagement:

1. It sells people unacceptably short.

2. It places 100 percent of the responsibility on you — their manager.

3. It creates employee entitlement and disrespect.

4. It becomes a means to an end instead of the means itself.

5. It's the wrong focus.

## What about Benefits, Bonuses, and Bribes?

Henry Ford flabbergasted the business world in 1914 when he doubled the pay rate of most of his workers to $5 a day, which is equivalent in 2010 dollars to $109.16 or $13.63/hour. He dubbed it "wage motive" and in the short term it proved profitable. Instead of constant employee turnover, Ford used wage motive to attract the best mechanics to Detroit, which raised productivity and lowered training costs. While it may have been profitable in the short term, over the years, it garnered an entitlement mentality that to this day runs rampant. Ford's attempt at motivating employees was merely a means to an end—an improved bottom line.

When two out of three workers do not know or identify with or even feel motivated to drive their employer's business goals and objectives, and 25 percent of people are just showing up to collect a paycheck, we should not be surprised to learn that employee benefits, bonuses, and bribes are not making an impact.

Now imagine you don't feel that connected to your company's mission, you're not motivated by your company's goals, you don't see a purpose for your role in accomplishing that goal, you don't see how you contribute or make a difference, and frankly you don't even give a damn about the company's success or your own. Do you think the gym membership will do it for your attitude? How about a little help with the work-life balance juggle? If the company offers you flextime and a telecommuting option, will that cause you to feel like you're an intricate part of the company's mission, or just lucky that you get to work in your pajamas? How about the breast pump? Will that connect you to the bottom line? What if they bribe you with bonuses, commissions, time off, or medical benefits? Will the money and time off entrap you, enrage you, estrange you, or engage you?

Benefits, bonuses, and bribes are not motivators, but when people lack a feeling of importance and relevancy in their work, a feeling of partnership with their boss, and a resilient and dauntless mindset, the missing benefits become a *de-motivator.* Consider the Peace Corps or Teach for America or any non-profit organization, for that matter: individuals courageously and emphatically working without the benefits, bonuses, and bribes in exchange for one of the most meaningful experiences of their lives.

## What about Happiness?

Studies show that happy sales people outshine their unhappy colleagues by 37 percent, while happy doctors are 50 percent more accurate in their diagnoses than unhappy doctors. So should we invest in people's happiness to compel them to be more innovative and more productive? And is there even a connection between innovation, productivity, and happiness?

The King of Bhutan thought so. In 1972, the King of Bhutan, a remote Asian nation of 600,000 people, offered an audacious concept to address his country's widespread poverty and illiteracy: "Gross National Happiness." He declared that GNH defines prosperity in terms of the well-being of the people, not just economic output. The four foundations of his GNH include sustainable development, environmental protection, cultural preservation, and good governance. Since lofting the idea of GNH more than 30 years ago, the country has experienced a drop in the illiteracy rate, a decrease in infant mortality, and a growth in its economy. Reports reveal that the nation's people feel happy. In fact, they're so happy that according to the 2006 Happy Planet Index (which merely estimates happiness because, let's face it, measuring happiness is not an exact science), Bhutan was ranked eighth happiest out of 178 countries and the happiest of any Asian nation.

Because the concept is so nebulous, it's hard to say that the focus on GNH really caused more people to read, fewer people to die, and more money to be made. On the one hand we have a moxie leader who prioritized people's happiness, in spite of success and in spite of whether success is even measureable. On the other hand, GNH may have made people happy, but it's questionable whether it generated their determined attitude, audacious approach, and uncompromising, perseverant action to their lives and their work. It may have just made them happier people, which in and of itself is a lovely thing, but not country-saving or for our purposes, company-saving.

Imagine if we followed Bhutan's model and adopted our own commitment to Gross National Happiness. The theory being that by prioritizing people's happiness first, economic prosperity would follow. By committing to GNH, we would ensure the ongoing development of people, an ongoing enrichment of the team, and a promise to treat people fairly and ethically. Who wouldn't be happier working in that kind of environment? That is certainly humane, but not the entire solution. We have all seen happy people who are happy with complacency and mediocrity. Moxie is never happy with complacency and mediocrity.

Many companies are investing in the happiness of their employees. Adobe offers positive psychology training, onsite cafeterias, and fitness facilities. American Express offers telecommuting, job-sharing, and paid sabbaticals. Financial firm UBS offers its people nap rooms and a Friday beer cart. It all sounds deliciously great until we scratch beneath the surface to ascertain the attitude, approach, and actions that these investments are actually generating.

The founders of White Castle had a simple philosophy: happy employees make happy customers. It's pithy, but not always true. What happens when an employee is happy but the customer is cranky? Will the happy employee just smile extra hard and cause the cranky customer to become happy? What if that doesn't work and the customer is still cranky? Soon the cranky customer will cause the happy employee to become unhappy. Instead what this employee needs is to use his moxie to deal effectively with the cranky customer, which will result in his own happiness in spite of the cranky customer.

Happiness is merely a byproduct of moxie. Happiness is not what causes people to operate with moxie; happiness just makes it easier for us to embrace and leverage a moxie mindset. But happiness alone does not automatically generate moxie movements. We've all seen happy people who don't go above and beyond for a customer or a project, who are not acting out of a commitment to make a difference, and who do not operate on the edge or attempt where others don't. They're just happy people. Maybe they took a class on the power of positive thinking. Maybe they like getting free beer at their company's TGIF social events.

Don't be fooled into a maniacal focus on making people happy. Happiness is a consequence of people using a moxie mindset. Your customers will be happy because of the enthusiasm, determination, resourcefulness, and resilience of the people who serve them, not merely because those people are happy.

### Inspire More Rob Mindsets

Rob, our ambitious NYNEX salesman, used a moxie mindset and his managers effectively influenced him to do just that. He was young and resilient. He didn't yet have a death grip on the status quo and was not riddled with a fear of change, failure, or the unknown. Ultimately, he did not know that he was not supposed to succeed. Because he was new to his job, he hadn't yet been influenced negatively by others in the group. Rob deployed his moxie before he could be infected by his colleagues' toxicity. As a result, he started to win. His wins gave credence to his approach and vaccinated him from their negative influences. Eventually Rob became a sales manager and he had the power to influence the moxie in others – from his boss to his peers to his own people.

Let's dissect moxie and our ability to influence it in the following chapters. We will soon understand how Rob and other successful leaders and contributors continue to generate moxie in spite of a world that attempts to bring them down with toxicity, complacency, and mediocrity.

### Putting It Into Action

- Ask each person on your team to tell you what they want to accomplish in their role.

- Ask them what difference their role makes to the team, the company, and to the customers.

- Ask people to identify for you their talents and abilities and then to specify how they are using those in their job.

- Now ask them which talents and abilities they feel they are *not* leveraging in their current role.

- Find a way to hand over control of an outcome to people on your team who normally are not in control of any outcome. Example, "Find a solution to this problem," or "You are in charge of planning the customer appreciation party."

- Recall a time when you acted like Rob. How did it feel? How long ago was it? What could you do today to once again harness the moxie factor like Rob?

**A Moxie Mindset**: Operating with the audacity, the chutzpah, and the guts required to succeed no matter what; approaching work with enthusiasm, courage, determination, and perseverance; facing situations with resourcefulness, resilience, brilliance, and relentlessness; acting uncompromising in your commitment; being maniacal in your focus and movement toward a goal in the face of any and all circumstances; encouraging and influencing others to do the same.

# Chapter 3

## Give Them a Battle Cry

. . . . . . . . . . . . . . . . . .

As I was boarding the Jet Blue plane on my way to Cancun, I realized I had forgotten to grab a spoon for the yogurt I had just bought. I asked the flight attendant for one and quickly learned that Jet Blue does not serve any food that requires utensils. But a few minutes later, the flight attendant handed me a plastic spoon. She said the pilot had overheard my request, and as people were still boarding, he got off the plane to personally get me a plastic spoon. Imagine my surprise and delight!

Why did the pilot go out of his way to get me a spoon? While it sounds like the start of a why-did-the-chicken-cross-the-road joke, it actually gets to the crux of people's moxie mindset. The answer is that the pilot was driven by Jet Blue's battle cry: "bring humanity back to air travel." And the pilot brought a slice of humanity to my air travel. As a result, I have not forgotten this superior service and my above-and-beyond experience and continue to retell the surprise-and-delight tale — as well as give my business to Jet Blue.

### Vision Statements and Mission Statements

Business consultants spend hundreds of hours and charge thousands of dollars helping businesses articulate their vision and mission statements. Ideally, a company starts by creating a vision statement to define how they envision the world in the future, and then they create mission statements that align with that vision. The *vision* is an organization's dream, the idea, the image of what the world should look like in the future or how it should operate differently than it does right now. "A world without hunger" is a vision. The *mission*, on the other hand, is an organization's goal that it has chosen to work on in order to contribute to that vision. For example, "To be the premier micro-financing organization in the world." Arguably, the vision and the mission are critical to an organization's strategy.

The problem, however, is that we get patronizing, impervious, confusing, aimless proclamations and formulaic declarations instead of action-inspiring, people-rallying charges.

In 1997 Scott Adams, the creator of the *Dilbert* cartoon, proved how leaders get mired in their own arrogant mission statements while forgetting the power to rally. Scott masqueraded as a management consultant named Ray Mebert who was hired by Logitech's vice-chairman to overhaul the company's mission statement, which at the time was written as, "to provide Logitech with profitable growth and related new business areas." Scott convinced the executives to adopt a new mission statement: "to scout profitable growth opportunities in relationships, both internally and externally, in emerging, mission-inclusive markets, and explore new paradigms and then filter and communicate and evangelize the findings." While mocking the executives, Scott was underscoring the absurdity of mission statements and the resulting disconnect between the purpose and the people who execute that purpose.

## The Battle Cry

"They can take our land but they'll never take our freedom!" cried William Wallace, the villager-turned-folk hero in Scotland's fight for freedom from Britain, as portrayed by Mel Gibson in the movie *Braveheart*. That's a battle cry.

"To run a different kind of company: the kind of place we'd want to work, that makes the kind of food we'd like to eat, and that strives for a healthier, more sustainable world – the kind of world we'd like to pass on to our children," cry Gary and Kit, the owners of Clif Bar, the energy bar company.

"To be the attorney you wish you had known last time you dealt with your attorney." That was my battle cry when I ran my own law firm. I wanted to practice differently. I wanted to incorporate both my strengths for analyzing and strategizing corporate law issues as well as my strengths for helping people succeed.

"To be the number one office by serving my agents, my company, and my community with relentless value, ruthless integrity, and uncompromising respect." This is the battle cry one manager created to keep focused on becoming an effective leader instead of a busy manager, to enable her agents to do the same, and to unabashedly pick up the phone each day to recruit new talent to her office.

"Organize, agitate, educate, must be our war cry," sang Susan B. Anthony, the prominent leader of the women's rights movement in the United States.

"Every one of them is as passionately committed to the Constitution and our government as I am. Once I understood they were people of good faith, as committed to this country as I was, it made my job easier," said Justice Sonia Sotomayor in a speech to the Chicago Bar Association during her first year on the court reciting advice that retiring Justice David H. Souter gave her. In other words, while the justices on the Supreme Court have varying beliefs, their shared battle cry is their commitment to the Constitution, the government, and the country.

Even the folks at Ma Bell had a battle cry when my grandmother worked there as a Ma Bell operator. During the height of winter, my grandmother was taking a cigarette break when she slipped and fell on the sidewalk outside of the building. A few of her colleagues came running over and asked her to move across the street so as to not jeopardize their accident-free streak.

And she did. The operators owned and therefore drove their "accident-free" battle cry.

A battle cry is the heroic exclamation we shout as we run onto a battlefield. Every day people show up at the office to run onto a proverbial battlefield to engage in proverbial battle. Sometimes that battle is for us, their manager, and sometimes it's on behalf of their team or the company. To ensure nothing short of victory, they need an exclamation to charge into battle together. No mission statement will do that. A mission statement can barely rally the nail that holds it up on the wall.

Skip the mission and vision statements. What every company, department, team, and person needs is a battle cry. We need something to jump out of bed for. Something to be excited about; something to show up every day and drive forward. Every person wants to make a difference, to be significant, to know that our work is important. We need a reason to rally. The battle cry gives us that reason to rally.

"To teach people entrepreneurship in all corners of the globe" is a battle cry that helps to drive the vision "a world without hunger" and the mission "to be the premier micro-financing organization in the world." Sometimes we can find the battle cry in the mission statement. For instance, Wal-Mart's mission statement is "to save people money so they can live better." This serves as a fabulous battle cry.

Harley-Davidson's battle cry is to "fulfill dreams through the experience of motorcycling." McDonald's battle cry is "to be the world's best quick service restaurant experience." One of Berkshire Hathaway's battle cries is "provide compassionate care for injured workers." PRIDE Industries, a not-for-profit organization headquartered in Roseville, California, has a battle cry: "to create meaningful jobs for people with disabilities."

Even people who collect garbage can create a battle cry. "Picking up garbage" is merely a job description. But "keeping the streets looking beautiful" is a battle cry.

## Give Them Something to Care About

The test of a good battle cry is whether it actually rallies people around something they care about. To them the battle must be significant, daring, imperative, and thrilling. And there can, and should, be more than one battle cry. Each individual should have their own battle cry and each team should have its own battle cry.

Let's revisit the Jet Blue pilot. Without knowing more, we can assume the following:

- The pilot is clearly aware of Jet Blue's battle cry to bring humanity back to air travel.

- The pilot is inspired by that battle cry and feels the battle is important and worth contributing to.

- The pilot feels he can make a difference in helping Jet Blue be victorious in that battle.

- The pilot is responsible for identifying opportunities and taking action to make that difference.

Would you go out of your way to fetch a plastic spoon for a customer? How about the people you work with — would they?

People will go out of their way when (1) they feel inspired by and passionate for a battle cry — they care about it, (2) they recognize how they can contribute in the battle, and (3) they feel responsible and enabled to take action to make a difference in driving that battle cry forward and being victorious in the battle. The Jet Blue pilot clearly acted in concert with his company's battle cry to bring humanity back to air travel. He perceived his role as one that could contribute to winning the battle. And then he felt committed to taking action to make a difference in doing just that.

Look around. Do you know what your leader's battle cry is? Do you have a battle cry? Do the people who work with you know what it is, feel inspired by it, and feel committed and able to take action to be victorious in the battle? This inquiry alone is exponentially more important than asking if people are engaged.

Here are five ways to assess their quest for victory in the battle cry:

1. Ask them what they believe they are working to accomplish – in the big picture. (Do they know your battle cry, your team's battle cry, or the company's battle cry?)

2. Ask them why they want to help accomplish that big picture. (Are they inspired by it? Do they feel it is important and meaningful?)

3. Ask them why winning the battle matters to them professionally and personally. (What's at stake for them?)

4. Ask them what actions they have taken that were not specifically assigned to them but that contributed to victory. (Are they encouraged to draw outside the lines?)

5. Then model it for them. Show them what it looks like to be inspired, responsible, committed, and in action.

## WSIC Mindset vs. WIIFM Mindset

Teach for America (TFA) has a battle cry to give all American children access to quality education, and the zeal for victory fires up everyone from facilities manages to senior executives at the organization. TFA leaders help people stay focused on why they should care about that battle cry by urging them to spend time in classrooms to see how they are making a difference.

To move people from indifference to unparalleled, from ordinary to astounding, from mediocre to magnificent, they need to be thunderstruck about the battle cry and by the difference they can make in that battle cry. They need to care about it, not just go into battle because something might be in it for them. When people don't care about the battle cry, they are left to care about themselves and what's in it for them. People quickly go from a "Why should I care?" mindset to a "What's in it for me?" mindset. For simplicity, let's call these the WSIC mindset and the WIIFM mindset.

In a WSIC mindset, people embrace the battle cry and then determine a way to make a difference in it. They do so by creating their own battle cry that furthers the organization's battle cry. From there people look for ways that their job, their role, and their contributions are integral in achieving victory in the battle. Finally, the magic happens because people feel responsible for taking action to make a difference in that victory. As leaders, we can influence this mindset by reminding people how they make a difference.

Google's battle cry is "to organize the world's information and make it universally accessible and useful." While Google wants everyone to embrace this, they are abundantly clear that people will care when they align their own battle cry with the company's. To that end, Google invites its engineers to create a battle cry. Each engineer is encouraged to spend 20 percent of their time working on something that excites them and furthers Google's battle cry. This cultural attitude promotes self-motivated individuals to pursue ideas and make contributions to the company's battle cry without the risk of those great ideas getting caught in a web of hierarchy. Gmail, Google News, Google Talk, and even the Google shuttle buses that bring people to work at the company's headquarters were all born out of what they call "20 percent time."

When people know the battle cry, care about it, and recognize that they can make a difference in it, they will step out of the comfort of the status quo and take action to contribute and make that difference, like the Jet Blue pilot did. That's the power of WSIC. Extraordinary managers help people to create WSIC-worthy battle cries.

But when people are fuzzy on the battle cry, don't care about it, or can't see how they can make a difference in the victory, they become perfunctory or worst case, won't take any above-and-beyond action. And when there's no WSIC, there's always WIIFM. Without a WSIC-worthy battle cry, people usually show up to work merely to make money. And when people work only to make money, they have a proclivity to see their work as merely a "means to an end." This leads to doing the bare minimum to earn that money. Doing anything above and beyond triggers the what's-in-it-for-me question. If I work one more hour or lift one more finger or fix one more light switch or sell one more product, what are you going to do for me? There's nothing to rally them other than money – an extrinsic motivator.

## WIIFM Mindset at Work

The *Boston Globe* newspaper was hemorrhaging cash. Without making drastic cuts, the paper was going to be forced to close. With a projected loss of $85 million, the *Globe* had been negotiating with its four major unions to accept wage and benefit cuts. At the eleventh hour, the largest union, the Boston Guild, said, "No." With this impasse, the paper imposed a 23 percent pay cut on all union members, to which the union responded by filing a claim with the National Labor Relations Board.

The what's-in-it-for-me mentality that pervaded the office was going to be its demise. Where was the leadership at the *Globe* that allowed this chasm between employees and management to grow so large that it would take a construction company to build a bridge big enough to connect both sides again? And why were the union employees risking the paper and their jobs? But scratch beneath the showdown and we can clearly see the forces at play here that encouraged the WIIFM mindset.

First, it seems everyone was being influenced by a human decision-making bias called "loss aversion." The *Globe* employees were so determined to avoid any option associated with loss that they were willing to risk losing everything. This desire to avoid losing leads people to do foolish things. Why would employees force their company, which was already lingering on the brink of financial collapse, into a court case with the NLRB? How would that save anyone's job, let alone the paper? It wouldn't. It's just a natural reaction to a situation that smacks of loss. And when there's loss, people want to know what they're going to get in return for that loss.

Second, it seems that a herd mentality had taken over. And when there's a herd, there's group polarization and no room for a balanced viewpoint. When people who share a belief get together to discuss that belief, they reach conclusions more extreme than the ones they held as individuals. Can you just picture the scene at a union meeting? "Those jerks!" "Yeah! They think they can take money out of our pocket." "Not a chance! They'll have to give us something pretty great to get us to concede!" Now imagine the scene in the management meeting. "Those entitled ingrates! They want their jobs? They'll have to concede and give up some of those benefits." And so it escalated on each side.

We also need to wonder how the leadership at the *Globe* fueled this WIIFM mindset. On one hand, it is honorable that the employees were so loyal that they stuck by the *Globe* for 20, 30, and some even 40 years. We could easily assume that it must have been a great place to work based on those numbers alone. But was it a great place or were the benefits so great – salary, pension, health, retirement, lifetime job guarantees – that they became golden handcuffs? If the leaders had created a place where people wanted to work and stopped bribing people to work there, they probably wouldn't have been in that predicament. I don't care how *bad* the newspaper business is, if people had harbored a moxie mindset they would have saved it. Unfortunately, they didn't. A few months later, the stand-off ended when the paper's parent company, The New York Times Company, threatened to close the esteemed newspaper. Employees begrudgingly voted to accept deep concessions on wages, benefits, and job security just six weeks after they had rejected the same concessions. While the concessions will save the *Globe* an expected $10 million a year and many jobs, union members are resentful. The bigger bully on the playground had more clout and won this round.

"What's in it for me?" This mindset is the downfall of every team on which we have ever worked and is causing the downfall of the *Boston Globe* and thousands of companies in similar situations. WIIFM is like radon gas that seeps into a home. Without detection it poisons the air, causing long-term, terminal illnesses. WIIFM is as toxic and impacting.

As evidenced by the situation at the *Boston Globe*, when people embrace a WIIFM mindset, the chasm between "US" and "THEM" grows wider. People pit themselves against the evil monster called "THEM," referring to the company and anyone representing the company, particularly management. US is thinking, "I want to know what I will get in exchange for going beyond my job title by even an inch." THEY need an employee; US agreed to fill that role and do the job in exchange for a paycheck. THEY should not expect any more from US unless THEY intend to incentivize US. When THEY ask US to go above and beyond the call of duty, US wants to know what THEY are going to do for US. What will US get for doing more than US originally agreed to do?

Without a battle cry, WIIFM clearly fans the entitlement flame.

WIIFM is the Darth Vader to the moxie mindset. It wreaks havoc on inspiration, perseverance, determination, and progress. And just like in *Star Wars*, once someone has gone over to the dark side, it is hard to come back. WIIFM infects deep into the soul of the organization and then spreads like a virus.

## WSIC Mindset

Our secret weapon, our chemo for cancer, our light saber in the fight against the WIIFM Darth Vader is the WSIC mindset – Why Should I Care? This is the question we must answer for ourselves and for people who work with us long before WIIFM creeps in. When we know the purpose, feel the importance of that purpose, and recognize how we can make a difference in fulfilling that purpose, then we care. And when people care, they become unstoppable.

President John F. Kennedy tapped the power of the WSIC mindset to rally and inspire America in the 1960s. In his January 20, 1961, inaugural address, JFK will forever be remembered for his aspirations of Americans and for demanding that we to step up to those great aspirations. First, he summarized the battle cry of the country: "Let every nation know, whether it wishes us well or ill, that we shall pay any price, bear any burden, meet any hardship, support any friend, oppose any foe to assure the survival and the success of liberty. This much we pledge – and more." He echoed back to us our feelings of the importance of that battle cry: "Now the trumpet summons us again – not as a call to bear arms, though arms we need – not as a call to battle, though embattled we are – but a call to bear the burden of a long twilight struggle, year in and year out, 'rejoicing in hope, patient in tribulation' – a struggle against the common enemies of man: tyranny, poverty, disease and war itself." And he acknowledged our significance in victory – that we could each make a difference. "In your hands, my fellow citizens, more than mine, will rest the final success or failure of our course." With the American people riveted by his every word, he answered the why-should-I-care question. They cared. And then he drove it home with the question that has memorialized JFK in history: "And so, my fellow Americans: Ask not what your country can do for you; ask what you can do for your country." That line resonated with the American people only because JFK reminded us why we should care.

Proctor & Gamble has figured out the power of WSIC, and uses it to rouse people to action. P&G's battle cry is "to improve the lives of the world's consumers." According to its Chief Operating Officer, P&G managers – not HR – recruit the talent. These managers recruit people who are inspired to fulfill P&G's battle cry. Then these managers deploy these people with a new battle cry – to go out to the field to visit retail stores and consumers' homes and obtain on-the-ground observations about how best to serve customers purchasing and using P&G products.

It's brilliant. P&G gives its people something to care about: improving lives, and then gives managers something else to care about: responsibility for hiring great people to execute on that battle cry, and then those managers give the newly hired talent something else to care about: understanding how consumers are purchasing and using P&G products.

## Triggering WSIC

To help someone think in WSIC mode instead of WIIFM mode, help them use this formula:

1. Identify a battle cry that is in concert with the battle cry of the organization, the department, or the team.

2. Assess whether victory in the battle is important.

3. Acknowledge the difference you make in achieving victory in the battle.

**First, identify a battle cry.** If we lead a department of the organization, identify the battle cry of that department. As an example, the leaders of the IT organization at Scotts Miracle Gro have defined one of its battle cries as: "to provide innovative, cost-effective IT solutions." If you are a manager in this organization, you better identify a battle cry for your team that aligns with that battle cry. And if you only manage one other person, create together a battle cry for a project you're working on that aligns with the department's battle cry.

Without a battle cry – a purpose for showing up to the battle and going in for victory – the people you work with will inevitably flounder. It's in the void that people start wondering why they are there and what's in it for them to keep showing up.

Rob, our ambitious NYNEX salesman from Chapter 2, now sells bar code scanning equipment and other mobile devices as a sales leader in the mobile technology industry. However, he advocates to his team that they do not sell equipment; they "create business process improvement." Clear about the battle cry, he and his team members get excited every time they discover a warehouse or notice a semi on the road from a company that is not a customer. They immediately write down the name of the company so they can follow up and assess whether the company is taking advantage of today's technology to improve their business processes. This battle cry has helped to keep people focused on their incredible passion for the problems they can solve with the company's technology, instead of attempting to be passionate about a year-end sales quota.

Next, assess whether victory in the battle is important to people. Is it something that they think about, worry about, get excited about, and are concerned about? Is it essential and imperative to the vitality of the organization, the community, the planet, or their happiness and fulfillment? Does the battle cry matter to them? Does victory matter? If it doesn't, can we help them find some aspect of it that does matter? For example, does fulfillment of the team's purpose contribute to one of their personal battle cries in some way? If we can't find a connection, we risk losing that person in a sea of wonderment about what's in it for them to keep showing up.

My dad was passionate about his company's battle cry. A salesman in the roofing industry, he was always on the lookout for an opportunity to "improve the value of a building by protecting its roof." Every time he entered a new building, he looked up in search of stains on the ceiling that indicated a water leak in the roof. He was particularly committed to making a difference for building owners, being one himself. Growing up in this family, we became accustomed to this routine. Instinctually whenever we walked into a new building, our entire family would look up in search of water stains on the ceiling. To this day, I can't help but notice ceiling stains in office buildings.

**Finally, acknowledge the difference people make in achieving victory.** What is their significance to the battle cry? People will care when they understand that they make a difference in that battle. Make reference to their many talents, abilities, and strengths that are integral to achieving victory.

## We Need to be Needed

If after your battle cry exploration, you discover that someone just doesn't care, don't rush to judgment. Look a little deeper and you might discover that they are just defending themselves from the feeling that they are not integral to victory in the battle. They are just not needed. Not being needed is the first step toward rejection, the abyss in any human relationship. When people feel they are at risk of being rejected, they will do the rejecting first. This protects their ego.

People need to be needed. They crave significance. They want to know that they are more than a disposable cog in a wheel. People are so starved to contribute and make a difference that when they feel needed, they care. They care about showing up. They care about their effectiveness and their performance. They care about the impact they are making.

When people do not feel needed, they may still care, but their fear of being rejected will smother that care. Soon they will start wondering why they care about showing up when no one cares if they show up. From there it's a quick slide down into speculating what's in it for them to care. And WIIFM sets in.

The crazy thing is that feeding this basic need to be needed is simple. It only takes an acknowledgement from you, their leader, that they are important to the team's victory in the battle. That's enough to fuel the ego. No matter how tough, detached, or indifferent people may appear on the outside, on the inside everyone is hungry to be needed.

This craving to be important, relevant, and essential to another or to a situation is ubiquitous. When the tragedy of 9/11 struck, people flooded New York City to help. When Hurricane Katrina wiped out New Orleans as we knew it, people raced to the scene to do something. When the 7.2 earthquake hit Haiti and killed hundreds of thousands of its citizens, people from around the globe inundated the area to feed that need to be needed. One doctor who flew to Haiti immediately after the earthquake to care for the injured appeared on CNN to share his experience. Through tears he said, "I am exhausted and emotionally drained but these people need me. There's no place I'd rather be." People are so hungry to feed this need to be needed that they often risk their own comfort and safety to do so.

When people are not needed, they don't show up, either physically or emotionally. This is the bane of voting in America. People consider the millions of others who are voting in an election and then conclude, "What difference will my one vote make?" If they can't see the difference, then they don't go out of their way to vote. When we have a large population that feels this way, we get voter turnouts during presidential elections of 55 percent on average, and only 35 percent during non-presidential election years. In 2008, 231 million people were of voting age, but only 132 million people voted. That means that more than 98 million people thought it would not matter if they voted.

When people focus on the stories of elections in which the winner was decided by just a few votes, their attitude changes because in those situations, each vote seemed to matter. They were needed. In 2009, Democrat Al Franken won Minnesota's Senate seat over Republican incumbent Norm Coleman after a statewide recount of the 3 million votes determined that Franken won by only 312 votes. A million and a half people suddenly felt that their vote was one of those 312 votes that actually made a difference. Their vote was needed.

## Confusing Busy with Meaningful

People feed their insatiable appetite to be needed and feel significant by creating a crazy busy schedule and then convincing themselves that their busyness proves their indispensability. They operate with a maniacal focus on their to-do list. They fill their schedule with a plethora of meetings, conference calls, and projects. They spend the day moving from one meeting to the next and one phone call to the next, feeling great and accomplished as they cross items off their to-do lists. Then they crash at the end of the day, exclaiming how exhausted they are and how hard they worked.

As a result and quite unfortunately, most people cannot articulate how something on their to-do list fits into the purpose of their job, let alone the purpose of the team or the organization. Without a battle cry, people are just being busy for the sake of being busy. They have confused busy with productive, effective, or meaningful. They don't even know how to prioritize because everything on the list is given equal importance. In addition, without a battle cry, they don't know how to delegate, defer, or say "No."

The problem with using busyness to feed the need to be needed is that our brain processes meaning before detail. It wants to know the meaning behind the details. And when our days are organized around the details of our never-ending to-do lists, the project plans, the action items, and the myriad of committee meetings, the details *become* the meaning. And when that happens, the details take on unnecessary significance. If you have ever worked with someone who made things overly important, you now know why – they lost sight of the big picture and were trying to bring meaning where there was none.

In the short term, this approach works to motivate – but in the long run it will fail to sustain. There comes a point when people will search for more meaning than the to-do list offers.

Soon enough, our brain will call the game. Without a battle cry, they may be busy, but there will always be something missing. That something missing will begin to gnaw on their motivation. When they realize that the details lack meaning, they will stop caring about the details. And like mold that grows in the basement, the WIIFM questions will fill the void. They will wonder why they are working so hard for nothing.

## Battle Cry Challenges

People rarely remember why they come to work each day. As a middle leader, you have a unique opportunity to promote the use of a battle cry to not only feed the need to be needed, but to prioritize the busyness and increase the effectiveness. You can change the game on your people. At the beginning, it will require you to help them craft their own battle cry – their own purpose, their own reason for showing up each day. If this conversation is met with reluctance, understandable; but if it's met with resolute derision, consider parting ways. You cannot afford to tolerate people on your team who only show up to attend meetings and cross things off a to-do list.

Sam Calagione, the CEO of Dogfish Head Craft Brewery in Delaware, knows the power of each person having a reason to show up. When he launched the company he committed to running a fun company where people aren't working for him. He believes that the people at Dogfish are the most effective, productive, and innovative when they are working for themselves. He encourages people to find their own reason for showing up, provided that it is aligned with and forwarding the company's battle cry: "to expose beer lovers to something other than big, industrial-brewed pale lagers." To that end, Sam goes to great lengths to demonstrate that people don't work for him. He never sits at the head of the table; his cubicle is no bigger than anyone else's; he shares the company's financials with the employees regularly; and he bonuses people on the financial health of the company because they have a direct impact on that health.

The most important way to move people into meaning is to start with your organization's battle cry. Your organization may be a team, a project, a department, or the whole company. Infuse that battle cry into people's strategic conversations. Show people what victory looks like. Remind everyone what they are showing up to achieve, clarify its importance, and reiterate how integral they are to victory. Then encourage them to identify their own battle cry that is in concert with the organization's battle cry.

## Battle Cry–Driven People

Just like companies need a battle cry to prioritize and succeed, people operate more effectively when they have their own battle cry from which to drive their behaviors. Everyone on your team should be able to answer the following questions: What is my purpose on the team and in the company? What problem do I solve? What difference do I make? What am I needed for? What am I working toward? Why should I care? Why should I show up?

Bernie Siegel's battle cry drives him to succeed in his practice of medicine. After growing up in Brooklyn, New York, Bernie was headed to medical school. He attended Colgate University and Cornell University Medical College, trained as a surgeon at Yale New Haven Hospital, West Haven Veteran's Hospital, and the Children's Hospital of Pittsburgh, and began treating cancer patients. In 1978 he discovered that his cancer patients were dying because they were not aware of their healing potential; they were too focused on the fact that they had a life-threatening disease called "cancer." His battle cry became "empower patients and teach them survival behavior." Driven by this battle cry, Bernie now writes books, lectures all over the world, empowers patients, and impacts medical education and medical care. Bernie shows up every day impassioned by his own battle cry.

People need their own battle cry. Encourage them to create one, such as "The Company's #1 Process Improvement Specialist," "The Team's #1 Project Success Strategist," "The Department's #1 Technical Assistant," "The Team's #1 Customer Strategist," or "The Company's #1 Navigator of Tough Client Situations."

The exact battle cry is actually irrelevant. It's more important that it rallies them personally, identifies for them the difference they make in the organization's quest for victory, and gives them a reason to show up and care.

Then recognize that your team needs its own battle cry as well. "We're the talent magnets." "We ensure the world knows how great our products are." "We're the aspirin for the IT headache." "We generate the innovative ideas." "We are the research specialists." You get the idea.

Invite people to be creative and change their title to be unique while truly describing the problem they solve at the company. Forget the eye-glazing job titles! What does "Business Analyst and Strategic Alignment Associate" mean, anyway? Welcome their creativity. Make it interesting.

When you were growing up, how many times did people ask, "What do you want to be when you grow up?" or "What do you want to do when you graduate from college?" Now think about how many times you were asked, "What difference do you want to make in the world?" Framed that way, we might have more people seeking opportunities to contribute versus chasing job titles and salaries. "What difference you want to make" is just another way to describe the battle cry.

Adopting a battle cry allows people to verbalize the contribution they are making and acknowledge its significance in the big picture. This exercise will also encourage them to up-level their own thinking about the role they play at the company and on the team, and reiterate for themselves the impact they make by showing up each day.

## WSIC Fuels the Moxie Mindset

Take a good, hard look at the people around you and determine if they operate with a WSIC inquiry or a WIIFM inquiry. If it's the former, keep fanning the flames. If it's the latter, identify a reason for people to care – a battle cry. And then if they care, fan the flames; if they don't, show them the door.

The members of the United Auto Workers Local 1112 in Lordstown, Ohio, were forced to identify a reason to show up that aligned with General Motors' battle cry. In the 1970s the 7,000 factory workers were insubordinate, defiant, and even rebellious. They were at war with management. Their bitterness was so pervasive that the workers sabotaged their own products. They intentionally slit the upholstery in and otherwise damaged thousands of cars during the manufacturing process. In 1972, the factory workers held a 22-day strike that cost General Motors $150 million. By the 1980s members of the union were so smug and supercilious that they opposed any concession the union leaders proposed. At one time, the members even picketed their own union hall to protest their leaders' proposed concessions. The term "Lordstown Syndrome" was coined to describe these mutinous factory workers. Management and the union deemed each other arch enemies.

The past 30 years have certainly changed the tune of the leaders of the United Automobile Workers and the leaders in General Motors management. GM's teeter on the brink of bankruptcy this past decade has exhausted the workers' conceit and arrogance.

Today, management and the union have joined forces against a new enemy: foreign competition. The workers have a new reason to show up – to keep the company alive by beating the new enemy. And the company has a new reason to appreciate its people – they need them to produce high-quality cars and help save the company from bankruptcy. The workers are stepping up to the challenge.

One factory worker explained the new attitude that has infused the plant, "We all realize we have to do our part to keep the company going." He said he shows up each day with a commitment to help General Motors prosper once again.

Since workers and management have discovered a new reason to show up, the plant has become a role model operation for General Motors. Member grievances filed against GM have plummeted by 90 percent since the 15,000 that were filed in the height of the hostility in the 1970s. Absenteeism has decreased. Leaders have resolved many workers' compensation claims. Members and management are working together to find solutions. Gone are the days of belligerence, antagonism, and animosity between factory workers and management. They each want the other to be successful. As a result, the Lordstown factory is now one of the most productive and efficient of all GM plants.

### Putting It Into Action

- What's your team's battle cry? What's your battle cry?
- Ask people why they do their job – what do they care about other than their paycheck?
- Ask people to craft a battle cry for a project.
- Have people share with you what difference they feel they make in the battle cry. How do they feel significant?
- Share with people their importance in a battle cry and the difference they make.
- Ask people what makes them excited to come to work and achieve victory.

- Ask people what they believe they are working to accomplish – in the big picture. And ask them why they want to help accomplish that big picture.

- Ask people why winning the battle matters to them professionally and personally. What's at stake for them?

- Model it for them. Share with people your battle cry and the difference you make.

# Chapter 4

## Fuel Their Self-Delusion

In one of my favorite Nationwide Insurance commercials, an enthusiastic insurance agent meets with a woman named Pam to interview her about her experience with her current insurance company. Seeming rather despondent and annoyed, Pam explains that she bought her policy online and hasn't heard from the company since. The Nationwide Insurance agent picks up the handset of a rotary phone that is strapped to him like an over-the-shoulder handbag and dials Pam's insurance company. Dramatically, he enthuses, "When Pam switches to Nationwide Insurance, we're not going to treat her like Policy 413. We're going to treat her like Pam. Get to know her. Be proactive. Oh, and rename the company, NationPam." Pam smiles broadly, nods with approval, and sighs contentedly while the agent sings, "NationPam is on your side."

That's exactly how to fuel self-delusion.

I had a NationPam experience recently when I was at Whole Foods looking for my favorite yogurt, Brown Cow's Cherry Vanilla. It was no longer on the shelf. In fact, I noticed that the entire Brown Cow yogurt brand had shrunk in shelf space. I approached Matt, the young man who was wearing a Whole Foods shirt, stacking eggs on the shelf nearby. I said, "Excuse me, Matt. I'm curious. Are you eliminating Brown Cow yogurt?" Matt shared, "We have found that Brown Cow does not move off the shelves like the other brands. Is there one that you like in particular?" I said,

"What a shame. I love Brown Cow because it isn't made with sugar and I love the Cherry Vanilla flavor in particular because it is so delicious." Matt said, "I'll bring it back for you." Stunned, I said, "Wow, Matt. Thank you so much."

Unbeknownst to Matt, he was actually demonstrating the unconventional, decentralized management model at Whole Foods, which inevitably spurs these kinds of exchanges. The management model ensures that the mindset of each store is as organic as the food they sell. Every store consists of about eight workgroups that are responsible for overseeing different aspects of the store, from produce to bakery to checkout. These teams are responsible for making key operating decisions, such as pricing, ordering, and in-store promotions. Unlike the standard supermarket practice in which national buyers dictate which foods make it to the shelves, Whole Foods' shelves are stocked with foods selected by the team responsible for those particular shelves.

Even the hiring process is organic. Every new member to the store is subject to a peer-based selection process in which that newbie is provisionally assigned to a team pending a four-week trial and a team vote. After the trial period, the team votes on that person's suitability and ultimately his or her fate. A two-thirds majority vote is needed to achieve a full-time slot on the team. This peer-based selection process is even employed at Whole Foods' headquarters in Austin, Texas.

This unprecedented approach in retailing is grounded on Whole Foods' belief that people who are most directly impacted by the consequences of decisions should make those decisions. As a result, the team members at Whole Foods don't work *for* Whole Foods, they work *with* Whole Foods. The autonomy granted to the people of Whole Foods feeds into one of the most basic foundations of behavioral motivation: we like to think it's all about us. And as a result of their model, Whole Foods team members can create NationPam experiences for their customers, who also like to think it's all about them.

## People Think It's All About Them

Every person thinks the world revolves around them. And it does. We are literally the only ones who know ourselves from birth to death, inside and out. Everywhere we go, there we are. We are the center of our universe and consequently, we operate from that standpoint. Wherever we stand, the world is literally revolving around us, at least in our minds. Every situation you are in is about you, because you are seeing it from your eye sockets, and from that view, you are the main character in every scene. It really is *all about you.* The idea that the world revolves around you personally is a delusion that each one of us embraces daily, and it fuels motivation.

Every one of us walks the planet clutching this self-delusion, and it actually serves us quite well. When we think it's about us, we feel important, significant, and needed. When the world needs us, we feel respected, admired, and appreciated, which feeds our need for esteem. This boosts our confidence and makes us feel self-assured, which naturally generates self-esteem and self-respect. When our confidence, self-esteem, and self-respect are high, we tend to perform better and achieve more. When we operate from the delusion that it's all about us, we produce, we achieve, and we succeed.

## Feeling Disposable

In a scene from the TV comedy *Will & Grace*, Karen was attending a cocktail party with Will, Grace, and Jack. While in a circle conversation with them, she is clearly inspecting the crowd at the same time. Upon seeing a couple enter the party, Karen announces, "Better people! Gotta go!" and she dumps her friends in order to mingle with this new couple. It's funny on TV, but not in reality.

When people are reminded that the world does not revolve around them, that they aren't needed to win the battle, and that the game will go on just fine without them, they feel dispensable and disposable. It's like a glass of water thrown in their face, reminding them that it's actually not about them. This reality check is deflating. Who wants to be told that they are nonessential?

When people feel disposable, they become aware that they are not needed for a project to succeed or for the company to survive or for the team to be victorious. It's difficult to get excited about work when we feel like it doesn't even matter if we show up. And more than that, this dose of reality impacts performance. Feeling dispensable generates self-doubt, which contributes to low self-esteem. And when our doubt is high and our esteem is low, our effectiveness suffers. We literally find it difficult to perform well when we don't feel good about ourselves. Sometimes we find it difficult to perform at all.

Consider Lisa, a manager at a large financial firm. She does a great job of letting her people know that the world does not revolve around them. Her flippant attitude toward the people on her team is communicated through subtle and not-so-subtle messages. For instance, in meetings she notoriously fails to introduce anyone on her team who is not in her favor at the moment. She literally and blatantly skips over them. Her passive-aggressiveness recently killed off Mark in a meeting. When Mark, one of her up-and-coming people, questioned why she did not introduce him to the group, she impatiently responded, "So I forgot you, get over it." Shortly thereafter, Mark quit. He did not want to work for someone who could not care less if he showed up and seemed not to notice when he did. Lisa continues to churn and burn through people because she seems to go out of her way to deflate them. As a result, in the last year alone, Lisa's entire team has turned over *five times*. Managers like this give the rest of us the reputation for being complacent and mediocre. It won't be long before the world will stop revolving around Lisa, unless of course, her managers are also complacent and mediocre.

## Meeting the Need for Esteem

People are driven on a daily basis to meet their need for esteem. They want to feel admired, respected, valued, appreciated, and regarded. When managers act like Lisa, the flippant financial firm manager, people's esteem goes hungry. And when it goes hungry for too long, people will go elsewhere to feed it, as Mark did.

Mary Kay Ash, the founder of Mary Kay Cosmetics, is famous for conducting her business as if the world revolved around her people. She insisted that leaders "praise people to success." Her mantra was "Pretend that every single person you meet has a sign around his or her neck that says, 'Make me feel important.'" Mary Kay's people felt important and as a result they worked hard for her and for their clients, which enabled the business to grow exponentially. In 1963, its first year of business, sales were $198,154 and 46 years later in 2009, worldwide sales were estimated at $2.5 billion.

Like Mary Kay, Paul Levy, the CEO of Beth Israel Deaconess Medical Center in Boston, chose to make his people feel important. During the heart of the 2009 recession, Paul brought his biggest challenge directly to his 8,000 employees: what to do about the economic freefall threatening to impact jobs at the Center. Understandably, people were nervous at the company-wide meeting, mindful that a layoff loomed. Paul stepped to the podium to share his commitment to protect all of the jobs at the hospital. He acknowledged that to do so, everyone would have to make a bigger sacrifice in terms of salary and benefits. Paul then made an esteem-nourishing request – he asked the 8,000 people in the audience to help him get through this economic crisis without having to lay people off. He sought their problem-solving ideas, and in so doing, he communicated his high regard, respect, and appreciation for their resourceful abilities and their commitment to partner with him to solve this problem together.

Immediately following the all-hands meeting, people began e-mailing Paul with ideas. One floor voted unanimously to forgo a 3 percent raise. One finance associate suggested working one less day a week. A nurse said she was willing to give up vacation and sick time. Paul received about a hundred similar messages per hour following the meeting. He laid victory or defeat in their hands – he made the world revolve around them. Paul allowed the people to make a difference, appreciated their commitment to success, listened to their contributions, and genuinely welcomed every idea. He shifted the focus from excuses to solutions and encouraged a cage-rattling change in order to be victorious in the battle.

But he could have figured out all of this on his own. Isn't he the CEO? Instead, he reached out to the people on the front line for their ideas, and accomplished two critical things that were not possible in his own head: (1) he received innovative, fresh, hospital-saving ideas, and (2) he made the world revolve around his people, which fed their need to feel valued, increased their esteem, and lowered their self-doubt. That's how Paul triggered their moxie mindset, saved the hospital, and earned his title of "leader."

## Participatory Bias

Paul Levy also tapped another powerful behavioral influence by asking his employees to help him solve the hospital's financial problems: participatory bias. In essence, people support that which they help create. They own ideas when they generate them. By asking his colleagues to generate ideas to solve the hospital's problems, he gained immediate support for the ideas because they generated them. If they don't support the ideas that Paul implements, they are essentially rejecting their own ideas, which is equivalent to rejecting themselves.

The ability to participate is a strong influence on motivation. People tend to support those decisions they help to make, those teams they help to create, and those solutions they help to generate. Having participated in the creation, people will defend to the death the creation. Their ego is at stake and they don't want to be wrong. Helping to create something influences people to support the creation rather than oppose it and be wrong for even getting involved in the creation to begin with.

Dusko Dragojlovic, an engineering director at global defense and technology company Northrop Grumman, leveraged the power of participatory bias. Dusko was leading a team of more than 1,000 engineers and technicians when he was faced with high talent turnover that was threatening his competitive edge in his sector. Dusko appealed to his managers, sharing with them that this turnover was actually threatening the entire company. Instead of pointing fingers at management and dumping the problem on them, Dusko worked with his people to create project teams to explore this issue and generate ideas and solutions. Dusko turned to people and in doing so, influenced them to support the solutions they generated.

Participation has an enormous influence on human motivation. People want to feel like their participation is needed, which then helps them to feel valued. The simple act of allowing someone to participate in generating an idea or a solution increases that person's effectiveness and self-value, which then results in an increase in their motivation to help implement that solution. Your key as a leader is to provide people with the opportunity to understand, explore, and participate, even when we don't need them to.

Susan Docherty, the head of the U.S. Sales, Service, and Marketing team at General Motors, intentionally involves others in decisions, even when she already has an opinion and knows where she wants the decision to go. She relentlessly inquires of her people, "What do you think? What would you do?" She often is rewarded with a fresh perspective and new insights from people who are not as close to the situation as she is. More importantly, she is rewarded with their support for the direction she ultimately chooses.

We are the leaders. We have the answers. We know what needs to be done, but telling people what to do or how to do it can be extremely de-motivating. It reduces self-efficacy, defined as "competence." To be great at leading others, we need to help people grow and function without us (even though that approach flies in the face of our own center-of-the-universe delusion). To do that we need to stop telling people how to do it and let them propose solutions. We may know exactly what needs to be done, but why not let them do some thinking for us? Like Susan Docherty, we may get new ideas and fresh perspectives that were never in our purview. When we skip over people because we are convinced that they don't have the experience or wisdom that we do to make such a decision, we ignore the possibility that they might offer a better solution to the problem than the one we conceived. In not allowing people to participate we also risk creating a team of people who are dependent on us to think. We limit our ability to take on new leadership opportunities when we make the success of the department entirely dependent on our existence.

The managers at India-based information-technology powerhouse Infosys Technologies routinely create many opportunities to leverage the need to participate. Senior executives launched a program called "Voice of Youth," which gathers up-and-comers for a seat on the company's management council. These ambitious twentysomethings are expected to debate, discuss, and critique all aspects of the business with others on the council from all levels of management. By inviting their young employees, the leaders at Infosys are giving them an opportunity to participate, which fuels their need for esteem and ultimately their motivation to support and implement the decisions made by the management council.

The managers at BBVA, Spain's second-largest bank, regularly invite co-workers to participate in each other's biannual review. In an effort to weed out potential managers who are coercive rather than participatory, BBVA leaders heed the opinions of peer sentiment. Peers are asked to analyze their co-workers' habits by answering 35 – 64 open-ended and fill-in questions. By allowing peers to participate, BBVA leaders are ensuring that its leaders and future leaders pass the test of being participatory all year long, not just at the biannual review.

## Illusion of Control

Think about the last time any person was 100 percent in control of their careers. It was during their hiring process. We wined and dined them. Most certainly we engaged in conversations with them about their career path and how we would be committed to helping them meet their career goals. We showed interest in them. Other people at the company showed interest. We likely introduced them to our boss and other colleagues, who gushed about all the benefits of working at the company. Then an HR professional made them an offer of employment accompanied by some final pitch about how they would have the opportunity to fulfill all of their career aspirations as part of the company. This individual skipped with glee, giddy with excitement, hope, and adulation, "They want me! They really want me!" The individual exclaims "yes!" only to quickly discover that that moment was the last time in which they were 100 percent in control of their career. Before the ink on their acceptance letter is dry, they have been shuffled off to join a group of people dubbed "employees," and the control they had during the hiring process to say "yes" or "no" has instantly vanished into the ether.

The illusion of control bias is the tendency for people to believe that we can control or at least influence outcomes that we clearly cannot. Essentially, when people feel in control of their work they are more productive and more effective. This psychological force is at play on our motivations even when we are not in control. We want to be in control or at least *feel* like we are.

According to a behavioral science study, happy people have a sense of personal control – the belief (the illusion!) that they determine their own destiny. This sense of personal control is not limited to the hours after work. Its greatest impact results from feeling this control at the office as well. So people are happy at work when they believe they determine their own destinies. What stands in the way of people determining their own destinies? When someone else determines it for them. The term "micromanagement" gets thrown at the boss when people feel like the boss is controlling their ability to make decisions and execute. The dead people we see every day walking the halls are those who feel no sense of personal control.

And being in control is just another way that people manifest their need to feel valued.

The illusion of control phenomenon explains why, according to the Kauffman Center for Entrepreneurial Leadership in Kansas City, Missouri, 437,000 people created new businesses *each month* over the ten-year period from 1995-2005. That number does not even include self-employed consultants or other sole proprietorships. People who work for themselves work harder and longer than most employees, but they have an illusion of control over their work. As a result, solo entrepreneurs for the most part feel exulted, invigorated, and ignited in spite of the long hours and stressful work.

Unaware of the power of this influence on all humans, mediocre managers give people very little control to implement and execute. They structure their day-to-day interactions to ensure that people are on a very short leash, lest they think for themselves and make decisions. People could make a mistake and the entire department might melt. Mediocre managers exercise control over these people by implementing and enforcing a variety of close supervision mechanisms such as standard operating procedures, corporate policies, exhaustive role definitions, and annual performance reviews. All in the effort to keep employees in line, but ignoring the fact that those employees are people who are famished to control (or at least *feel* like they control) the way they contribute.

Google attempted this once too. In its early days, as the company was growing up, it tried to establish a supervisory structure typical in traditional software companies. It soon discovered that this structure was squelching the "I think I can" mindset and instead creating a "No, you cannot" bureaucracy. The excessive oversight was suffocating innovation, the very feature that gave Google its edge. Within a matter of weeks, the leaders ripped out the structure and replaced it with an anti-authoritarian team structure. Today, most Google employees work in small teams and the leader of the team rotates among team members. Most team members work on more than one team, and no one needs permission from the HR department to switch teams. Google's philosophy – people should *commit* to things, not be assigned to them – fuels the desire people have to feel in control.

Even more extreme than Google is W.L. Gore, the chemical company famous for Gore-Tex, which prides itself on a complete lack of management layers and organizational charts, and very few titles and no bosses. Gore operates similarly to Whole Foods and Google, with small, self-managed teams. Each team has two common goals: make money and have fun. The leaders of these teams are grown organically out of associates who make disproportionate contributions to a team's success. Peers vote with their feet. If an associate demonstrates a capacity to execute and an excellence in building teams, then peers will follow. Through its support of this free structure, Gore leverages the human motivation to want to feel in control. It's merely an illusion of control when we realize that associates are reviewed by their peers (whose assessments determine compensation), but the illusion of control exerts great influence.

When I was recruited to be a senior associate at Fenwick & West, a Silicon Valley law firm, one of the key attractions was their free agent structure. At Fenwick, associates are not assigned to partners. Instead partners are required to approach associates with opportunities to work with them on a particular corporate transaction. As free agents, we literally had the power to say "yes" or "no" to that opportunity. I loved the control over my workload, the type of transactions I wanted to work on, and the partners with whom I worked. As associates, we clearly felt in control at Fenwick. In reality, however it was merely an illusion of control because at the end of the day, in order to justify our job and make our bonus, we needed to bill a certain amount of hours each year. And we were ostensibly striving for partnership, which required the partners' approval, so we were motivated to please them. As a result, we said "yes" more often than we said "no." However, the important aspect with this structure is that we felt like we had the freedom to turn down opportunities if we were buried or if we didn't want to work with a certain partner, and we justly felt like the partners had to treat us with respect in order for us to do their work. As associates, we prided ourselves on the control we had, even if it was merely an illusion.

Jarden Home Brands, the niche consumer products company responsible for brands such as Diamond, Pine Mountain, and Ball, leverages the influence of illusion of control to attract people to join the company. Jarden allows people to define their own roles and build them from the ground up. This gives Jarden employees the opportunity to grow their own personal careers while helping the company to grow. With this approach, Jarden is putting the control over career development in the hands of the people who are most directly impacted by the consequences of those decisions. It's an illusion of control, however, in that Jarden will support the development of careers that support Jarden's overall battle cry. If someone were to define their career aspiration to become a circus clown, Jarden would certainly show them the door.

A career in sales is attractive because of the illusion of control. Even though the career comes with inevitable rejection, salespeople are in control of their own success. They can earn as much or as little as they want. That too is an illusion; they are often restricted by territory, product line, and margins, among other things.

## Delegating the Decision-Making Prerogative

The most powerful way to combine the influences of control and participation is to give someone the power to make a decision. If you allow me to make a decision, you are demonstrating respect, admiration, and appreciation for my opinion. I am now motivated to not only make a great decision to prove you right in your respect, admiration, and appreciation, but I am motivated to work hard to ensure success of that decision because my ego is on the line. I am empowered because you allowed me to control and participate in the decision. I will now go out of my way to support that decision and make sure it succeeds.

As we saw at the beginning of the chapter, Whole Foods allows people to make decisions selecting products for the shelves and people for their teams. As a result, people are more willing to promote the sale of those products and support the success of their new team members. It's a brilliant use of two powerful motivators.

The leaders at Zappos also get it. The online retailer prides itself on outstanding customer service. To that end, Zappos operators are encouraged to make decisions on their own that drive the company's commitment to create a personal emotional connection with the customer. They refer to it as "P-E-C."

Zappos' famed customer service is the result of a customer call center where the people are motivated to fulfill the company's commitment to "wow" the customer. This motivation stems from their leader's philosophy. Zappos CEO Tony Hsieh has a happiness theory that could easily be dubbed a moxie theory. It involves creating a balance among four needs: perceived progress, perceived control, relatedness, and connection to a larger vision. People at Zappos work hard, control how they contribute, create relatedness to each other and to their customers, and understand how they can make a difference in the fulfillment of Zappos' larger vision of wow-ing the customer. As a result of these four factors, Zappos people do extraordinary things for customers without being bribed, monitored, strong-armed, or threatened into doing the right thing for the company.

Unlike most call center operations, Zappos does not provide a script from which operators must read. In fact, Tony likes to draw attention to the lack of specific policies for dealing with each customer service situation. Because Zappos managers are committed to serving human beings instead of committed to a bunch of policies to keep those human beings in line, the call center operators use their own best judgment to provide customer service. Is it always the best possible judgment that the managers would have made in that situation? Perhaps not, but the one mediocre or even bad decision pales in comparison to the thousands of great decisions that that operator made on behalf of the company, most of which could never have been scripted. By delegating decision-making prerogative to people, Zappos managers reap the benefit of people motivated to succeed on behalf of the company.

During one of his speeches, Tony shared an example of the extraordinary things people do when we let them. A customer's husband died in a car accident shortly after she ordered boots for him from Zappos. She called to ask for help with the return, and the next day she received flowers from Zappos. The operator who had assisted the woman ordered the flowers without even checking with her supervisor. The widow was so surprised and impressed – and touched – that she told her family and friends at the funeral about her extraordinary experience. Proving once again, people just want to contribute and control the way they contribute.

Mediocre managers don't get this. Why? Because they are too busy feeding their own need for respect, admiration, and appreciation and they don't have the wherewithal to look beyond their own world-revolves-around-me delusion.

The freedom granted to the customer care team at Zappos would make the mediocre managers at other customer care teams recoil in horror. Contrast the customer care team at Zappos with that of a well-known Fortune 500 company that does not allow its customer care people to go off script for any reason. Any decision not covered by the script must be elevated to a supervisor for input. The failure to do so is grounds for termination. The customer care team is not empowered to make any decisions on behalf of the company. To ensure their strict adherence to these policies, their phone calls are monitored and audited weekly. Operators are regularly written up for attempting to make a decision that would help the company maintain a good relationship with one of its customers. This approach shows no respect, admiration, or appreciation for the people on the team to make a decision in the best interests of the company while serving the customer. Instead, the leaders of this customer care team are manically focused on maintaining all control.

The world of retail provides us another great example of how to de-motivate people by ignoring the illusion of control and the participatory biases. I walked into an Abercrombie & Fitch store and fell in love with a jacket, on a mannequin. Apparently everyone else loved it too, because there were none left on the hangers. I started to undress the mannequin, ready to hand over $130 for this great jacket when an associate came running over to inform me that the clothes on the mannequins were not for sale. She said that headquarters would not allow her to sell anything off of the mannequins even though the mannequins were promoting clothes no longer available in the store and even though I was ready to give them my money. The associate shrugged. She had no power to make a decision to contribute to the success of the store. She could only follow the strict instructions of her boss, who was nowhere to be seen.

Most retailers keep their store managers on a similar short leash. They tell their store managers exactly how to display merchandise in the windows and on the floor. From the style to the color to the size of each item, retail store managers and their people are required to follow literally every instruction communicated from headquarters. Even when the store associates and managers have some new ideas or insight into what is or is not selling in their location, those managers are not allowed to use that knowledge if it conflicts with instructions from the main office. Managers in headquarters control people because they don't trust that they will make a good decision. They are more committed to every single store operating exactly the same than they are in leveraging the insights and wisdom of the people who are making those stores run.

The leaders at Bed Bath & Beyond (BBB) take a different approach. They are an example of influencing people by granting them with decision-making prerogative. BBB store managers are called "Merchants" and the store clerks are called "Associates." Each Merchant is given a broad structure for the store, for example, bedding goes in the back of the store and kitchen supplies go in the front. After that, it is up to the Merchants and their Associates to determine how to best display merchandise based on their ideas, insights into their customers, their expertise, and their experience. The Merchants and Associates are invited to make the decisions that will contribute to the store's success, and then they are held accountable for the success of those decisions as measured by the success of their store.

The structure at BBB leverages the illusion of control and participatory biases. The BBB Merchants get to participate in the success of their store and *feel* like they are in control, even if it is just an illusion because ultimately the managers at headquarters can trump them at any time. It works beautifully. Because those Merchants are allowed to participate in decisions about product positioning and display, they work hard to ensure those decisions are successful ones. The Merchants and Associates feel like they make a difference with their work, which feeds their need to feel valued and respected for those decisions. As a result, the Merchants and Associates are motivated to succeed, which allows BBB stores to boast a profit higher than most retail stores in their category.

## The Self-Delusion Bias

The underlying bias that is influencing the illusion of control and participatory biases is the self-delusion bias. Studies show that when people feel good about themselves, they tend to achieve more. Accordingly, as a leader of people you will be best served by feeding the self-delusion in others, and as a contributor to other leaders, you need to recognize where your own starving self-delusion is getting in the way of your success and theirs.

Again, the secret is to realize that every person who crosses your path every day thinks it's all about them. Spend one hour observing strangers in a public place and for each person you see, say, "She thinks it's all about her." "He thinks it's all about him." The reality of it is staggering.

It's obvious why there is so much conflict in the world. We all think it's about us. When one person puffs his chest out a bit bigger than us and says, "No really, it's my rule, my property, my reign, my decision, it's all about me," we get annoyed, frustrated, and angry. *Don't they realize that it's not about them, and that it's really all about me!? Well, I'll show them it's about me and not about them. I'll create a policy that will force them to obey me first. I'll have him fired and show him who is stronger. I'll start a hostile takeover and demonstrate who really has more power. I'll build a bigger army and then they'll know that it's all about me.*

Suddenly, new policies are born, bad decisions are made, and wars are started.

The key to succeeding as a middle leader, however, is to stop and realize that it's human nature for everyone else to act this way. Everyone under the sun operates as if the world revolves around them because – ready for this? – it does. Who are we to burst their bubble? When our natural instinct is to be flabbergasted that someone could do the things they do or say the things they say, it's better to pause and remember, "Oh, yeah, they think it's all about them." It will give us an ounce more patience to deal with whatever insane thing that person just did or said. When someone is making it all about them, stop and consider that perhaps we forgot to make it about them and they are just trying to feed their own need for esteem.

When I first graduated from law school, I joined the tax department at Coopers & Lybrand (now PricewaterhouseCoopers), one of the big accounting firms in San Jose, California. The leaders at Coopers had decided to hire a team of six associates fresh out of law school, and I was one of them. They informally nicknamed us "The Dream Team." We were brought in to do research and analysis of tax laws and to raise the caliber of tax advice that partners could offer their clients. Secretly, we loved being called "The Dream Team," although we never verbalized it. We got paid more. We got treated differently. We felt special. As a result, we worked hard to fill the big shoes required by the title "Dream Team." We executed above and beyond expectations. That's what people on a Dream Team do.

One problem. The leaders forgot about the impact on everyone else who had been slaving away at the firm long before The Dream Team came along. The morale at the firm was already in dire straits. The addition of The Dream Team only made matters worse. The chasm grew wider as feelings of resentment hung in the air. The partners forgot to feed the need that all non-Dream Team people had to feel valued, respected, and appreciated – the need for esteem. Within a few years The Dream Team was disbanded but not before causing additional damage to office morale.

This is the biggest obstacle to internal "High Potential" programs proffered by Leadership & Development teams in corporations. Suppose I feel like I am working as hard as the woman next to me, and yet she is handpicked to participate in the company's special high potential program while I am not. What does that say about me? Managers in charge of the high potentials will argue that it doesn't mean anything about me; instead it just means that the other woman's performance shows more potential. Regardless, the impact on my self-esteem is costly as I realize (or perceive) that the company clearly does not see potential in me. The managers do not recognize, appreciate, or value my contributions.

To prevent this situation, many companies treat their high potential programs like a secret society of Skull & Cross Bones, refusing to publicize what the program is, what it means to the careers of people who are in it (and what it means to those who are not), and what exactly happens in the high potential program. Other companies are beginning to realize the wider impact of this elusiveness. They have changed the name of their high potential programs to "High-Ready Leaders Program" or "Ready-Now Leaders Program" to clarify that people selected for this program are ready to take on new levels of leadership immediately and are being trained to do just that. They are hoping the new name will communicate that others will have the chance to participate when they are ready as well.

But the problem with this entire dance goes well beyond its name. Through the ongoing promotion of these programs, there is an unspoken message that not everyone in the company has high potential. Furthermore, managers are declaring to people that they are only going to invest in the development of people who have recognizable high potential. The others can fend for themselves.

What a missed opportunity. Like moxie, everyone has high potential. As Dr. Quirk says about children's self-esteem, there's nothing to develop, but individuals and their managers simply need to get out of the way of suffocating that potential. High potential programs and "Dream Teams" not only get in the way, but make loud declarations that accelerate the bursting of the self-delusion bubble that would otherwise allow people to tap into their own potential. And at the end of the day, do you wonder why a manager would hire someone who does not have potential?

## When Esteem Goes Hungry

When people do not get their need for esteem met externally, they must generate it internally. When they are unable to generate their esteem internally, it's called a lack of self-esteem. Without self-esteem, confidence plummets, causing their productivity, performance, and effectiveness to suffer negatively. To combat plummeting confidence and rising self-doubt, people will go out of their way to make it about them.

We see people make it about them when they create rules and policies – written and unwritten – and make themselves the gatekeeper of that rule or policy. This allows them to feel in some way that it's about them. It results in "No, I cannot process this paperwork. It has not been completed properly. It needs another signature. That's the policy and I'm in charge of that policy." "No, you cannot enter here." "No, that ticket won't work." "I'm the only who can approve that." "Why? Because I said so." Suddenly we have bureaucracy and red tape clogging the flow and dampening bright spirits, all in the name of feeding someone's need for esteem.

When people discover that it's not about them, then they conclude logically that it must be about someone else. And when it's about someone else, their need for esteem goes hungry.

To feed their hungry esteem, they often sabotage, consciously and unconsciously, other people's efforts in the process in order to make it about them again.

Cynthia discovered the sabotaging impact of hungry esteem when she became a student teacher in Mrs. Jones's third grade class. Mrs. Jones had never worked with a student teacher in her class before and was unprepared psychologically and emotionally for the change. Predictably her esteem suffered a blow when Cynthia took over the class as the apprentice teacher.

Third graders are always infatuated with their teacher. Mrs. Jones's students were no different. Mrs. Jones's students fed her esteem daily. She was the star of the class, the center of these kids' universe. She was the reason they loved school. She was the reason they progressed. On a daily basis she made a difference to these kids, and they valued, respected, and appreciated her with their exuberance for school, their passion for answering questions, their test scores, their smiles, their outpouring of love and affection for her. Their world literally revolved around Mrs. Jones. And in Mrs. Jones's mind, no one could impact these kids like she could.

Until Cynthia came along.

The kids took to Cynthia instantly. They adored her humor, her great smile, and her warm personality. They learned from Cynthia in new ways. They showered Cynthia with appreciation and affection in ways not dissimilar to how they appreciated and adored Mrs. Jones.

Mrs. Jones sat in the back of the room day after day realizing that the world no longer revolved around her. Her students did not need her to learn or love school. And because she was not getting the immediate reward from her students that she got in the front of the classroom, she did not feel respected, valued, and appreciated for her work as their teacher. In fact, she was forced to battle her own feelings of irrelevancy and uselessness. Mrs. Jones had never shared her classroom before, so she had no experience in generating her own esteem. But without the requisite self-esteem, Mrs. Jones's confidence as an effective teacher began to waver. Cynthia at the front of Mrs. Jones' classroom was like a big neon sign reminding Mrs. Jones that it was not all about her and that her students could thrive without her. Someone else could do just as good a job as Mrs. Jones.

Mrs. Jones' bursting self-delusion caused her to sabotage Cynthia's success as a student teacher. Hungry for confirmation that she mattered, Mrs. Jones began to make it all about herself to prove that she mattered, much to Cynthia's chagrin. She did this in order to confirm that she Mrs. Jones was still needed and that the classroom's success did indeed revolve around Mrs. Jones. Mrs. Jones stopped supporting Cynthia.

In addition to her sabotaging success, Mrs. Jones began to perceive Cynthia's actions as unappreciative and disrespectful. Not because they were, but because Mrs. Jones's feelings of irrelevancy and uselessness caused her to defend her territory and in doing so to filter Cynthia's words, behaviors, and actions as offensive. Mrs. Jones began to question Cynthia's teaching, her methodology, her lesson plans, and her effectiveness. On a daily basis, Mrs. Jones would come up to the front of the classroom and hijack the lesson from Cynthia, embarrassing Cynthia and confusing her students.

Cynthia's esteem was a different story. Instead of taking any of this personally, she realized that the sabotaging was merely a manifestation of Mrs. Jones's suffering. Cynthia stepped back from the situation and into Mrs. Jones's shoes to understand her experience. Once Cynthia realized that Mrs. Jones was feeling irrelevant and unappreciated, Cynthia was determined to help feed her need for esteem. She began referring to Mrs. Jones's work with the students, including Mrs. Jones periodically in the class discussion, and asking Mrs. Jones to participate in various activities with the students. In their after-school debriefs, Cynthia acknowledged Mrs. Jones' great work with the students using specific examples. Each day she highlighted different students, commenting on how much progress they had made and acknowledging the impact that Mrs. Jones had had on that progress before Cynthia came along. The new teacher genuinely demonstrated respect, value, and appreciation for Mrs. Jones. These efforts did not go without results. After a few weeks of Cynthia helping Mrs. Jones to feed her need for esteem, Mrs. Jones began to feed her own esteem. Before long, Mrs. Jones was supporting Cynthia's success once again.

Educational institutions do not have a monopoly on starving esteem. The abundance of unnecessary bureaucracy found in corporate America can also be seen through the prism of this esteem starvation.

## Let Them Think It's All About Them

As middle leaders, it is vital to people's success that we make it all about them. There are many ways to do that. Let's look at a few easy ways to do this immediately: eliminate multi-tasking, remember names, ask the Second Question, stop calling them "employees," and draft communications from their perspective.

**Eliminate Multi-Tasking.** I recently observed a manager who sat behind her desk whenever she held a meeting with someone on her team. During the meeting she would be distracted by each e-mail that popped up on her computer screen. In addition, each time her phone rang, she excused herself to take the call. She was clearly plagued with the world-revolves-around-me mentality. Not surprisingly, people were left feeling like everyone and everything else was more important than they were.

This manager defended herself saying that the matters she was working on were critical to her business. She had to answer the calls and e-mails immediately. We demonstrated for her that through her actions she was deflating confidence where she needed it most – with people. Finally she acquiesced and tried it our way. Each time she had a meeting, she turned off her phone, walked out from behind her desk, and sat next to the person. Two things happened. First her actions demonstrated her focus on the other person, making them feel respected, valued, and appreciated, thereby fueling their need for esteem, which boosted their self-delusion and self-confidence. Second, without distractions, she became more engaged in the conversations and with the people she worked with. A simple change of scenery made a world of difference.

**Remember Names.** People love the sound of their own name. When we use their name, we instantly demonstrate to people how we respect, value, and appreciate them. And when we not only use their name but remember it the first time, we make it about them. Just when they start to feel a bit like they are blending into the crowd, perhaps their esteem is beginning to flat-line, we arrive and remember their name. Bam! We've just made it about them by the simple act of remembering their name.

Reuben Mark, former CEO of Colgate-Palmolive, knew the importance of using people's names to connect with them. He once attempted to get all 35,000 Colgate employees to wear identification tags with their first names in large type to allow people to use and remember each others' names. Reuben knew it would make it easier for managers to connect with people. This was just one of the many ways that Reuben intentionally used actions to influence people's experience at work. Sure enough, Reuben was ranked 15 on the CNBC Portfolio's Best American CEOs of All Time.

As Reuben Mark appreciated, remembering names without some memory aids can be challenging. While identification tags and name tags are great in the moment, the way to remember them without that crutch is to attach a story to the name. Recall from Chapter 3 that our brains process meaning before detail, so give the name a meaning and you will easily remember the detail. Stories are our secret weapon because they paint a picture that makes the information memorable. So, adding a story to the name will increase our memory's success. For example, I met a man who has gray hair and loves to cycle and whose name is Chuck. My grandfather's name was Chuck, he loved to cycle, and he had whitish-gray hair. Because I have made that association for my brain, I always think of my grandfather when I see Chuck and I have never forgotten his name.

**Ask the Second Question.** My good friend Cherryll Sevvy introduced me to her theory of the "Second Question." Most people ask one question and then hijack the conversation with their own story, similar experience, or commentary. For instance, typical people may ask the standard first question, "What do you do?" When they hear the answer, they instantly jump in with, "That's interesting. I have a friend who does that." Or "I used to do that." Or some comment like, "I bet the market has not been good for you."

The self-confident, self-assured person does not need to entertain, impress, and be interesting. Instead they focus on being *interested* and connecting with the other person by staying interested in them. People who are committed to connecting always ask a Second Question, such as, "How did you get into that career?" or "What's a typical day like for you?" or "What is that experience like?" or "How does it feel to run that department?" or "What's it like to work with new clients?" My favorite Second Question is "What do you love about your job?" People love talking about themselves, and in the process I learn so much about them with this straightforward Second Question.

We stand out as managers when we ask people the Second Question. By the simple act of asking one more question, we are making it about them, even in just that conversation. People love talking about themselves and because we are asking them to talk about themselves, we are feeding their need to feel important. By inquiring genuinely into their experience, we are respecting, valuing, and appreciating who they are as individuals. The key, however, is to be sincere and interested, to listen intently to their responses, and then to follow up.

Rather than doing it as if we're checking something off the list, it's important to carve out a few minutes to ask people the Second Question, to really inquire about them. People can tell when we are insincere. A "How's it going?" as we pass people in the hall does not count as sincere curiosity. We need to demonstrate our curiosity by challenging ourselves to ask the Second Question, whether it's about a personal or professional matter. Most people do not take this extra step to connect, so doing this one thing will set you apart from managers everywhere.

Asking is one thing, but listening is another. We must force ourselves to slow down long enough to not only ask but to be interested in the answer. This requires us to pay attention without thinking about the next meeting or conference call. If we listen with a commitment to ask the Second Question, we'll compel ourselves to listen to the first answer.

Want to take this game to the next level? Remember something about the conversation. Commit to keeping notes about the people you interact with daily. Names and birthdays are entry level, but to remember something about the conversation and their answers to your Second Questions is a whole other game. Just by remembering something about the people we work with, we demonstrate our respect for them. What an easy way to stop making it about us for a moment and to feed their self-delusion and self-confidence.

Then we get bonus points for finding and sharing an article or a book based on something we discovered about people in our Second Question game. Imagine how valued they will feel when they receive an article referencing something we discussed. It's so easy to make it about other people in everyday conversations, and yet so easy for most managers to belittle the importance of it.

**Stop Calling Them Employees.** One manager kept referring to her team as "staff" until someone observed that "staff" sounds like a skin disease. Not inspiring at all. The word "employee" is sterile. It allows us to create an "us vs. them" scenario. It's "us" managers against "them" employees. Employees create problems, act entitled, and must be engaged, as if we need to change the batteries and flip the switch to turn them on. People, on the other hand, solve problems, earn and appreciate, and just need an opportunity to contribute. When we refer to someone as an "employee," we are not singling them out as a valuable, important individual. We are not recognizing their distinctions from all others. Instead, we are grouping them with a bunch of other second-class citizens. And in so doing, we don't make the world revolve around them. We make them just like everyone else, and no one wants to be just like everyone else.

ING Direct CEO Arkadi Kuhlmann never used the word "employee" when interviewed by a *New York Times* reporter for an article. He referred to the people who "serve with him" as "associates." And recall earlier in this chapter, we noticed that Bed Bath & Beyond refers to their folks as "Merchants" and "Associates," not store clerks.

Similarly Barnes & Noble calls everyone a "Bookseller," even the person in the storeroom. This title acknowledges the true contribution people make in doing their jobs. They aren't just stocking shelves or sweeping the floor; they are each contributing to the sale of books. The people who work behind the counter are not cashiers, they are booksellers. The people who stock the shelves are booksellers. The people who clean the floors are booksellers. They all participate in the store's success at selling books, and their titles reflect that. Even something as simple as giving people a title that acknowledges their impact and importance to the business fuels the self-delusion and feeds the need to participate and contribute.

Like Barnes & Noble, many leaders implement title changes in order to demonstrate respect and appreciation for a person's participation in and contribution to victory. For example, changing "Receptionist" to "Director of First Impressions" acknowledges that the person answering the phone is in charge of the first impression that a caller has of the company. Changing the title from "Assistant Manager" to "Director of People Success" acknowledges that the individual is responsible for others' success, not just assisting the manager of the store. It changes the focus for this person from "I'm just waiting in line to become manager" to "My role is to serve the people in the store and to support their success in whatever way I can." It elevates the importance of the role for this person, the manager, and for everyone in the store.

These distinctions generated by language alone break down the wall that separates "us" managers from "them" employees. It acknowledges that we work with people who contribute and solve problems instead of creatures called "employees" who need things and create problems. This is a simple way to express our respect, value, and appreciation for people's contribution to the battle and impact in the victory.

**Craft Communications from Their Perspective.** Even our memos reek of an "It's-not-about-you-people-it's-all-about-us-leaders" attitude. We draft messages in ways that make it all about the good of the company or the customers. What we fail to do, however, is draft it from the viewpoint of the people reading those memos. Why should they give a damn? What does that notice mean to them personally, not abstractly? For example, one inattentive leader sent this e-mail to his people: "I need you all to update your sales forecasts in the database for me by the end of the day so I can get the information to my boss, who needs it in the morning." Notice the difference you feel reading this same communication with a different message: "I am confident that each of you will astound even yourselves this quarter with your success. I want to support you in your commitments to make a lot of money. In order to do that, I need to work with our procurement department to ensure that we have enough products on hand to meet your needs. Please update your sales forecasts in the database by the end of the day so I can get our projected product requests in to procurement before any other team in the company." Remember, people just want to know why (the battle cry) and how they fit into that why (the self-delusion).

As managers with moxie, we are no different than the people we work with. We too rely on the world-revolves-around-me self-delusion, but we must check ours at the door if we want to influence the intrinsic motivation of others. To them we must revolve the world around them.

## Spark Self-Delusion; Avoid Self-Deflation

In the office, in the family room, in the supermarket, our best strategy for winning with people is to spark their self-delusion and avoid their self-deflation. We spark self-delusion when we make it about someone else. We avoid self-deflation by *not* focusing on what's wrong with them and instead shift the focus to what's right about them.

PRIDE Industries, the largest employer of people with disabilities in the United States, cannot afford to focus on someone's disabilities. They're a not-for-profit manufacturing fulfillment house with a battle cry to create opportunities for people with disabilities. About two-thirds of the people who work at PRIDE have some disability. But the company is running a business. As such, the middle leaders have to focus on each person's *capabilities*. Of each person, they ask, "What can this person do?" and then they find a job for that person based on his or her capabilities. Can you imagine what your company, let alone corporate America, would look like if we approached each person as a walking capability rather than mark each person with a flaw, weakness, or area that requires improvement?

Every person wants the spotlight on them, but only to draw attention to their good parts. We want to believe that not only is it really all about us but that we've done a marvelous job of covering up any imperfections and allowing our assets to shine through. Logically, the most efficient way to kindle this self-delusion in others is to turn up that spotlight on those positive features. And the fastest way to kill that self-delusion is to direct that spotlight on those imperfections. In an instant, self-delusion will be replaced by self-deflation.

Parenting coaches advocate for catching kids doing something right instead of constantly looking for ways that they've screwed up. Applying this concept to the people we work with is the fastest way to fuel their self-delusion. Catch people doing something right instead of what every mediocre manager does – catch them doing something wrong.

When people are self-deluded to think that it is all about them and that they really are that great, their ego inflates and their self-confidence soars. They may even think, "It's about time someone noticed!" By spotlighting their strong points, we are showing them respect, admiration, and appreciation for those strong points. We are validating their value. This feeds their need for esteem, which results in them wanting to let those good qualities stand out even more. This is how we can influence people to achieve more using what they already have.

I received a card from my Director of Operations and its impact continues to influence my behavior. It read, "Dear Ann, Just wanted to send you a quick note to let you know that you are the best person to work for EVER. Thank you for all of your support. I am excited to be back." (She had taken a few months off to complete a certification program.) Her note of recognition not only made my day, but it continues to influence my behavior going forward. I pause before sending an e-mail to her and I ask myself, "Is this how the 'best person to work for EVER' would handle this situation?" That is the power of the spotlight to fuel self-delusion and influence another's behavior.

## Self-Awareness Results in Self-Deflation

The fastest way to go from self-delusion to self-deflation is to move the spotlight from assets to liabilities. We know we have liabilities, weaknesses, imperfections, and flaws, but we think we are the only one who knows about them. When someone lets on that they know our secret, our self-delusion begins to deflate. Inevitably, we are concerned that this knowledge is the precursor to rejection – our greatest fear. And when we are not only reminded of our limitations but know that you know about them, we become especially self-aware of our limitations. This self-awareness results in self-doubt and pokes holes in our self-confidence, ultimately leading to self-deflation.

Self-awareness does not encourage us to work on our weaknesses – there's nothing motivational about working on our weaknesses. Working on weaknesses is deflating. Seventy-five percent of New Year's resolutions fail by January 3 because resolutions are classically about fixing something that's wrong with us, not working on something that's already right with us. But no one wakes up in the morning excited to fix things that are wrong them. Focusing on weaknesses just asphyxiates motivation, energy, and excitement.

Instead, self-awareness causes us to become insecure. It's hard enough to be productive and effective when we actually feel good about ourselves, let alone when we feel bad about ourselves. Therefore, we achieve less when we focus on our weaknesses. It's a vicious circle.

Mediocre managers are heavily committed to this fix-the-weakness approach. Every year they engage an assessment tool to clearly identify people's weaknesses. Then they help them create a plan to address those weaknesses throughout the year.

Yes, that's inspiring. Sign me up to drag myself in to work every day to a place that does not respect, value, and appreciate me and that reminds me on a daily basis that I am not as great as I thought. Wow, can't wait to get to the office to work on those weaknesses! That should be fun.

No wonder people hate Mondays. The whole recipe creates short-term relationships.

Worse than the mediocre, focus-them-on-their-weaknesses managers are those with their own unmet esteem needs. They insist on feeding their esteem and making themselves feel better by disparaging others. In describing different team members, they'll say, "She thinks she knows everything," or "He acts as if he is all that," or "That new kid on the block is a little too brazen."

Yes, that is horrible. We should not work with people who feel confident about themselves and their contributions. We need people on our team who have low self-esteem and rotten confidence so we are all on the same playing field. That will make the rest of us feel better about our own low self-esteem. Please get me a team of people who feel like losers, pronto!

Knowing what we do about the forces behind our motivations, the amount of office gossip that swirls in the halls should not be surprising. If people are harboring their own unmet esteem needs, what is the fastest way to feel better? Compare themselves to someone else whose life is more unbearable. Find the first drama-laden rumor, and they can breathe a sigh of relief that at least their life doesn't look like *that*. Learn about a personal train wreck and smile and say, "See, they thought they were so great. They aren't. Serves them right for flaunting their success!" Or run home to watch a dose of reality television. Whew, that makes them feel better about themselves. At least their mediocre life isn't that bad after all. That thought alone generates a slight increase in their self-confidence ... but only temporarily.

## Don't Deflate Them

People are inherently negatively biased — they are already deflating themselves. Perhaps it dates back to the caveman days when people had to be thinking of the worst-case scenario in order to protect themselves. Wherever it started, the bias to the negative does not serve people anymore. The saber-toothed tiger is not waiting outside of Starbucks and it certainly is not waiting outside the office door. Arguably, being negative still protects people from other dangers, but it stunts their growth and ultimately their fulfillment at work.

Here's the reality. People already know what's wrong with them. They're clear about their limitations, drawbacks, and the areas in which they are not that proficient. Reminding them that they need to work on those limitations only gives power to the problem – it does not inspire them to be great and work harder. Let's stop deluding ourselves that people will fix these limitations or that they ever can be fixed, for that matter. Instead, your success rests in covert cognizance and realistic resourcefulness.

Be covertly cognizant – know your people really well by observation and by subtle inquiry. Just by paying attention we can identify the person who is disorganized, the person who is too focused on details and misses the big picture, the person who skips details altogether.

Next, discern whether the limitation is due to a lack of knowledge, skill, or ability, or whether the limitation is due to a lack of desire. Can the person learn the skill like a child learns to read, or is it a lack of desire like my own lack of desire to learn computer programming? The important distinction is what activity makes that person light up, even if they aren't that great at that activity yet, and what activity makes them recoil, even if they are really great at it? One person may exuberantly generate creative ideas and strategies for the launch of a new product but may procrastinate, grumble, and avoid the research necessary to follow up on those ideas. One person might really love to do research but they aren't that proficient at it yet. They need some new knowledge, training, experience, or simply practice. Another person might be really great at research but might loathe the thought of it. You need to know your people this well. And you do this by observing them and by asking them.

Mediocre managers become maniacal about assessing people, telling people what's wrong with them based on that assessment, and then how they expect those people to fix what's wrong during the coming year. My favorite mediocre manager story is about Eve, who actually wrote on a young man's performance improvement plan that to fix what's wrong with him he needs to engender Eve's trust. What the heck does that mean? Shame on Eve's manager, who allowed this plan to actually be delivered to the young man.

No wonder he changed roles at the company as soon as he could. Who wants to work with two mediocre managers, let alone one?

The bottom line is that you are the boss. You have the power to point out limitations, deficiencies, weaknesses, and flaws. You also have the power to force people to do what they don't want to do. You could make them do the research. You could obligate them take a class to learn a skill. But if forcing them to work on the limitation does not spark their self-delusion, you will only be aiding and abetting their self-deflation. Then rest assured you will not have this person on your team whether in body or spirit for very long.

Alternatively, if you identified through observation and inquiry the areas where a person wants to develop, then you will fuel their self-delusion when you help them create a plan to develop those areas. Because you paid attention to what areas that person wants to develop and you are helping them to do so, that person will feel like you are making the world revolve around them.

Anne Mulcahy, former CEO of Xerox, identified her successor when she formed a partnership with Senior Vice President Ursula Burns. That's all it took for Ursula to step to Anne's side for the challenge of helping Anne turn Xerox around. In Anne's words, Ursula helped Anne transform Xerox for a new era. Over those eight years, Anne developed and mentored Ursula to seamlessly and effectively assume the role of CEO of Xerox upon Anne's retirement. It has been touted as one of the least tumultuous power transfers in Xerox's history.

After your observation and inquiry and your identification of people's avoided limitations – the ones they don't want to develop, then you have a choice: ignore your observations and inquiries, or become realistically resourceful. You ignore them by forcing people to fix limitations they are not enthused to work on. Or you become realistically resourceful by supporting the development of the embraced limitations – those that they are excited to work on – and backfilling those avoided limitations by other assets on your team.

"You are my deficits," my friend Helen always says to me. I like to be in front of people and think strategically, whereas she likes to research and focus on details. My strong points are her weak points and vice versa, which is how we were drawn to work on a project together. We backfilled each other's avoided limitations. The people on your team can be each others' deficits as well, but they need you to help them identify, distinguish, and then move the puzzle pieces around to do the backfilling.

We can create a workaround for avoided limitations by finding another way to get what we need, not flagellating people until they do what we want them to do, even if they don't want to do it. For instance, imagine that Bob is horrible at spreadsheets and reports. His organizational skills leave a lot to be desired. Every time we assign him a report, he cringes, he procrastinates, and he delivers a product laden with errors and a week behind schedule. Let's end the pain. Assign the report to another team member who is excellent at spreadsheets and reports and is drawn to doing them.

Now if we determined through observation and inquiry that Bob liked to do reports but just needed some new skills to improve, then that would be helping him develop an embraced limitation. But Bob hates reports and is miserable doing them. This is his avoided limitation. Let it go and assign the work to someone else. If report-generating is the bulk of Bob's job responsibilities, then Bob is in the wrong job and we should end everyone's misery and reassign him to another role, either on the team or in the company.

## Helping People Feel Heard and Felt

Observation and inquiry are essential to sparking self-delusion. While observation is natural, it's the inquiry part that flummoxes most managers. There are two keys to inquiry – helping people feel heard and helping people feel felt. We will cover this in more depth in Chapter 6, but it's important to understand the concept because if we aren't good at listening, we jeopardize self-delusion.

We help people feel heard when we not just listen to the words that come out of their mouths, but we actually hear what they are saying. We understand their perspective, even if we don't agree with it.

We help people feel *felt* when we understand how they feel and then we communicate that understanding. Mark Goulston teaches this "help people feel heard and felt" technique in his fantastic book, *Just Listen.* Goulston says that people need to feel felt and the best way to do that is to step into their shoes and imagine what it must feel like to be them, and then to verbalize those feelings as you feel them. As an example, to a colleague who is mad as hell that his boss transferred a great client to another team, we could say, "I can only imagine how upset you must be to have worked so hard to build a relationship with that client only to have it reassigned." We are not apologizing nor are we taking responsibility. We are just helping that person feel felt.

Now let's put them together. Suppose someone shares with us that their report is late because the server went down and lost their information. We can help them feel *heard* when we say something like, "So the computer system hiccupped and destroyed your great work, which is why the report is delayed." We then help them feel *felt* when we acknowledge how they must be feeling as a result of what they just communicated. "I can only imagine how frustrating that was."

This is an extremely powerful tool. When we stop long enough to understand what people are communicating and then attempt to imagine how they are feeling based on what they communicated, we are making the entire world in that moment revolve around them. Fan those self-delusion flames!

This approach is especially helpful when we are met with a foul mood. When people harbor a foul mood, their self-delusion is at an all-time high. They *really* think it's all about them and they are nasty about it. Their expectations were not met, something did not go according to plan, and they think the world is conspiring against them. The best way to deal with their emotional inflexibility is to acknowledge their bad mood and recognize the space they are in. The worst thing we can do is to ignore them, berate them, or belittle them. To do this will move them quickly from angry self-delusion to pathetic self-deflation. Neither is ideal.

It takes practice and emotional resilience on our part not to be triggered by their tantrum. It's a natural instinct to initially be on the defensive, as if their tantrum or foul mood is a personal affront, especially when we are operating in our own world-revolves-around-us mode. The key is to make it about them in order to help diffuse their impending outburst.

The widely popular book, *Happiest Toddler on the Block*, describes a process of mirroring a child's upset in order to diffuse it. This works equally well with adults. When a toddler has a temper tantrum, they want attention. They want to feel heard. Our best response is to demonstrate that we hear them. Here's how it works. Suppose three-year-old Cooper is mad. If his anger level is at an 8, then we want to mirror his feelings but at a level or two below his. And because he's in a mini-meltdown, he needs us to articulate it for him. With level-6 anger, we say, "Cooper wants that ball right now!" Cooper stops and looks at us. We got his attention. We repeat and continue, "Cooper wants that ball right now, but Cooper can't have the ball right now." As we continue we begin decreasing our own level of anger and start slowing our pace, saying, "That must be frustrating. Cooper can have the ball when Hunter is done playing with it." This works to calm Cooper down (and save his brother Hunter from getting punched in the face).

This same technique works on adults to help us create the "Happiest Person at the Company." If Sara is on our team and she calls us upset and yelling, we need to mirror her feelings back to her. First, pause and remember that her upset has nothing to do with us. She wants to be heard and she doesn't feel heard. She wants the world to revolve around her and it's not, and she's mad about that. We can help her feel heard by mirroring her feelings. "You want to attend that workshop but once again it has been postponed. You must be so exasperated!" Then keep it all about Sara but move her to a more productive conversation. For example, "What can you do instead? What's the next step?"

On the one hand, it's maddening to think we have to deal with temper tantrums at home and at work. But the need to feel heard is ageless and timeless. Emotional resilience challenges everyone, from babies to adults. We can fight it or we can help people move through it quicker – and then focus on something more productive.

The key to being an extraordinary manager (and human being) is to not get triggered. It would be so easy to get annoyed by Cooper and irritated by Sara. But that would just be making it all about us again. In the midst of their tantrums, people have no interest in how we think the world revolves around us. At that moment, it is revolving around them. If we start making it about us, we just cause them to dig in their heels even deeper. We need to put our ego aside and remember that their rants have nothing to do with us; they have everything to do with the fact that they are not being heard or not feeling felt. And, as great managers, we can do something about that simply by getting our ego out of the way and showing compassion.

Imagine how much better it would be to walk the planet if we showed this same compassion for the people who crossed our paths each day. Our emotional resilience would ensure that we don't take personally other people's foul moods. We would remember that rudeness and road rage have nothing to do with us. They are manifestations of angry self-delusion. They are instances of people just acting out their own lack of feeling heard and felt.

## Putting It Into Action

- Create a task force to help you solve a problem.

- Practice asking people for their opinion and feedback on decisions, even when you know the answer or have made a decision.

- Invite people to participate in finding a solution or creating a new idea.

- Intentionally put away your cell phone when you enter a meeting instead of leaving it on the table buzzing with messages.

- Make a point to remember people's names and important information about them. Ask about their lives each week.

- Practice asking the Second Question in all of your conversations personally and professionally. Notice how drawn people are to you when you act interested instead of interesting.

- Check your e-mails and memos to determine if they all about you or all about other people.

# Chapter 5

## Pause for the Applause

. . . . . . . . . . . . . . . . . .

It was a gorgeous spring day and I was cheering for Jack, my 11-year-old stepson who had just learned to ride a bike. He was bravely rolling down steep hills at the park. I was cheering while tears ran down my face. He had found his balance and was riding a bike for the first time in his life. Carly, my precocious, fearless 8-year-old stepdaughter, was attacking the hills on her bike without hesitation. She learned to ride a bike the prior year.

After 20 minutes of whooping and hollering for Jack and his enormous accomplishment that day, Carly rode over to me and, without apology or embarrassment, requested, "Can I get some woo-hoos, please?"

We are all like Carly, starved for recognition. But before we scoff at this strategy and sweepingly characterize people as feeble and fragile in need of some therapy, let's understand the importance of recognition in our ability to influence people's motivation.

As we explored in the last chapter, people are constantly seeking to fulfill their need for feeling valued, respected, and appreciated. The latter too often gets ignored. And the simple act of recognition is the easiest way to help people meet this need. My stepdaughter just wanted to be recognized. She was afraid of being forgotten. The lack of esteem is as great a de-motivator as the presence of it is a motivator.

But why is their lack of feeling appreciated your problem? Because you are the conduit through which people will meet their various needs. And when people don't get their need for appreciation met, they will change their behavior in order to get the appreciation they need. For example, if we love Felicia's fresh perspective and the new ideas she shares in our weekly meeting but fail to acknowledge her contributions, she will eventually stop contributing. Without recognition and appreciation, people feel ignored, which is just another form of rejection. We all go to great lengths to avoid feeling ignored and being rejected.

Not only do we need to be appreciated and acknowledged but the fact that we need it at all comes with baggage. Asking for appreciation feels needy, vulnerable, even borderline pathetic. While we think it's cute that Carly wants woo-hoos, our fear of what others think of us stops us from asking for it ourselves. But deep down we wish we could be 8 again, and genuinely request, "Could I get a woo-hoo, please?"

## The Scarcity of Recognition

"We don't recognize people for doing their jobs," she heard the HR woman shrilly whine on the other end of the phone. Ella was speechless. Ella leads a team of salespeople and engineers at a Fortune 500 technology company. Chris, one of her technical assistants, recently worked an entire weekend during his vacation to ensure the successful launch of one of their client's systems. On Monday morning, Ella called HR to initiate the formal process of recognizing Chris with an *Above-and-Beyond* award for his extraordinary efforts.

The HR representative explained that Chris was a salaried employee not an hourly employee, and that "supporting clients in system launches" falls under his job description. "We don't recognize people for doing their jobs," she repeated.

Wow. When did thanking people for working hard require a policy manual? The real question we should be asking is when did HR forget that the "H" stands for "Human"? When nitwits like this are in charge of people, it's no wonder that appreciation is scarce.

Clearly this HR buffoon was suffering from a lack of feeling like the world was revolving around her, so she was making it "all about her" by pointing to the rules. But she was getting in the way of Ella's commitment to appreciate a team member. So Ella went around her and created her own *Above-and-Beyond* award to recognize Chris for his above-and-beyond efforts. Ella ensured that HR's absurdity did not deprive her of the opportunity to help Chris feel appreciated and to encourage him to continue to go above and beyond again and again. Ella wrote a check for $500 out of her personal bank account, knowing she was making an investment in Chris, not bearing an expense. In addition, she sent out e-mails to Ella's boss and her boss's boss recognizing Chris' unheard-of efforts, being sure to copy Chris and the HR nitwit.

When once asked by a reporter how many people worked at the Vatican, Pope John Paul XXIII (1881-1963) responded, "About half, I think." Aware of this legendary mockery looming over his people, the century's new pope, Pope Benedict XVI, ordered the first-ever bonuses to be issued to recognize those who do in fact work hard to keep the bells tolling.

The bottom line is that recognition triggers success and strengths in people. If it is so powerful, why aren't we leveraging it? In addition, if it is so easy, why aren't we doing it on a daily basis?

## Does Recognition Cause Complacency?

Let's explore the argument that praising people makes them complacent. There are two presuppositions underlying this concept. One, people should know when they are doing a good job, and two, telling people that they are doing a good job will only cause them to stop doing whatever it is they are doing because they already accomplished their goal — getting it right and getting paid for getting it right, perhaps even earning some bonus or other reward. To fully understand the holes in this argument, we need to dig deeper.

People are not working to make you happy or to please you. Their goal is not to do a good job or to finally figure out how to get a job done right. These are all accomplishments that can be checked off a list. At the core of all of these accomplishments is the ultimate objective: to avoid rejection. This is an ongoing quest that can never be checked off some list.

If you acknowledge and appreciate someone's behavior or action, they are clear that they are not being rejected. And logically, if that behavior or action helped them to successfully avoid rejection, then they know they can continue avoiding rejection by repeating that behavior or action.

If, on the other hand, their behavior or actions are met with your silence, then people are left to make up stories about that silence. If they make up a story that your silence is just another form of rejection, then they will equate their behavior or actions with causing that rejection. They will quickly change their behavior or actions to something that does not cause them to be rejected. Or they will keep their behavior but reject you for rejecting them.

Bart subscribes to the complacency theory. Instead of recognizing his people, he is silent when he approves and reprimands when he does not. How fun. A guessing game at work – does my boss's silence mean he likes me today or hates me? That's very productive, Bart.

Another leader admitted that he is a product of his own generation in which recognition was scarce from both his parents and his boss. His boss' theory was that if he doled out praise, people would get too confident. Yes, we certainly don't want a bunch of confident people on our team. A bunch of people who are dispirited and discouraged because they feel inept and fearful about their jobs is a much better foundation upon which to build a powerful team.

Think about it. Isn't it better to have to peel people off the ceiling rather than pick them up off the floor?

## More Anti-Recognition Theories

Arguably we are just too busy to spend time recognizing people. But that's a cop-out. Let's dig deeper to see what's really going on with our inability to dole out praise and recognition.

As we have seen numerous times already, every person – managers and employees included – is combating their biggest fear: rejection. And when we the managers are considering recognizing someone else for their contributions and accomplishments, this fear lingers like a gremlin on our shoulder. It doesn't magically disappear. It loiters and gnaws, "Does someone else's success mean our failure?"

We engage in a covert comparison whenever someone else accomplishes and succeeds – even someone who is on a lower pay grade than us. We compare our accomplishments and successes to theirs. We ruminate, "If that person did something great and we didn't, does that mean that we are not successful? Will their success cause others to reject *us* in favor of them? Perhaps if I don't acknowledge their success or progress, I won't draw attention to it and prompt others to reject me." Ahhh! The crazy mind games we play.

And when we are not feeling confident about ourselves and our own managers have not recognized or appreciated us lately (as a result of whatever crazy mind games they are busy playing), we are particularly susceptible to this fear of rejection. With our fear of rejection on overdrive, we quickly make scarce any recognition, appreciation, or acknowledgement.

Another argument against recognition is the one that gets thrown in response to the younger generation's request for woo-hoos: way too much coddling. By generalization, Millennials grew up getting blue ribbons just for showing up. Because preserving self-esteem was of the utmost importance, no one lost and everyone was a winner. Managers in the Gen X and Boomer generations consider this approach detrimental. "If only those Millennials tasted failure they would be more resilient," they share with me exasperatingly. "If only someone would put them in their place." But why is it better to have a bunch of people whose self-esteem has taken a beating before their 22nd birthday?

Managers argue that it's ridiculous and energy-consuming to constantly create a celebration for people just because their parents did. But let's put this in perspective. People are not asking for a party every time they show up or complete a project. They don't need a 21-gun salute for typing up the agenda just the way you wanted it. A simple acknowledgement that they did the work would suffice.

One VP of Compensation shared his concern that if we recognize people, they will demand more money for their work. How shortsighted. Once more, people don't need a dinner held in their honor for completing a report on time. They are so hungry for an ounce of gratitude that the last thing they are thinking is, "Oh, you like that? Then pay me more." People just need acknowledgement. That acknowledgement will feed their need for esteem and will stop the rejection gremlins from sending their neurons in a change-the-behavior-or-change-the-scenery flurry. As we explored previously, money becomes a factor only when people lack esteem –feeling valued, respected, and appreciated for their work. When people don't feel valued, respected, and appreciated for their work intrinsically and we as managers have done nothing to help influence those feelings, then yes, money does become the focus and a lack thereof becomes a de-motivator.

### Mood Congruity

Let's start with an understanding of how our brains work so we can see how recognition and appreciation impacts people neurologically. And then we'll see how easy it is for us to use recognition to help people alter their own performance.

Walking through San Francisco's financial district, I saw a woman who looked familiar. I stopped in my tracks racking my brain trying to figure out how I knew her. My mind was in overdrive searching the mental files for this woman's name or context. Where in my life had I met her before? Suddenly I got it. She looked just like my fifth grade teacher, Mrs. Trout.

This is the association game. I am associating what is in front of me with people and situations I have experienced in the past. If I make a mistake and start ruminating on it, my brain will scan the mental files searching for other mistakes I have made that look similar to this one. Let's say my proclivity for disorganization caused me to miss a deadline, which cost my firm a deal. If I chew over that one mistake, my brain will automatically start looking for memories of other instances in which my disorganization caused me to fail. I will suddenly remember the time I had to pay late fees on a credit card because I couldn't find the bill. And that memory will remind me of the time I stayed up all night to complete my tax return because I was so disorganized. And that will remind me of the time I pulled an all-nighter in college preparing for an accounting exam. The downward spiral will be in full throttle. I will be so focused on my shortcomings and failures that in that moment, I will reject myself into paralysis, unable to do anything right.

If the next day I learned that I had been hired to keynote a leadership conference, the association game will work in the opposite direction. That one success will quickly remind me of a myriad of other familiar successes, from my standing ovations to my overjoyed clients to my success as a corporate attorney to my top-of-the-class law school graduation. Suddenly, I can do no wrong. I am unstoppable.

What is going on with all these reminders and resemblances? Why do our brains work so hard to find familiar faces, places, foibles, and victories?

We are influenced by something called "mood congruity" in which a focus on a current failure or setback will trigger a recollection of our past failings, while a focus on a current success or victory will trigger a recollection of past successes and victories. Whether we walk through the day weighed down by our collection of failures or high on our collection of successes, will dictate how productive, effective, and even enthusiastic we are that day. Weighed down by failures, we become sluggish, dejected, ineffective, and pessimistic. Conversely, when we operate high on our collection of successes, everything seems easy. We're in the flow and we are on fire.

Ever our champion, the neurons in our brain automatically look for associations to arm us with information on how best to deal with a person, place, or experience in front of us at that moment based on what worked or didn't work for us in the past with a similar person, place, or experience. Arming us with this information helps us survive from moment to moment without having to process everything that crosses our path as if it is completely new. Our brain is connecting the current event to past events that seem similar and informing us immediately what emotional response to have.

Neurons are similarly triggered by our thoughts. Positive thoughts trigger neurons to find past experiences of similar positive thoughts, which provide us knowledge of how to quickly process through whatever we are thinking about. Negative thoughts trigger neurons to find similar negative thoughts. In essence, our brain creates self-perpetuating cycles.

Triggering neurons is fun and even helpful when it's a familiar face or place. It's not so fun, however, when it impacts our outlook on the day, our work, or our life. The good news is that we each get to decide if the brain's habitual game of association should be our downward spiral or our morning juice. The great news is that as managers, we can heavily influence this game.

## Triggering Their Neurons

Obviously the champion brain is a far more powerful place from which to operate than the browbeaten brain. As leaders, we have the power to trigger the neurons in our favor but we also risk triggering them to work against us.

It's easy to trigger the neurons against us. Simply ignore the power of appreciation and watch as you wreak havoc on people's endurance. When you focus only on the final result without applauding intermittently, you jeopardize sustainability. At a marathon, bystanders don't withhold their applause until runners cross the finish line; they applaud all along the route. The same must hold true at work. People cannot sustain momentum without being appreciated and recognized along the way. Let's explore the basis for this to fully grasp the importance of appreciation and recognition in your arsenal.

## Fear—the Foundational Need for Appreciation

People are hardwired to hold themselves back. While it's easy to blame a lack of willpower or even laziness, it's actually fear that causes people to sabotage success. People fear failure, success, the unknown, and even the known. And at the center of all those fears lies the fear of rejection. As a result, most of what people do is not generated out of a desire to gain approval but out of a need to avoid rejection. Left to their own assessment and evaluation, people will sabotage their success by relying on their brain's ability to play the association game. Without any outside influence on that association game from you, they must rely on past experiences to help them determine how best to avoid rejection.

A lack of recognition, feedback on progress, or appreciation will trigger the neurons to find past instances in which they similarly experienced a communication or recognition scarcity. Before long people are fixating on the complete lack of recognition they have endured over the years. If they associate "feeling rejected" with that lack of recognition in the past, then they'll make the same association today and feel rejected as a result of your lack of recognition. And when people feel rejected, they change something immediately to stop feeling rejected. They'll either change their behavior or change their scenery, neither of which is desirable to you.

As the manager, why would you want to gamble someone's success on their neurons and their prior experiences with other managers? That's the chance we take when we fail to recognize, appreciate, and acknowledge people's progress and contributions. We force them to reference past experiences to determine if your lack of communication is equivalent to rejection. It's so easy to convince those neurons to work in your favor that not doing so is just unnecessary risk and a missed opportunity, breeding grounds for mediocrity. Be cautious, however, not to confuse recognition with a once-a-year performance evaluation, which is merely perfunctory and has zero impact on behavior, let alone neurons.

## Intentionally Recognizing Others

Whenever you find yourself editing an acknowledgment or shortchanging some form of recognition, send up the red flag. It's just rejection gremlins influencing your decision to recognize others. Make that the opportunity to intentionally recognize, to go out of your way to do just that. Because of underlying fears, a show of recognition often feels uncomfortable, even vulnerable. But you are committed to rebuff mediocrity, so you need to face the discomfort and recognize anyway.

For painless practice, recognize people outside of work and start with acknowledging people you will never see again. I once recognized a train conductor, "Your personality commands respect. Thanks for making the ride so enjoyable." She beamed. I moved on. So easy and yet so impactful. I thank wait staff for going out of their way to steer me clear of mediocre items on the menu. I share my appreciation for people who go out of their way to help me in stores, restaurants, gas stations, even the YMCA. I clap after each fabulous spin class or aerobics class. I want the instructor to know what a great job she did. I'm amazed at how people rarely do this. Pay attention to people who do their jobs with enthusiasm and passion – and then say something. That's it. You don't need to pay them more for the burger and fries or the gallon of gas. You don't need to give them a job. You don't need to do anything more for them. It will make an enormous difference to their neurons just to have you verbally notice their efforts. That's how you stand out in a crowd. That's how you stand out as a leader in the middle.

Planet Sushi is a great Japanese restaurant in New York City, and every time a guest walks in, every staff member turns toward the door, acknowledges the new guest, and hollers in unison, "Konnichiwa!" which means "Hello!" in Japanese. They are welcoming people to their work and their enthusiasm is sincere.

My stepkids greet me similarly. If I haven't seen them in a few weeks, they welcome me with a running hug. Wouldn't it be great to be greeted like that at work every day? A welcoming holler from your colleagues and a running hug from your boss – simple acknowledgements that everything is brighter now that you're here.

Because we instinctually stifle comments of recognition, it will take cognition and intention to stop stifling and start recognizing. One way is to create easy structures for recognizing individual and group wins – big and small. The team at COACT in Toledo, Ohio, gathers at 8:00 every morning for 15 minutes to hear about each other's successes from the day before. Whether it was a meeting scheduled for a client, progress made on research, or follow-up calls completed, this routine allows people to receive public acknowledgement of their efforts and their successes.

At the dinner table with my stepkids, we created a routine to recognize each person's accomplishments of the day. Instead of asking, "How was school today?" and hearing for the umpteenth time, "Fine," we ask them, "What are three great things that you made happen today?" We quickly discovered that this question generates far more revealing and interesting answers. And everyone sits taller, proudly announcing their accomplishments in a public forum, as we cheer and woo-hoo.

## The Basics on Recognizing and Appreciating People

Recognition is an intentional show of respect and appreciation for another's skills and abilities. By acknowledging someone's work, by recognizing their impact, by thanking them for an accomplishment, we can easily trigger the neurons and feed the need for esteem.

We help people trigger neurons to identify success associations with applause. Applauding alone will not make everything wrong turn right, nor can we just applaud our way through problems. But since we know how the brain works, let's make it work in our favor. Activating the success associations in people's brains is one of our secret weapons. People will be far more effective when they work from an "I-can-do-nothing-wrong" standpoint than an "I-can-do-nothing-right" standpoint.

There are many ways to applaud the successes of people, and each of these will in turn teach them to start applauding for themselves. In so doing, you will express appreciation for their contributions instead of highlighting their shortcomings. Here are a few ways to start the clapping:

**The Weekly Snapshot.** One way to recognize people is to require them to put their accomplishments in writing. At the end of every week, have each person on your team produce a one-page snapshot of the week, and call it something like "The Weekly Snapshot." It shows in a snapshot the progress they made that week and where they are going the next week. In the Snapshot, people should list (1) their achievements during the week, (2) the projects they are still working on, and (3) any questions they need answered to move forward or other issues that are becoming a roadblock. Not only are we kept apprised of what each person on our team is up to, but we don't even need to search for accomplishments and achievements to acknowledge – a week's worth are identified on paper for us. In addition, the simple act of writing down achievements will help people to trigger those neurons in their favor. Of course, we can do some acknowledging after reading the Snapshot to play backup support to those neurons. In all it will take two minutes to read a Snapshot and one minute to make a comment recognizing a certain accomplishment.

In addition to a structured recognition discovery tool, you will have in your possession evidence of progress and accomplishments for an entire year for each person on your team, thereby cutting in half your effort in completing their annual performance reviews. And if I were on your team, rest assured I would want you to know what I've been working on – I want to stand out from the crowd.

**Sing Their Praises to Others.** Another way you can recognize people and trigger their neurons simultaneously is to sing their praises to others at work. Doing so offers a double benefit – it makes them look good while making you look good at the same time. Ella used this strategy to recognize Chris for going above and beyond during his vacation in spite of the HR nitwit.

Similarly Lynn uses this strategy relentlessly. She is constantly sending e-mails to her boss and her boss's boss to recognize her team members' accomplishments. For example, Ed, one of Lynn's salesmen, forwarded an article to Lynn in which Ed's customer highlighted Ed's solution in their own monthly newsletter. In the article, they gushed about the impact that Ed's product has made on their business. Lynn immediately sent the article via e-mail to Lynn's boss and Lynn's boss's boss and copied Ed on the e-mail. Lynn gave kudos to Ed for the great work he did to grow the opportunity and the relationship with this customer over the past year. Lynn did not take credit or even partial credit, did not use the word "we," did not downplay Ed's accomplishment, and did not let her ego or own fear of rejection edit her acknowledgement. She put the spotlight entirely on Ed. In doing so, however, Lynn created her own unstated kudos for not only for being a great leader who recognizes others, but also for the fact that Ed, a stellar contributor to the company, is on Lynn's team. Lynn's impact on Ed's performance went without saying.

A Victory Log is a list of accomplishments that gets updated weekly or monthly. The inventory includes anything from personal wins like relationships to professional successes like getting a job or winning a new client. You can certainly encourage people to create a log, but you can elevate its importance and effect by inquiring about the log each week. Humble people wait to place big victories on their log, but you can change this. Ask them if they won an appointment that week, completed a report, got an answer, or moved some project forward. Those are all victories, small as they may be, and they belong on the Victory Log. When people reflect on the past year they will not give credence to "winning a client appointment" or "completing a project," so the victory is lost. However, when we look at the past week or even the past eight hours, those victories become worthy of acknowledgement and applause. The neurons begin working to find similar victories when we reflect not just on the year, but on the week and the day. That's how we help people generate their own applause and trigger their own neurons.

Pause for the Applause. Like the Victory Log, this strategy requires a little training, as people are not inclined to do it. Too often people modestly shun the spotlight when others offer a "Great job!" or "Thank you!" or "Congratulations!" Meekly, they'll dilute the applause with "It was nothing" or "I got lucky" or my favorite, "Just doing my job." In your quest to rid your team of mediocrity, your job is to draw attention to instances when people do this and then educate them on the impact on their own neurons when they downplay their accomplishments this way. Strongly request that they just say, "Thank you." Their neurons will automatically look for other applause and soon their feelings will match the acknowledgements.

A WIN file is a file specifically dedicated to collecting acknowledgements and recognition. Have everyone on your team create a WIN file to amass thank you and congratulation cards and e-mails, certificates, pictures of accomplishments, letters of recognition, and their Victory Log. Anything that will remind them of their wins should go into their file. Encourage people to open the WIN for a juice boost. Listening to the exploding applause will make their neurons go crazy.

**Decorate with Applause.** Every office and every cubicle at the Barnes & Noble headquarters is stacked with books. They have no trouble remembering not only what business they are in but the books they have helped to bring to the public. Similarly, every office and every cubicle at the Toys 'R Us headquarters is stacked with toys. They too have no trouble remembering what they do for a living and what toys they have worked on to bring to life.

Take it one step further. Encourage people to decorate their work space with reminders of their successes, such as certificates of accomplishment, thank you letters from clients, awards, pictures of family and vacations, trophies, etc. My office has a framed picture of the largest check I have ever received from a client, which is right next to the picture of me skydiving, the picture of me riding my bike down the coast of California, and pictures of me with different family members. It may seem narcissistic, but it helps me walk into a celebratory environment every day, instead of sterile office stacked with piles of paper.

**Gifts and Tchotchkes.** We had a booth at an HR conference in which vendors met potential leads by attracting them to the booth with company-branded tchotchkes and other giveaways, such as pens, calculators, mouse pads, notepads, and other trinkets. One attendee was walking through the aisles pushing a baby stroller filled with tchotchkes he had collected from each booth at the show. I stopped him and inquired what he was doing with all of those items. He proudly declared that he was the manager of his company's finance organization and he was bringing them back to the team as gifts to show appreciation for their great work. On the one hand, we couldn't imagine being on his team and receiving a pen from another company as a thank you gift. On the other hand, we couldn't help but respect his pride and his commitment to recognize people in a cost-effective, fun, and innovative way.

After participating in a team offsite during an entire Sunday and then driving 10 hours to a meeting the following week, my team was working hard. I gifted each of them with a massage at a local day spa. While yes, they were doing their job, and yes, they were getting paid to do that job. I wanted to communicate to them my enormous appreciation for the effort it took to rearrange their personal lives to accommodate our quirky schedule that month.

**Put It In Writing.** I write handwritten thank you notes. I write so many handwritten thank you cards that I believe I have single-handedly saved the U.S. Postal Service from bankruptcy and created a resurgence in the paper industry. It takes time. It takes effort. I never just write "Thank you." I mention something personal that I appreciate about the gift-giver. I compliment. I gush. I work diligently to include more of the word "you" in my thank you notes than the word "I." People appreciate that I go out of my way to thank them. I often get thank you e-mails and phone calls in response to my thank you cards.

Thank you notes and cards fuel the self-delusion that we all have that the world revolves around us. By applauding them with pen and paper, I am making it about them. At the same time I am feeding their need to feel appreciated, respected, and valued. This double whammy makes thank you notes an incredibly powerful tool. One successful entrepreneur I know challenged herself to send out five handwritten thank you notes a day until her business doubled – and then she upped the ante to ten.

One of the Vice Presidents at American Express writes a personalized thank you note on each performance review recognizing the individual's efforts and appreciating their contributions to the company's success.

**Be Specific.** Recognition communicated in the moment is powerful; recognition in the moment laced with specific details is hugely impactful. For example, a "Thank you" is not nearly as impactful as a "Thank you for your great work on the report you gave me last week." "I appreciated that you took the extra step to follow up with the customer." "Thank you for organizing the meeting so efficiently. Everyone benefited from your leadership." Bam! Instant fanning of the flames.

After my wedding, I sent the standard handwritten thank you cards to all of our guests, but instead of "Thanks for coming and for the gift," I decided to include a rave about the specific gift we received and how we were using it. For example, "Thank you for the toaster oven. We love it! Every morning we enjoy preparing our toast with it and we think of you fondly!" Far more impactful than "Thanks for the gift" or "Thanks for the toaster." Even the guests who gifted us with money were told exactly what we had spent the money on and how much we loved what we had bought with their gift. The specificity of the thank you makes it ever more meaningful.

**Hang it on the Wall.** AMC Theaters in the Monmouth Mall in New Jersey puts their recognition on a plaque, like many companies do. But to generate even more meaning from their "Employee of the Month" recognition, the AMC managers hail one person as the "Difference Maker of the Month." Think about how simple and yet brilliant this is. They have combined two human motivations: to make a difference and to be recognized for making a difference. By publicly recognizing someone on the team for making a difference, the AMC managers are communicating that making a difference is important to the team's success. In addition, they have a year's worth of "Difference

Makers" hanging in a place where the general public – their customers – can see it too.

At Gailene Cowger's real estate office in Orland Park, Illinois, she uses her office door to publicly cheer for agent's sales. On a simple 8 ½ x 11 piece of paper, she includes their headshot, a picture of the house they sold, and an exclamation such as "Sally sold this house in 8 days!" Before she posts the page on the door, she announces it at the Monday morning team meeting. One gentleman who did not know the order of her routine asked her, "When does my picture go on your door for the house I sold in 10 days?" He was asking for his "woo-hoo" and demonstrating once again that people are hungry for recognition.

**Remember Them.** One or my favorite things to do is to remember people beyond their birthday. I like to remember some conversation we had, some interest they are pursuing, some project they are working on. Then as I flip through magazines and newspapers, I keep one eye peeled for articles to rip out (my "flip and rip" strategy) and mail to them with a note attached: "Thought of you when I read this. – Ann." What an easy way to recognize what is important to another person, while making them feel special by letting them know that we remembered them. In addition to feeling acknowledged and remembered, people are often surprised by my effort. We loved surprises as kids, and we love them as adults. When we remember someone on our team and then go out of our way to surprise them, we not only demonstrate our appreciation for them, but we have made the moment about them. A double bonus!

**Notice Them.** Take notice when people are not themselves. Recognize when they seem distracted, upset, or just off. If you don't notice when they are off, you are inadvertently making the world revolve around you and not them. Very simply make an observation: "I've noticed that you seem off today. Is everything OK? Is there anything we can talk about or anything I can do?" "I've observed that you are not your typical vivacious, energetic self today. Is everything OK?" This is even better. You are communicating your appreciation for who they usually are, while also making the world revolve around them with your concern that they are not that way today. "You seem a bit on edge today. Did I do something to upset you? Did something else happen that we can address?" We are noticing. We are checking in to see if we own any responsibility. We are recognizing while fueling their self-delusion. One caveat: As long as we notice, recognize, and appreciate them when they are themselves as well as when they are not, we won't be training them to be "off" just to get us to pay attention and notice them.

**Skip the Birthday Cake, Feed Their Instinct to Win.** One of Jan King's first acts as the new president of a 50-person publishing company was to abolish "Cake Day." Jan realized that "Cake Day" was appreciating people for getting older, not for their contributions to the company's success. In addition, it was costing the company time and money. Jan replaced the birthday celebration with a different kind of celebration: a numbers celebration. Every month, instead of getting together to sing "Happy Birthday" and eat unhealthy cake, she brought her entire company together to review the financial statements, to celebrate the month's successes as evidenced by those statements, and to strategize about what the company and its people needed to do to surpass that success the following month. Jan knew that people needed applause and congratulations, but it wasn't for turning a year older, it was for their efforts. They were hungry to understand how they impacted the bottom line. By sharing numbers with them instead of birthday cake, she not only fed that hunger, she demonstrated her appreciation for the important role they played in the company's success yesterday and tomorrow.

## Signs That People are Starving for Recognition

So how do we know when people are starved for recognition and appreciation? There are a few telltale signs, each of which is evidence that their need for appreciation and recognition has gone unmet, thereby forcing them to meet the need another way. People create interesting, if not maddening, ways to get these needs met, resulting in unnecessary drama, spotlighting, talking, and other attention-grabbing efforts. All in an effort to be recognized and appreciated.

**They Talk Incessantly.** Isn't it amazing how much people like to talk about themselves? They talk incessantly without asking any questions of their listener. Before condemning them, I am reminded that this is just a manifestation of a lack of applause in their world before they crossed my path. I dined with a friend recently and not once did she ask me a question about me. She didn't even pretend to care. She clearly was not interested in knowing about my experiences of late. I immediately felt personally rejected and started to make her wrong for it, essentially rejecting her back. Then I thought about her life and what was going on that she must holler for attention. She'd had twins three months prior. Instantly I connected the dots. She was starved for attention. She had been listening to babies for three months straight and just wanted someone to listen to her. So I obliged. I asked a lot of questions and listened relentlessly. My friend still recalls what a great dinner we had that night and how she cannot wait to see me again.

**They Look Like They Just Rolled Out of Bed.** When we ignore people enough, they assume they are being rejected. As we saw earlier, people dread rejection so they will change their behavior or scenery. However, when people feel helpless to change their actions (because in their minds, nothing they try works to get your attention) or change their job, they accept the rejection as valid. What comes with valid rejection is the feeling that they don't matter. And when someone feels they don't matter, they stop caring. They may stop caring about their hair, their dress, and their health, not to mention their performance. When someone shows up to work looking like they just rolled out of bed, it is an indication that they have stopped caring as a result of being starved for attention. When their hair goes unbrushed, their clothes look like they were worn to weed the garden, and they gain a lot of weight, these are telltale signs of how someone feels about themselves. Putting our judgments aside, pay attention to these signs; they reveal a lot about what is going on underneath the surface. Are there things you can do to help them feel appreciated and reject rejection in order to influence their intrinsic motivation?

**They Create Drama.** People who frequently create their own drama are annoying. It's as if drama follows them. And it does. Why? Because they aren't getting attention without it. When their train wreck occurs, we turn all of our attention to them. But when there is no train wreck, we don't. We literally train people to create drama to feed their need for appreciation and acknowledgement. People want to be noticed. No one likes being unnoticed and ignored.

When people create drama or share their drama stories, note that they are merely starved for attention. You can help people get the attention they need, but first you must coach them to stop the drama. Clearly it takes diplomacy, encouragement, commitment, and, not the least of which, patience to confront someone caught in a drama trap. Your best strategy is to offer them constructive feedback without causing them to immediately defend and attack, two reactions to sensing the onset of rejection. We will explore this essential skill in detail in Chapter 6.

**They Gripe.** Just as some areas in nature really do abhor a vacuum, so too do people. When people are not getting their need for appreciation met through recognition or acknowledgement, they may work harder to produce and succeed, but after a while, their satiation will succumb to filling the vacuum with griping.

Clearly there must be a lot of managers not celebrating people because the corporate world is bursting at the seams with people who gripe. And people who gripe hate to gripe alone. They want to share their gripe with others, which just escalates the gripe.

People love to gripe about all the things that are wrong in their world – not with them, of course – with the company, the colleagues, the boss, the economy, the administration, the stock market, the Republicans, the Democrats, the weather, and the planet. They focus on all the things that have gone wrong and how they got the short end of the stick – again. Their success neurons have not been activated in a while. And just like our approach to drama, we need to nip this one in the bud, as its poison is far more contagious than drama-sharing.

**They Reenact *Lord of the Flies*.** At the extreme, when people are not getting their need for appreciation and acknowledgement met, they turn on each other, especially if they feel like others are getting the recognition and appreciation that they themselves crave. Symptoms include backstabbing, biting comments, withholding of information, and exclusion from the clique. Girls in middle school have a particular dexterity in covert bullying, but people in corporate America are just as versed in this human epidemic.

At a law firm where I worked, I witnessed this firsthand with one of the best lawyers in the office. She was stunningly beautiful, she was wicked smart, she was brazen, and worst of all she did not care what anyone, especially the other women at the firm, thought of her. (In reality, she was rejecting everyone else before they could reject her.) She was out to prove something – that she was the best. Let's call her Mary. Everyone at the office had a theory about Mary. It went something like this: She's a witch. She could not be that smart and look that great; her father must have pulled some strings for her position. She's too skinny. She wears white T-shirts too often under her suits – what's up with the white T-shirts? She must be sleeping with the managing partner to be moving up the ladder that quickly. No one ever acknowledged the amazing number of IPOs she completed, the happy clients, and the business she brought into the firm.

Think the rest of the office was starved for a little attention and recognition?

**They Go Elsewhere.** People notoriously leave their spouse because they do not feel appreciated. They may leave physically through an affair or a divorce, or they may just check out mentally or emotionally. Similarly people will leave their boss, either physically or in spirit, when they do not feel appreciated for their work. This is not to imply that the unappreciative spouse or boss is at fault for the cheating spouse or checked-out employee. But take note that appreciation is the cheapest, easiest, and fastest-acting regenerating way to contribute to a relationship. It is so significant that the absence of it literally contaminates the relationship.

Every interaction between two people either contributes to or contaminates that relationship. Consider the veracity of that statement and then ask yourself why you don't always choose the former.

**They Stop Showing Up.** Recall that when efforts go unnoticed, people will change behaviors or change scenery to get noticed and to avoid rejection. Each change is detrimental, especially if you appreciated the effort and were counting on it in the future. Nancy, a volunteer at a non-profit, stopped returning phone calls and e-mails. She became extremely difficult to work with because no one could get any effort from her, let alone any information. She stopped showing up to meetings altogether. To avoid the rejection of not being noticed, Nancy changed her behavior and her scenery. The volunteer manager suffered in the short term and missed an opportunity in the long run.

## Sabotaging Our Recognition Efforts

When we actually do recognize people, we must be careful not to take it back, even unintentionally. If our action or inaction communicates something contrary to the words in our recognition, we risk doing more damage than we did without engaging in recognition. People hate lip service – they know when our lips are moving in one direction but our feet are going in the opposite.

**Throw Them Under the Bus.** No matter how much effort we give toward recognition and appreciation, throwing people under the bus will eradicate all of the contributions we had made to that relationship. This includes blaming people, stepping aside so they will take the fall, not defending them, even allowing others to assume that people were at fault or did not execute.

I witnessed an HR director at a Fortune 500 company recognize and appreciate a project leader on her team in one e-mail and throw him under the bus in another less than five minutes later. Thalia sent an e-mail to her project lead and copied the people on the project leader's immediate team congratulating everyone for getting the program up and running so quickly. So far, so good. Recognition and appreciation. Check, check. People were sighing with relief and patting themselves on the back for averting disaster, for she had a reputation for losing her temper. Not five minutes later the team was copied on another e-mail in which Thalia jumped through the message to slap the project leader across the face. One of the participants in the program was confused (due to his own user-error, of course) and asked Thalia what to do. Without picking up the phone to call the project leader or e-mail him individually to find out how to respond, Thalia forwarded the participant's e-mail to the project leader, the entire team, her boss, and her boss's boss literally screaming at him over e-mail for causing confusion. Five minutes later, the confused and user-error-prone participant sent a follow-up e-mail to let Thalia know that in fact it was user-error and that he had solved the problem. Thalia then sent another message with an apology and a bunch of smiley faces. What a waste of initial recognition and appreciation, and a waste of people's time and energy. All because Thalia forgot to take a deep breath. She is constantly contributing to and contaminating her relationships, usually in the same conversation.

**Take Credit for their Work**. Wanda had slaved for months on the report. She had interviewed hundreds of people about eliminating waste and improving efficiencies in the office. She proudly delivered the report to her boss, Joe. Pleased with Wanda's work, Joe sent the report to his boss, Carl, who would be presenting it to the CEO at the team meeting the next day. At the meeting, Wanda was on the edge of her seat bursting with pride and prepared to answer questions about her report. As they sat down, Carl distributed a copy of the report to everyone in the room, including Wanda and the CEO. The title page read, "Eliminating Waste, Establishing Efficiency by Carl X." Wanda had to pick up her jaw off the table and her ego off the floor. Without batting an eye, Carl presented Wanda's report as his own. Wanda's immediate boss, Joe, did not say anything and neither did Carl – not before, during, or after the meeting. Joe told Wanda to let it go. Wanda did, but it was also her respect for Joe and Carl that she let go. She stayed at the company for another five years, but in body only. She gave them her time, but she refused to give them her passion, enthusiasm, ideas, or excitement. They had stolen her work and never even bothered to say "Thank you." Wanda was experiencing, unfortunately, the drip of Carl's insecurities on her. Clearly, he was lacking recognition and appreciation so he chose to take Wanda's.

**Ignore Them**. In the 1985 movie *The Breakfast Club*, Ally Sheedy's character, Allison Reynolds, was someone starving to be noticed. She showed up to an all-day detention at the school library with four other students who were being punished for misbehaving. Allison, however, had not misbehaved. She didn't do anything to get herself into detention; she was not required to be there. Allison showed up because, as she confessed, she had nothing else to do that Saturday. Over lunch, the characters shared the nasty things their parents did to them. One boy said his dad hit and yelled at him; another said his parents unduly pressured him to succeed. Allison said, "My parents ignore me." The teens all agreed that being ignored was even worse than being pressured, beaten, or yelled at.

Randy's boss once told him that she trusts him with their top clients. Randy is the best there is. Randy knows how to do the job even better than Randy's boss does. So she talks to Randy maybe once a month, if that. She feels there is no higher compliment she can give Randy than to give Randy independence and let him just run. While Randy appreciated the acknowledgement last year, time is fading the good feelings. He is now referencing past experiences of being left to fend for himself, and he recalls feeling rejected following a similar lack of attention. He now convinces himself that his boss is ignoring him. If his boss cared about his career, she'd pay attention to him; if she liked his work, she'd say something. Inevitably, Randy begins to check out because Randy's boss keeps forgetting to check in.

As managers, we often forget about our steady performers when we're consumed with fawning over our high performers, cajoling the low performers, and wading through everyone else's drama. We can't ignore them and assume they won't feel rejected. You may not feel rejected in a similar situation, but you need to stop measuring other people based on your perspective. You haven't the slightest idea what experiences and related baggage they bring with them. You cannot afford to make assumptions, especially with the people you count on to consistently show up.

**Lip Service.** One way to sabotage applause is through lip service. We take it personally when someone says one thing but does another. It's an insult and a backhanded rejection.

Derek was the CEO of a paper manufacturing business. He hired Simon to manage the six production workers who make the business run. While Simon reports directly to Derek, Derek likes to regularly walk the production floor to check in with the people who touch the paper that gets sent to their customers. He diligently reads all of Simon's reviews before they are delivered to the workers and he listens relentlessly to the off-the-record feedback from his workers and Simon.

Much to his dismay, Derek quickly discovered that his new production manager is just a manager, not a leader. None of the workers respects him; they merely tolerate him. On top of which, Simon doesn't want to be a leader. He wants to work with paper, not people. Derek offered to help transform Simon from a leader to a manager, but Simon was not interested. Simon knows the production business really well, but doesn't enjoy managing people. He is similarly just tolerating his role managing people.

Feeling stuck with a small team and defined roles, Derek has not made any changes over the two years since he made this discovery. He has done nothing to redefine roles and move Simon into a position that allows him to impact the business without impacting the workers. Derek literally hopes everyone just learns to play better together.

The problem with not doing anything is that Derek is sending a conflicting message. On the one hand, he listens relentlessly and really cares what people think, but, on the other hand, he is not doing anything to address their concerns and the situation. He cares what they think ... but not that much. He is not walking his talk. He is just moving his lips.

**Failure to Communicate.** Joanne resigned from two companies as a result of feeling unappreciated, only to be showered with appreciation and offers of more money by her managers on the way out the door. In addition, without fail on her last day at each company, she was sent off with a going-away party in which her colleagues and managers poured on the appreciation and recognition for all of her contributions. She thought, "How interesting. Where was all of that love and adoration when I was on the payroll? Maybe I would have stayed longer."

I once read about an octogenarian who threw her own memorial because she wanted to hear her eulogy while she was alive. She wanted to experience all of the appreciation and recognition showered by her family and friends.

At every turn, people are literally starved for appreciation and recognition. As middle leaders, we can easily do something to feed them.

## Using Applause to Fuel Self-Delusion

The tale of the three bricklayers illustrates the importance of knowing how our job fits into the bigger picture. Three men were laying bricks. When asked about what they were doing, the first bricklayer said, "I'm building a wall." The second one said, "I'm building a church." And the third one said, "I'm building the most amazing cathedral that will bring people and their God together." None of them said, "I'm laying bricks."

You could thank them for laying bricks. That would be appreciation. Or you could instead thank them for building the most amazing cathedral that will bring people and their God together. The former is simple appreciation. The latter is appreciation that fuels self-delusion.

People don't show up excited to push paper, create reports, attend meetings, send e-mails, and answer customer calls. The work of their jobs is not what fuels them. People are fueled by the knowledge that what they are doing is contributing to something greater than laying bricks and pushing paper – their battle cry. Their work has purpose and meaning, the purpose and meaning that they assigned to it. And as a leader who has the power to influence their intrinsic motivation, you can remind them of the impact and importance of their job. Each time you proffer appreciation, you can simultaneously feed the need for appreciation and fuel the self-delusion that it's all about them.

Frankie and Jeanne, renowned restaurateurs in the New York area, are connoisseurs of not only great food, but of using applause to fuel self-delusion. They have been operating restaurants and catering businesses for over 25 years, most recently as "Landmark Hospitality." Frankie and Jeanne are crystal clear that they cannot do this without the people who touch their customers every day – the wait staff. These people are literally walking billboards for their restaurants.

"Creating memories" is the battle cry that rallies on a daily basis the people who make Landmark Hospitality one of the most enviable and profitable in the restaurant and catering industry. Every team member wears a classy, silver bracelet engraved with the words "Memory Maker" to remind them of their important role in achieving victory in the battle.

Because the wait staff is often the only human contact that Frankie and Jeanne have with customers, they routinely applaud their people. They applaud not only to appreciate their contributions, but to fuel the self-delusion that the success of the restaurant rests on their shoulders. They use applause and recognition to remind people of the difference they make in that success.

Applause at Landmark Hospitality begins with the menu tastings. All wait staff members are involved in the tastings, and their feedback is welcomed and encouraged. In addition, every person on the team is required to attend monthly strategy sessions where they look at the financials for the month. They are not exposed to all of the financials – that would just be distracting. They are given the financials they directly impact – the weekly food sales and expenses. Each month, people are eager to know "How did we do? What went well and what could we do better? What needs to be addressed?"

Frankie and Jeanne continue to applaud and fuel the self-delusion by granting staff members the power to surprise and delight customers. All servers are provided with business cards for the purpose of developing long-term relationships with customers. In addition, staff members are invited to enchant their customers with special chef tastings available each night. And they are able to comp dishes at their discretion. Of course all comps impact the food expenses number examined by everyone at the end of each month, so the team holds each other accountable to ensure that no one is abusing this power.

People who work for Landmark Hospitality feel their contributions are recognized and appreciated and at the same time they feel like the success of the restaurant revolves around them. As a result of using applause to fuel self-delusion, Frankie and Jeanne enjoy industry-low staff attrition. But of course their attrition is low. Why would someone want to leave a job when they feel appreciated regularly for being an integral part of a business's success?

## Putting It Into Action

- Practice saying "thank you" and specify what it is you appreciate. For example, "Thank you for calling the client right back." "Thank you for creating the agenda so clearly."

- Recognize someone's effort by sending an e-mail to their boss and their boss's boss and copying that person. Don't take any credit. Just acknowledge their effort and the contribution to the team, to the department, and to the client.

- Practice acknowledging people outside of the office who provide you with great service.

- At the end of one day, write a list of people you acknowledged that day and what you acknowledged them for.

- Institute the "Weekly Snapshot" for people on your team.

- Require people to make a "Victory Log" for you to see every quarter.

- Encourage people to decorate their cubicles with evidence of their success.

- Write two handwritten thank you notes each day for one week.

- Create a plaque for "Difference Maker of the Month."

- Formally recognize people's special efforts in newsletters and on your intranet.

- Get to know someone by asking questions and Second Questions, then skim magazines or newspapers looking for an article or book to send them based on that conversation.

- Ask people about the best recognition they have ever received – this will be very telling about how they like to be applauded and recognized.

# Chapter 6

## Lift the Fog

. . . . . . . . . . . . . . . . .

In 1993 Chinese Northern Airlines Flight 6901 was en route
from Beijing's Capital International Airport to Urumqi Airport
in Xinjiang, China. The Chinese pilots were flying a U.S.-built
McDonnell Douglas MD-82 airliner. They were attempting to land
in heavy fog when an audio alarm went off in the cockpit warning
the pilots of their dangerous proximity to the ground. But the
pilots were baffled. They had no idea what the alarm meant, and
just before landing, one crew member asked another in Chinese,
"What does 'pull up' mean?" A dozen people were killed when the
plane hit power lines and crashed moments later.

The literal and figurative fog resulted unnecessarily in
the deaths of 12 people. The McDonnell Douglas engineers who
designed the MD-82 airliner never imagined that anyone would
have been confused by the phrase "pull up" following an alarm.
The Chinese pilots, on the other hand, had never seen the words
"pull up," especially following an alarm. Had they survived, they
may have argued that the situation called for the words "You're
about to crash" following such an alarm. One situation, two
sides of the story. One life-threatening condition, two different
approaches to solving it.

In law school we learned that every case has two perspectives.
In life I have learned that every situation actually has at least
seven perspectives – mine, the other party's, and the point of view
of the five random third-party observers. And if we asked 10 more

people to share their perspectives of any given situation, we would get at least 10 new interpretations. In other words, there are as many perspectives as there are people on the planet. And everyone thinks their point of view is the correct one.

## Communication — The Missing Link

Every communication between two people either contributes to or contaminates that relationship. There is no in-between. This is excellent news! And it's also precarious. We have the opportunity to contribute to our relationships with people every single time we open our mouths. But we also run the risk of contaminating them with our communication – or lack thereof.

Rob, our fearless salesman from NYNEX, had an interaction in his early days at the company that demonstrates how to contribute to and contaminate relationships in one conversation. Rob had just been promoted to Manager at the young age of 24 when he got into an altercation with Vin, a District Manager at the company. Rob's boss called Rob into his office and said, "We're going to call Vin together and you're going to apologize." Realizing that the relationship was important to his career, Rob acquiesced. With Vin on speaker phone, Rob apologized. Vin said, "Well thank you. I appreciate that. You know, Rob, this is one of those areas that you will learn, we've just always done it this way." Irritated, Rob blurted, "That's the problem, Vin. Just because you've always done it that way doesn't mean that there aren't better ways to do things! If it was stupid 20 years ago, it's even more stupid today." Bam! Poison delivered. Relationship contaminated as quickly as it had been nutured.

## The Importance of Communication

Want to make someone feel paranoid, fearful, suspicious, and mistrustful? Just stop talking to them. Not speaking when communication is desired, required, or needed is as toxic as contaminated communications. The lack of communication is the fastest way to destroy a relationship – personal or professional.

When you stop communicating, there is a void that people fill with fabrication. People will make up stories as to why you stopped talking to them and then look for evidence to determine which story is correct. In this story-fabricating game, people wonder whether your furrowed brow means you are unhappy with them, upset with someone else, or simply have a headache. Without information to the contrary, people usually choose the former.

And the fog rolls in.

During the merger of Hewlett-Packard and Compaq, the leaders of the two companies announced that 10,000 employees would be laid off in six months. They did not say from which department or organization and they did not identify the individuals. They just said that somewhere, sometime soon, some people will be laid off. For the next six months, people walked around fabricating stories. They imagined that they were on the list, imagined their boss knew something and wasn't sharing it, and imagined who else had a target on their back.

The leaders at HP offered this looming layoff promise because they knew Wall Street wanted to hear that they were cutting costs following the merger. They communicated to Wall Street, but they neglected to realize the impact of not communicating to everyone else. They underestimated the influence of fear. Because people were afraid – afraid for their jobs, afraid of the looming changes, afraid they were about to be rejected, their intrinsic drive was influenced negatively. With this one communication, the leaders laced the next six months with fear, anxiety, paranoia, and dread, but not much execution and implementation. Without any further communication, the people could only worry about their jobs instead of doing their jobs. The leaders' half-baked communication campaign paralyzed a workforce for a few pennies on their stock price.

## 7 Keys to Lifting the Communication Fog

1. Walk in Their Shoes

2. Listen Like Your Job Depends on It

3. Speak to be Understood

4. Set Expectations

5. Give Feedback

6. Ask for Feedback

7. Suspend the Story

*1. Walk in Their Shoes.* Research scientists at the MIT Agelab in Cambridge, Massachusetts, have invented a Boomer bodysuit to allow companies to empathize with the experiences of the 50+ generation. The bodysuit, which has been named AGNES (the Age Gain Now Empathy System), restricts mobility and free range of motion, and limits joint function, balance, and vision. By limiting every joint in the body, AGNES allows researchers and product designers to create the experience of being old. They are literally stepping into the shoes of this generation in order to create solutions and products appropriately.

Irrefutably the most powerful thing we can do in our relations with others is to see the world from their perspective. When we "walk in their shoes," we pretend we are on the other side of our communication, experiencing it from the other person's viewpoint, imagining what it would be like to receive the communication that we just delivered. When we walk in their shoes, we attempt to hear the communication from their perspective. We endeavor to understand where they are coming from.

Consider the path they traveled before reaching the conversation with you. Have they spent their entire career at the company? Or did they just graduate from college? Do they deal directly with customers or push paper all day long? Are they positive or negative? Are they distrustful of management or part of management? Are they outgoing or introverted? What's important to their success?

I was dancing with Susan from the procurement department at one of our clients, and we were clearly stepping on each others' feet. She was standing in the way of a contract that everyone else in the department had already agreed to. I couldn't figure out why she and I kept butting heads until I stopped to see the world from her perspective. First, the leadership department that wanted the contract never involved Susan. So right away she was feeling left out and deflated. They should have boosted her ego and self-delusion by allowing her to weigh in on the contract. Then I realized what was important to her. Being part of procurement, she is charged with keeping costs low and ensuring diversity in the company's vendors. Once I appreciated her perspective, I was able to not only communicate from that perspective but help her look like a hero. I offered her a justifiable discount and offered to provide her with our women-owned business certification. She was delighted, and we became partners.

It's irrelevant whether we agree with another person's perspective; we just need to understand it. When we seek understanding first, we can avoid miscommunications. This alone will diminish frustrations on your end and theirs. In addition, understanding their viewpoint will promote compassion. Instead of mulling, "That's ridiculous to think that I would intentionally sabotage their career!" we will pause to consider, "I wonder why they think I would sabotage their career? What have I done that has inadvertently communicated that? I wonder what experiences have they had with me or other bosses that have taught them that this is how managers treat people?" Our frustrations and their fears and anger will dissipate when we stop to understand their perspective.

Walking in their shoes also demands that we stop to consider how the other person is receiving our communication. Is there a chance that they will misinterpret what we have said? Will they be offended, even if we didn't mean it? Will they clearly understand what we said? And if they don't understand, will they ask questions to clarify or just nod to appease us? Are they missing pieces necessary for comprehension? Are they the type who will make up stories to fill in those gaps or ask clarifying questions? All of this is "walking in their shoes."

Every time we open our mouths, we should be speculating about how the other person might interpret what we say. With an overload of information ricocheting around people, we must go to great lengths to ensure that our communication is clear, intentional, and effective.

If we are really committed to another's success, we cannot expect them to read our minds.If we say something is "urgent," do they know that we want them to drop everything to work on it immediately? If we say something is "important," will they know that we just want it done by the end of the week but not at the expense of other priorities?

Even without any chance of miscommunication, building that bridge to another's viewpoint will not only expand our own perspective, but generate compassion for another's journey. The exercise might even welcome new ideas for us.

The leaders at Hyatt Hotel Corporation are cognizant of the benefits of walking in their shoes. When the leaders discovered that most people in the corporate offices in Chicago had never actually worked in a hotel, they decided to change that. In 1989, they officially launched "Hyatt in Touch Day" to compel the corporate employees to walk in the shoes of the hotel employees. Now a yearly ritual, they close the corporate offices and dispatch each corporate employee to one of Hyatt's hotels around the country to join the staff. The corporate employees spend the day opening doors, hauling luggage, serving lunches, pouring drinks, checking in guests, and cleaning rooms. Through this experience, the corporate team at Hyatt is literally stepping into the shoes of the hotel staff members to gain new perspectives and insights into their own business.

The concept of the reality show *Undercover Boss* is similarly grounded in the "walk in their shoes" concept. Each week the CEO of a large organization goes undercover to experience what it's like to work for him. He disguises himself with a new name, a new haircut, and sometimes a pair of glasses. Over the course of a week, the incognito CEO assumes the role of a new employee to discover what it's really like to work for his own company. The CEO is stepping out of his corner office to literally walk in other people's shoes.

In one episode, the CEO of 7-Eleven, Joe DePinto, went undercover for a week to become a store clerk, a night shift clerk, a pastry maker, and a delivery driver. Before embarking on this journey, Joe reflected on his decision to go undercover and shared his belief that to succeed as the leader, he needed to better understand the people who directly serve the company's customers. To do that required him to actually experience what they experience, not just receive a report on it. So he went undercover to taste it firsthand.

Joe was blown away by the people he worked with that week. Their commitment, enthusiasm, and hard work humbled him. In particular, he discovered many opportunities to improve the store, various processes, and the investment the company made in people. Through this experience, Joe gained a whole new appreciation for the people on the front lines. He returned to headquarters, called an all-hands meeting for the corporate employees, shared his experience with the people in the stores, and announced his commitment to serving them better. Joe walked in their shoes and he will never be the same again.

2. *Listen Like Your Job Depends on It.* The average person speaks at a rate of 150-200 words per minute, while the average listener can comprehend up to 400 words per minute. What lies

between is a lot of idle time for the mind to wander and meander through a plethora of thoughts. And when the mind takes a siesta, no one feels connected to the conversation.

Every person wants to be heard and understood. As we have seen throughout this book, people are constantly feeding their self-delusion and working to avoid rejection. Feeling heard and understood meets these needs.

But every day, people are subjected to others who do not listen to them – their spouse, their kids, their boss, their colleagues, their vendors, their elected officials, even their dog. And when they look extrinsically to feel important, relevant, and not rejected, not being heard is the fastest route to deflation and rejection.

Ultimately our responsibility is to not negatively influence their intrinsic drive. When we don't listen to people, we do just that. Conversely, when we listen, we help them feed the delusion and avoid the rejection.

But we can't just listen to them; we have to listen like our job depends on it. Because it does.

There are three kinds of listening: Muddled Listening, Squabble Listening, and Relentless Listening.

*Muddled Listening.* We listen while we are also driving, reading e-mails, cleaning our office, walking the dog, daydreaming, or simply thinking about what we will make for dinner. Essentially, we are only half-listening. According to John Medina, author of *Brain Rules*, the brain naturally focuses on one concept at a time; it is not even capable of multitasking. Now imagine how wretched we are at listening in a multi-task mode.

*Squabble Listening.* When we are engaged in a discussion, debate, disagreement, argument, or other difference of opinion, we are listening solely for the purpose of getting our argument in order. We wait for our turn to respond and to convince the other person of our point of view. We can barely stand to wait for the other person to be done talking so we can make our brilliant point.

*Relentless Listening.* This occurs when we are listening intentionally, actively, and enthusiastically, completely committed to understanding the other person's point of view. We are using our auditory senses to step into their proverbial shoes in order to understand their perspective. Only when we are committed to understanding and we are unrelenting in our listening do people ever feel heard.

Relentless listening is hanging on their every word. To do so we must use retracing, inquiring, paraphrasing, and empathizing with the speaker's feelings. All of this of course must be done with the utmost sincerity, which cannot be betrayed by body language or a tone that communicates otherwise.

Retracing words is the first key to relentless listening. We literally repeat a few words back to them to show we are listening and to keep track. For instance, if I say, "I was so frustrated, upset, and angry when the company ..." Nod, say a few "uh huhs," "ohs," and "hmmms," and then insert a clarifying "Frustrated and upset?" It's not paraphrasing; it's actually repeating some words back to the other person.

Retracing also helps to keep you focused. As you know, when people are starved for attention and we pay attention to them, they tend to verbal vomit. But the attention span is limited to about 15-20 seconds without some interaction. This makes relentless listening a huge challenge because the mind naturally wanders. You hear something they say and it triggers a thought about dinner or your kids and suddenly you look like you're in the conversation but you're really not. Our brains are processing so fast that it takes great effort to stay focused. Retracing creates the interaction our brain requires to stay engaged in the conversation.

The next tool we have as listeners is to ask questions to clarify the speaker's meaning and intent. Inquiry will help you discover the backstory to their communication. Asking questions also helps to keep you and the speaker engaged in and focused on the conversation because, like retracing, it requires interaction.

"How did you decide to do this?" "What did you hope was the outcome?" "What has the experience been like?" In addition to supplying you with backstory and intent, you can use the Second Question technique from Chapter 4 to emphasize your interest in the other person and make the world revolve around them.

Asking clarifying questions stops people from treating you like their therapist, especially as they get caught up sharing a story to a rapt audience – you. Questions break the impending monologue and keep them focused on the important points. Alan Weiss, renowned guru to the consulting industry, regularly and unapologetically interrupts people by asking, "What's your question?" Not warm and fuzzy, but in doing so he demonstrates that he is listening ardently and just wants you to get to the noun and the verb.

After using retracing and inquiry, start paraphrasing what you've heard. Do this by saying, "If I understand you correctly, this is the problem, this is who it involved, this is when it happened, this is where it happened, and this is how it happened. Is that correct? Is there anything I'm missing?" Don't parrot their story word for word. Paraphrase it to ensure that we got the meaning right and to express our understanding. This is critical in the effort for people to feel heard.

Finally, to really lift the fog in communications and relentlessly listen to them like no other manager, let alone leader, has ever listened to them, you want to help people to "feel felt." As we explored in Chapter 4, we help people feel felt by empathizing with them. "Wow. I can only imagine how frustrating that must have been for you to work so hard on the report and then for me not to even look at it." We don't need to assign blame and we don't need to defend ourselves; we just need to communicate that we get what they just experienced. Helping people feel felt requires us to not only jump into their shoes, but to also jump into their skin.

Relentless listening may seem like a lot of work and somewhat scripted at times but it is a powerful tool that will be a contribution – a gift – to your relationship with others. Rarely do managers listen to people as if the relationship depends on it, let alone their job or their success. I would venture to say that your boss doesn't even listen to *you* like this. But because you are committed to being extraordinary, not mediocre, you cannot afford to listen any other way.

*3. Speak to be Understood.* At company meetings, Jeffrey Katzenberg, CEO of DreamWorks Animation, intentionally explains financial performance using language that artists can clearly understand. He remembers his audience – the creative minds that populate the film production company, and then he speaks to be understood by them. He doesn't have to. He could talk about the financials in MBA-speak to prove how smart and educated he is, thereby making the world revolve around him. Instead, he makes the world revolve around everyone in his audience by speaking to be understood.

People say I speak too fast. Defensively (and jokingly), I say they just need to listen faster. In that one comment, I make it all about me, and in so doing I impart a message that it's not about them at all. I don't want to feel rejected by their judgment of me, so I reject them first by letting them know with my snide comment that the world revolves around me, not them. In so doing, I not only let the fog roll in, but I inflict frustration and deflation and allow my ego to win.

But it's not my audience's responsibility to keep up with me. Whether I am speaking to one person or 1,000 people, I am 100 percent responsible for my communications, including the rate at which I speak. It is not about me. It's about them. And when I go out of my way to ensure they understand my communications by speaking in a way that is easily understood, I remind them that the world, even in just that conversation or just that speech, truly does revolve around them.

Can you imagine what work, let alone the world, would be like if every communicator owned the responsibility to deliver communications that are understood? We would have less hatred, cruelty, and war. Mediocre managers are committed to merely delivering a message. Extraordinary managers are committed to the other person receiving and understanding that message.

Here's the secret: Never assume that your message was delivered.

Rather, use words, body language, and voice to engage, re-engage, speak purposefully, be intentional, get to the verb, check-in, and clarify. "Could you repeat back to me what you heard so I can make sure I have said it clearly and covered everything?" The onus is on you. It is your responsibility to help your listener understand. Not theirs.

*Tell Stories.* One of your best strategies for delivering a point while enrapturing your audience is storytelling. No matter what message you are trying to deliver, your listener's brain needs a story to engrain the message. As we explored in Chapter 3, the brain processes meaning before detail; it craves emotions before theory. How often have you heard a great speaker, and while you can't remember what they said, you loved their story about the cow or about their mother? Stories help to create that emotional aspect and bring meaning to our points. People pine for understanding, and stories help to paint that understanding in bright, bold, vibrant colors.

Most people fail to leverage the power of stories to connect with others about work. But put them at a party with friends and they'll share stories all night long. Or listen to them exchange weekend stories on Monday morning in the hallways, and they seem like natural connectors with their storytelling prowess. Put that same person in front of his peers at a team meeting and watch as his fears of being rejected paralyze his tongue. Immediately, he resorts to citing financial numbers, pontificating about corporate goals, and tossing out the company's meaningless mission. Eyes glaze over and yawns are stifled as the speaker misses the opportunity to connect with his audience and appears to care more about himself than about his listeners.

The most captivating speakers are the ones who use personal, revealing stories to create understanding. Sam Duncan, CEO of OfficeMax, captivated us with his personal story as he kicked off a diversity conference hosted at the OfficeMax corporate offices in 2009. He had us all on the edge of our seats by sharing with us the story of his childhood, revealing how he came to be passionate about diversity and inclusion at his company. He painted for us with his words a picture of his childhood, how he met his wife, how he served in the army, how his career brought him to OfficeMax and about the diverse people he had the privilege to meet at each turn. Sam did not drone on about statistics, numbers, or mission statements. He connected with us in the audience through his story, and while it was ultimately about Sam, he made it about us by delivering his message in a way that was easy to understand and remember.

Here's the next secret: Always assume that you are responsible for a miscommunication. When a miscommunication occurs, assume that the error was on your end of the communication. If someone is left confused, assume that you spoke in a way that was not clear, understandable, or memorable. Granted, it is far easier to roll your eyes, place blame, pass judgment, and dismiss the confused. But that is merely a way to reject them before they reject you. No one likes to admit they made a mistake, let alone erred in communicating. By owning the responsibility, however, you are investing in your relationships and cementing your commitment to contribute to – not contaminate – them.

*4. Set Expectations.* Influencing Tenet #4: People just want to be winners, not losers. So show them how to win. The easiest way to help others win is for everyone to understand expectations from the beginning. Then refer to Influencing Tenet #5 – We each crave control – and give them the ability and the control to meet those expectations and win.

One of the biggest causes of fog between people is missed expectations. Following any communication, expectations are established, usually implicitly. I walk away expecting one result, while you walk away expecting a similar result or perhaps something completely different based on your assumptions. For example, in Singapore, service providers say, "It will be a while," in response to how long the wait will be. This frustrates Americans, who assume based on their experience with the phrase that "a while" translates to "many hours." To Singaporeans "a while" means five minutes. That's a missed expectation.

In a 1990 Columbian airlines Avianca Flight from Bogata to New York, air traffic controllers put the plane in a holding pattern over John F. Kennedy International Airport as a result of congestion at the airport, fog, and wind. During the hold, the aircraft exhausted its reserve fuel supply. When air traffic controllers asked the crew if it could hold a bit longer, the pilots replied, "We're running out of fuel, sir." Moments later the plane plunged into the small village of Cove Neck, Long Island, about 15 miles from the airport. The pilots never declared a "fuel emergency." Instead they asked for a "priority landing," which to Spanish-speaking pilots and controllers, indicates a severe emergency. But not to the English-speaking controllers. They were listening for the words "fuel emergency," which they never heard. The controllers did not equate "priority landing" with having a fuel emergency. The Avianca pilots' miscommunication made it impossible for air traffic controllers to give them correct priority status.

While people's lives are not always in danger with miscommunications, deadlines usually are. Imagine that you want a report done by the end of the day. Someone on your team moves mountains to have it completed and in your hands by 8:00

pm because they heard "end of the day" and to them that means "by the time they leave at the end of their day." You, however, needed that report for a meeting at 5:00 pm. In your mind, 5:00 pm is the end of the workday. Now, you storm out of the office, empty-handed and frustrated. The person on your team is now confused and similarly frustrated because they toiled for hours all afternoon to complete it but in spite of their diligence, they failed. They missed our expectation and we missed theirs.

Missed expectations permeate relationships. Bosses continue to assign projects to people, completely unaware of workloads, while overwhelmed employees keep adding to their pile without asking about priorities. Expectations about deadline, let alone about outcome, are unclear and the fog rolls in. While it is easy to blame people for not inquiring about priority, we could also blame you for not clarifying priorities.

More than avoiding or accepting blame, here is why setting expectations is so crucial in any relationship. By working on the expectations, including the boundaries and the outcomes, you are setting up the other person for success. You are making their experience a priority. You are making it about them. In addition, you are circumventing the situation whereby their fear of rejection causes them to fail to ask for clarification and then fail in meeting your expectation, thus fulfilling their own prophecy. The rejected and dejected do not recover easily, let alone execute effortlessly. And all of this drama creates ineffectiveness which can be avoided by setting clear expectations at the beginning.

Expectations are essential. Let's get in the habit of setting expectations with our own leaders and with the people we lead. Clarify tenaciously the who, the what, the where, the when, the how, and most importantly, the why of every project, meeting, and assignment. "What else is on your plate at this time?" "Just to be clear, what time do you want me to deliver this report to you? Do you want it in draft form or in final form?" "To clarify, what does the client expect from us as an outcome?" "To clarify, what do you expect from me as a participant of this meeting?" "To clarify, how shall I prepare for our meeting with you and the team?" In Chapter 9 we'll explore one of my favorite questions from the Grow Model, "What outcome would make this meeting/conversation a success?"

Clarifying expectations from the beginning not only lifts the fog but contributes to the relationship again and again.

*5. Give Feedback.* For flights up to 10 hours' duration, the Federal Aviation Administration tolerates errors of no more than 2 nautical miles per hour of circular error on 95 percent of a plane's flight. In other words, an airplane can be off track 95 percent of the flight time provided that the error is no more than 1 nautical mile on each side of the intended flight path. That means that a plane is on the originally programmed flight path only 5 percent of the flight. To stay within the FAA Regulations, the pilot must constantly engage with air traffic control to course-correct.

Consider that you are air traffic control and the people on your team are the pilots. Without the constant flow of feedback, they are sure to miss their destination. You must communicate with them regularly to get them the information they need to stay on track. People depend on feedback in the same way that pilots do; without it, neither has any idea if they are on course or not.

In order to course-correct, people, just like pilots, need the feedback to be specific, immediate, and on-the-job. Feedback that is given once or twice a year does little good on the flight to Hawaii or the project for the marketing group. Yearly performance evaluations are at best a dashboard of where people are. They don't offer any behavior-impacting advice. Suppose the dog chewed your favorite shoes last week; yelling at him today won't cause him to behave differently, it will just cause him to be confused. If a pilot is going to miss the runway by 100 yards, feedback next month, or even the next day, is useless. Similarly, what good does it do to give people feedback in June about a presentation they made in February? Who can remember what the speech was about, let alone how they performed? If you want to significantly impact people's behavior, you need to give them feedback immediately, when the behavior and the feelings are fresh.

There are a few reasons we hesitate offering feedback and none of them is worth the fog they create. First, we are too busy doing our very important job, but not making the time just communicates that the world revolves around us, not them. Second, we don't know how to give feedback, but that's just a cop-out. We didn't get this far in our careers by not doing things we don't know how to do. Finally and at the crux of it all is that we want people to like us, not reject us. Giving feedback, especially critical or unfavorable feedback, suddenly becomes a reflection of our character instead of merely an observation of their behavior.

While people need feedback regularly to do their jobs well, they don't always welcome it. People hear unfavorable feedback as criticism, and criticism feels like rejection. Naturally, they take it personally and become defensive. Whenever someone tells us that we are doing something wrong, our own fear of rejection triggers an immediate, defensive reaction.

As leaders, we have a unique opportunity to position feedback as a contribution rather than censure. We just need to add compassion, diplomacy, dedication, and empathy. Asking permission, setting the stage, and making observations are great ways to do just that.

*Ask Permission.* You can minimize defensiveness by first asking for permission. Asking permission sets the stage without catching people off-guard. In addition, when they agree to receiving feedback, they tend to support hearing it. As an example, "Would you be open to some feedback?" "Would you like to hear my perspective?" "If I have some observations that I think might contribute to your success, would you like to know them? If so, what would be the best way to communicate them?" "I have some thoughts on your performance that might benefit you. When would be the best time to share them?"

By giving people the opportunity to say "yes" or "no" to receiving feedback and when to receive it, we are leveraging the illusion of control and the participatory biases that we explored in Chapter 4.

*Set the Positive Stage.* Once they grant permission, start the conversation with a positive declaration about your commitment to their success and to the success of the relationship or the success of a project. For example, "I know you really care about doing a great job for me." Then reveal your own commitment, such as "And I am committed to your success on this team," or "And I want you to be ready to take on the next leadership opportunity." Then put to rest any fears they may be experiencing that you are rejecting them, by adding, "And I want you to know how much I appreciate all of your hard work." Then, having set the foundation, you can declare your commitment to contributing to their growth and development with feedback. "To that end, I have some feedback that might benefit both of our commitments."

*Observation, Not Judgment.* Here's the key to giving powerful feedback. It's merely your observation; it's not your judgment of their character or some other conclusive verdict. Two powerful phrases for giving feedback: "I've noticed ..." "I've observed ..." and "My experience is ..." For example, "I couldn't help noticing that ..." "I have observed lately that you ..." "My experience being on your team is ..."

Then share the consequences of the behavior you have observed. "The problem this causes is ..." "You might not realize it but it is having an impact ..." As a result of your actions ..." "The consequence has been..." "You come across as rather ..." or "The effect on others is ..."

Next, pause to walk in their shoes and gain their perspective on the situation. "What is your perspective?" "What has your experience been?" or "What do you think of the situation or my observation?" Give them an opportunity to respond – and get ready to listen like your job depends on it. You are listening to understand their perspective, not debate, laugh it off, scoff at it, or question it. Just to understand it. Ask questions for clarify, but above all, stay committed to understanding their viewpoint.

With an observation of the situation (your perspective) and an understanding of their experience (their perspective), you can now explore with them some options to address the situation. "Based on my observations and your perspective, let's see what we can do to address it. What ideas do you have?" Problem-solving is more effective when people who own the problem are involved in solving it. Granted, you could tell them exactly what to do differently but it is completely unnecessary to prove how smart you are. People learn better when they discover rather than when they are told. Asking them to participate in generating a solution will leverage the participatory bias and they will tend to support the ideas that get generated. After pausing and listening relentlessly to their ideas, you can always offer your own. "I encourage you to ..." "I recommend ..." "I suggest ..." or "I request ..."

The formula is:

Would you be open to some feedback? *[ask for permission]*

I am committed to your success and I am confident that you are as well *[acknowledge each of your commitments]*

I couldn't help noticing ... *[your observation]*

The consequence/impact/result is ... *[describe the impact]*

What's your experience/perspective ...? *[check-in, walk in their shoes]*

So what you're saying is ... *[listening relentlessly]*

Let's see what solutions we can create to address the situation ... *[explore]*

Based on my observations and your perspective, I recommend ... *[contribute your recommendations]*

*Deliver Positive Feedback Too.* We have assumed thus far that our feedback is going to be constructive, an area that screams for improvement. However, we need to communicate positive feedback as much as constructive feedback. As we saw in the last chapter, people are starved for appreciation, admiration, and respect. To help feed this need, we can use positive feedback to recognize people and spark their self-delusion instead of their self-deflation. Even an offhand comment can deliver a powerful high-five. For example, "That's one of the things I like about you. You ..." Then describe the behavior you value as a way of reinforcing it and encouraging its recurrence. When was the last time someone gave you positive feedback this way? It's so rare that this approach alone will set you apart from the mediocre. It will distinguish you as the person everyone wants to work for.

*6. Ask for Feedback.* Have your managers ever asked you, "So how am I doing? What can I do better to serve you?" Would you look for the hidden cameras if they did?

The CEO of ING Direct employs this strategy year after year, and he reaps the rewards. Every December, Arkadi Kuhlmann gives ING employees the opportunity to vote anonymously whether he should be CEO for another year. Why does he ask? Because, as Arkadi shared with *The New York Times*, "I don't want to serve here unless I've got the commitment of people genuinely wanting me to serve." He admits that if the ING people are as important as he says they are, then they should have a say in whether he continues to lead.

Arkadi emphasizes that, the vote is not about being popular. A vote in his favor is a vote of confidence for the company's battle cry and a vote of confidence for his ability to lead people to victory.

Interestingly, Arkadi phrases the question in his annual voting ritual as follows: "Would you vote for me *to serve with you* for another year?" Notice that he does not focus on his position as the CEO. He doesn't mention anything about "running the company." He sincerely sees his role as one in which he has the privilege to serve with people in the accomplishment of a mission.

By calling for the vote and asking to serve with them for another year, Arkadi communicates a few important things: (1) he doesn't take his job for granted, (2) he is accountable to ING people to walk his talk, (3) he recognizes and appreciates their opinion, (4) he is committed to combating complacency and forgoing the status quo, (5) he is not afraid of failure or being rejected; he is more committed to serving, and (6) he is modeling for all other leaders in the company the importance of asking people for feedback.

Arkadi's colleagues and the directors on the ING board think he's nuts. He's well aware of this. But he is nuts in furtherance of his battle cry — to serve with people to accomplish the company's objectives. Being "nuts" separates the moxie from the mediocre. In spite of (or arguably, as a result of) his being "nuts," ING continues to rise under his leadership.

Most companies run hierarchically. Leaders are in charge of the people below them, but they don't operate as if they are accountable to those people. Asking for feedback underscores your accountability to the people you serve.

There are two reasons why we rarely ask for feedback from our peers or the people we lead. First, like the people receiving our feedback, we too hate criticism, and second, because of who is offering the feedback, we tend to discount it.

Let's start with the fact that we hate criticism. As we have explored many times thus far, we each have a deep fear of being rejected, regardless of who is doing the rejecting. Feedback that is anything other than glowing praise must be a criticism. And criticism is essentially a rejection of some aspect of us. Instinctually we go on the defense. That's just human nature.

Larry announced a new promotion to encourage the sales team to drive sales of the company's new product. Larry announced the details of the bonus on a conference call with all of his sales managers. A question was raised about leads that had been identified prior to the start date but sold during the promotion period. Larry and his HR representative mutually agreed that sales resulting from those leads would indeed qualify for the bonus. Following the announcement, Grace, one of Larry's smartest sales managers, called Larry to clarify that the sale to her team's biggest client (which was closing the following week) would qualify for the bonus promotion. Larry contradicted the answer that was given in the conference call. "No. The bonus will only be triggered by leads identified and entered into our database after the start of the promotion and closed before the end of the year." Stunned, Grace shot off an e-mail to Larry and copied the HR representative questioning the contradiction and the policy, cautioning that it would drive the wrong behavior. Larry called Grace immediately, furious over her "offensive" e-mail. Grace was dumbfounded. "I'm confused. What was offensive about my e-mail? I was just trying to clarify the policy and offer my perspective." After a heated debate, Larry finally revealed his true fear when he said, "Are you trying to make me look dumb by highlighting my mistake?"

What if we didn't look at it as criticism and instead looked at it as a rare opportunity to understand another's observations and a contribution to our own development? With this mindset, we can embrace and appreciate observations, feedback, and even outright criticism. When we stop operating on autopilot and consciously let go of the need to defend, explain, or justify our behavior, we have can actually benefit from feedback.

The key is to pause and be grateful for the chance to hear another's viewpoint, listen without interrupting, and thank them for their contribution. One of the side benefits of taking this approach is that when we stop resisting, the other side stops criticizing. Simply say, "Thank you for your observations" or "Thanks for being honest with me about how you feel. I appreciate the feedback." We don't have to agree with feedback, but we should be grateful to know another's perspective. It gives us the choice and the power to do something about our behavior or their perspective – or nothing at all.

The second reason we don't ask for feedback is that we don't value the source. We are all influenced by something called "value attribution." We attribute value to an idea, suggestion, comment, or feedback based on the person offering it. As a result, we assume that feedback or an idea that comes from a lower-level employee does not have as much value as it would if it came from our boss or an officer of the company.

To prove this theory, one of the best violinists on the planet, Joshua Bell, once dressed as a street performer to play his $3.5 million violin for passengers in a Washington, D.C., subway. He found a corner of the platform and casually started playing. He was his masterful self, but people did not notice. They judged him on his outfit and the surroundings, not on the sound of his music. More than a thousand people walked by without so much as a glance at the world-famous violinist presenting a concert for them. Joshua normally performs to sold-out crowds around the world, but the subway riders could not see beyond the picture in front of them. It told them a different story. They attributed less value to his performance that day because they perceived him to be merely a street performer playing in subway station for free. Had they paid to attend a sold-out performance in one of the best concert halls in the country to hear the world-famous Joshua Bell, their perceptions would have been starkly different. Then they would have attributed enormous value to the quality of Joshua's performance based on a different perception.

This same value attribution impacts our perception of the feedback we receive. If we receive it from the "wrong" person, such as someone two levels below us or from someone we do not respect, then we tend to discount and discard it, even if the feedback is 100 percent accurate. On the flip side, if we receive feedback from someone we regard highly, such as the CEO, we may accept that feedback blindly, even if it is 100 percent inaccurate.

Similarly, the influence of value attribution affects our ability to consider suggestions and ideas from people we work with. If we perceive someone to be of high quality, we will attribute that perception we have of them to the value of their ideas. Conversely we are more likely to discount an idea coming from someone whose value we have discounted.

No matter how much we despise the thought of being vulnerable and risking rejection, asking for feedback helps us lift the fog in our relationships with others. And because people are dictated by their self-delusion (that the world revolves around them), they will deem our asking as an acknowledgement of their importance. And finally, because of the influence of participatory bias, our request for their participation will compel them to support any subsequent attempt we make to improve – the relationship, the communications, or ourselves.

Ed Koch, Mayor of New York City from 1978-1989, was famous for asking, "How'm I doing?" when he greeted people on the street. It became his catchphrase. How intentionally he was listening to their answers is subject to debate, but at least he was asking the right question.

7. *Suspend the Story.* I e-mailed one of my oldest friends to schedule a time to get together, but she never e-mailed me back. We had gotten into a spat the previous year and were in the process of reconnecting. When she didn't e-mail me back, I made up a story that she no longer wanted to reconnect. We were not going be friends after all, I told myself. A week later she called out of the blue saying she was thinking about me and wanted to reach out. When I asked her about the e-mail, she said she had recently changed her e-mail address and never checked that old e-mail. I just shook my head, amazed that I didn't pick up the phone and call her to get together. I had been caught up in holding up my story instead of suspending it.

When we miscommunicate, fail to communicate, or create missed expectations, people are left to wonder, filling in gaps with their stories. And when people fabricate stories, conflict becomes inevitable. The only way to address conflict is to confront the other person. But we must be wary because confrontation amplifies the fear of rejection, thereby causing people to automatically defend themselves. There is an opportunity for us to contribute to someone even while confronting them, provided that we remember their fear of rejection and we suspend our own stories.

There is a powerful phrase that will allow us to confront without condemning: "What happened?" No judgment. No accusation. Just curiosity. This invites the other person to explain and share their perspective, including any fabricated stories, allowing us to identify the communication breakdown. When we approach conflict with curiosity we initiate a dance instead of a standoff.

When we make assumptions about people and situations, we leave no room for alternative explanations, hence the standoff. Instead, drop your own assumptions and defenses, and genuinely wonder what a reasonable, rational person must have been thinking to act or behave in such a way. "I'm curious ..." "I'm wondering why ..." "I'm interested to learn ..." are excellent curiosity phrases. Bear in mind, your body language and your voice must match your curiosity, so don't scowl or roll your eyes when you say, "I'm wondering ..." And don't add condemning words to your curiosity phrase. "I'm wondering why your head is screwed on backward today," will not likely garner the contribution to the relationship you are committed to.

My dad was the quintessential salesman and he used curiosity to start every confrontation. His famous line was, "Help me understand. I'm confused." But rest assured, my dad was rarely confused. He was sharp, savvy, and insightful, always checking his facts. But he knew miscommunications happened more often than not, and he knew he would escalate the confrontation by appearing as if he were on the attack. So he checked his ego and began by asking questions. He would look directly at the other person, assume an open, inquisitive, curious expression, and say, "Help me, I'm confused. I thought we agreed … What happened?" This inevitably put the other person at ease, inviting them to share their side first. My dad was stepping into their shoes to fully understand their view instead of launching into an attack that he knew would just put the person on the defensive and shut down all communication. With a complete understanding of the other side's perception of the situation, my dad could now dance with that person instead of duel.

As Sergeant Joe Friday said in *Dragnet*, "Just the facts, ma'am." That's the focus with your first statement. Skip the dramatic fairy-tale, rich with heroes and villains. The other person will just poke holes in it because they are on the defense. Rather, describe the facts as you experienced them using objective observations – and skip the accusations. "I'm wondering why you didn't show up to the meeting." "I'm curious why you didn't return the customer's call by the end of the day as we had promised." "I thought we agreed that you would complete the report by Monday morning." Then throw out the white flag that allows the other person to salvage their dignity when they lob an excuse: "What happened?" State it as a straightforward inquiry, not a veiled indictment. Ask if you are presuming there is a really good reason it didn't happen and you are on the edge of your seat for what that could possibly be. We are curious, wondering if perhaps we have missed something. We don't want our words, our body language, or our voice to betray our genuine curiosity, especially if a small part of us might also be thinking, "What's *wrong* with you?"

At this point, you must now be feeling like a therapist to the stars. Remain flexible in whatever happens next. Continue to listen relentlessly. Don't forget to fan their self-delusion so they know your world revolves around them, even if just that conversation. Be curious as if an Oscar-winning movie were unfolding in front of you. Stay steadfast in your vow to understand what happened from the other person's point of view.

Once they have satisfied your curiosity and you have engaged in relentless listening, it is your turn to share your perspective. Be sure to forcefully but delicately interrupt any interruptions. Avoid being condescending or pejorative, lest you fuel their defensive fire. Add your own perspective with "I" language. You are sharing your point of view and observations, so communicate that. By doing so, you are clarifying that you are not making dogmatic rulings or final judgments; you are merely stating your perspective of a situation. "From my point of view ..." "The way I see it ..."

It is critical to avoid any statements that paint the other person with a sweeping generalization. "You are always late." "You never do what I ask." Use these and watch a shield of armor appear as the other person goes into battle ready to defend themselves. Instantly they will be thinking of the one time they actually showed up on time or did more than was expected. They will distract the focus by arguing that our "always" or "never" is incorrect.

When we confront an impending conflict by suspending our story in favor of hearing theirs, we demonstrate our commitment to the success of that person and to our relationship with them. Add a genuine curiosity for their experience and an authentic sharing of your own point of view, and you will successfully create a bridge in that relationship. You are demonstrating through your words, your body language, and your voice that you are committed to addressing the conflict and that in spite of the conflict, you still respect and value the other person. But if you approach people ready to accuse and convict them of their poor judgment, rest assured you will trigger their fear of being rejected by you. With this insecurity, they will immediately go on the defensive.

Most people avoid conflict altogether at work and at home. They would rather be right than related. They would rather cut off the relationship than risk being rejected by confronting a situation and having to own any responsibility for it. It happens every day at the office, in our families, and in our communities. People are more committed to protecting their ego than they are to protecting the relationship. They would prefer to reject the other person by avoiding them, making up stories, and cutting off the conversation and relationship altogether. This ensures that they will never be rejected by that person.

The way people deal with conflict breeds mediocrity. From the receptionist to the CEO, people are run by their fears, more committed to avoiding rejection and protecting their egos than they are to the success of relationships.

Confronting conflict is an area that is starved for "business as *unusual*." This is your opportunity to rise above the madness, to stand out from the pedestrians, to stay devoted to the bigger picture. This is your opportunity to be a breath of fresh air. In so doing you will not only contribute to your relationships, you will also be a role model for others to do the same. That alone will make you more than just their boss or their manager; it will make you an extraordinary leader.

A great way to practice this dance is with children. These short people are honest and loving. They aren't going to reject you for confronting a conflict in a powerful, committed way; they are going to be grateful that someone wants to listen to them. Practice engaging with children, especially teens, using genuine curiosity.

## Curiosity is the Key to Lifting the Fog

Even without conflict, curiosity is a powerful tool to contribute to any relationship whether it is brand-new or years old.

Instinctually upon seeing another person, we size them up using our past experiences with similar-looking people. We fill in gaps by making assumptions, fabricating stories, and passing judgments based on what they're wearing, what they say and how they say it, their actions, their behavior, and their choices. We forget to be curious, opting instead to rely on our assumptions, stories, and judgments. And the fog creeps in.

In reality, our perceptions of people give us little genuine understanding of them and instead erect walls between us. We barely know the people we are related to, let alone the people we work with. But attempting to get to know them, we create a connection, lift the fog of assumptions and stories, and contribute to the relationship. Curiosity is key.

I am a huge fan of Table Topics (www.tabletopics.com), a game centered around a box of questions that force people to ask questions out of curiosity. For instance, "What was your best vacation?" "What was one thing you learned as a child that helped to influence your career choice?" "What is your favorite season?" "Would you rather live in a tree house or on a boat?" The company of the same name has customized the game for a variety of participants. There are now many versions of Table Topics: Family, Teens, Couples, 60s, 70s, and 80s, among others. We use Table Topics at the dinner table every night, regardless of who is at the table. It is far more interesting to hear about people's ideal vacation than to talk about the weather or the dreaded "How was school today?"

As an experiment, I placed a box of Table Topics on each table at my wedding reception without any instructions or mention of the game, eager to witness what would happen with the curiosity game. To my surprise and glee, our guests devoured the game. As soon as they sat down, they were diving for the question cards, distributing some to everyone around the table, and inviting each other to share their responses. One table was even writing everyone's different answers down on their set of cards. At the end of the night people didn't fight over the flower centerpieces, they fought over the boxes of Table Topics. They all agreed that it was refreshing to use interesting conversations to turn strangers into immediate friends, rather than make idle bar chat with strangers who are destined to remain strangers.

The CEO of Financial Engines in Palo Alto, California, uses Table Topics to create connections with his team. Whenever someone walks into his office, he asks them to pull a question from the box, and they both answer it. What an enjoyable and effortless way for the CEO to contribute to his relationships by using the power of curiosity to connect with people.

Susan Docherty, the leader of the sales, service, and marketing team at General Motors, plays musical chairs to keep her curiosity about people alive. Susan tenaciously sits in a different chair at each meeting. In her career she has seen too many leaders sit in the same chair, think the same way, and talk to the same people. This is a recipe for insularity and staleness. Susan resolved that when she became a leader with a big team, she was going to be disruptive, unpredictable, and dynamic. Sitting in different seats is one of the ways she disrupts the predictability of the meetings and connects with different people on her team. Her curiosity for others and their perspectives keeps her and her meetings fresh and innovative.

## Putting It Into Action

- When someone brings to you some drama or gossip, wonder aloud about the backstory to that story.

- When sending out an e-mail, writing a memo, or leaving a voice, consider how it will be received, not how you perceived it was communicated. What is the recipieny's perspective or viewpoint?

- Over-communicate about the progress of a project or a decision, even if all you have to say is, "The jury is still out," or "I haven't looked at it yet," or "The department head is looking into the legalities of the project before we can move forward."

- Spend time observing people in action or better yet, doing their job with them. Get on the phone if you are in charge of a customer service call center. Get to the plant floor and screw some bolts into a machine if you are the production manager. Start sweeping or cleaning the toilets. Not only will you experience their world, you may discover some things that could be improved to make them more effective, or make their jobs easier.

- Practice your relentless listening with your significant other and young people in your life. Retrace their words, paraphrase, summarize, and confirm what they've said.

- Practice helping people feel felt by saying "I can only imagine ..." or "That must have been ..."

- Observe how many times a day you are engaging in multi-task listening — driving, conference calls, taking out the garbage, or walking the dog all while talking on the phone.

- Take responsibility for a miscommunication that has occurred. Consider how you contributed to that miscommunication with your message or delivery, and then own it.

- Set clear expectations at the beginning of each meeting, each conversation, each conference call, and each relationship.

- Give feedback regularly by first asking permission and then treating the feedback as a contribution to their growth and development, not a reprimand or retribution.

- Make observations with people – avoid passing judgment.

- Ask for feedback from others, including your peers and people who report to you.

- Suspend your stories about people and their intentions. Encourage others to do the same. Say, "I don't think we have all the facts." "Let's wait to hear from them." "I'm sure there is a good reason behind all of this."

- Before convicting people, ask "What happened?" with the most genuine form of curiosity.

- Purchase a copy of TableTopics for your office.

# Chapter 7

## Crush the Patterns

. . . . . . . . . . . . . . . . . . . .

In the fifth inning of the third game of the 1932 World Series between the New York Yankees and the Chicago Cubs, with the score tied 4 - 4, Babe Ruth stepped into the batter's box. He was one of baseball's greatest hitters of all time, and had already hit a home run in the first inning. Everyone thought it implausible that he would hit another.

With the count at two balls and two strikes, the Cubs were jeering, and in turn, Ruth was taunting the Cubs with his theatrics. He dramatically pounded his bat on home plate and then pointed the bat to the center field bleachers, indicating his intent to hit the next pitch right there. This hubris enraged the Cubs pitcher, who employed all of his speed and power to hurl his fastest ball to the plate in an attempt to strike out the great batter. With one crack of the bat, Ruth hit a line drive into the center field bleachers, exactly where he had pointed.

Following the game, a sportswriter asked Babe Ruth, "But what if you hadn't hit the ball to the spot you indicated?" Ruth looked incredulous as he replied, "I never thought of that." Babe Ruth hit 714 home runs in his history-making career. He frequently practiced this concept, called "framing."

## Framing

People make choices in part on the way a problem or situation is presented. In fact, depending on how a situation is stated, people will actually make inconsistent decisions when presented with the same situation that is simply framed differently. As an example, "After one year on this new diet, 75 percent of the people lost weight." Fantastic! I will be in that 75 percent!" Or "After one year on this new diet, 25 percent of people did not lose any weight." Automatically we think, "Yikes. I might be in that 25 percent. That would be maddening to suffer on a diet for a year and not lose any weight. I'll try a different diet."

We can influence people's choices merely by reframing the choice. For example, if the marketing group told Dari that she has a 20 percent chance of failing if she goes with Strategy A, she will hesitate. No one likes to fail – failing is just a slippery slope away from rejection. But if the marketing group reframes the choice for Dari so that it is presented as an 80 percent success rate if she goes with Strategy A, then she will likely not hesitate at all. By putting Strategy A in a more desirable frame, the marketing group has influenced Dari to look at Strategy A differently. That's reframing.

Another example is often used by great account managers. Instead of saying, "I've got some bad news. Our solution has been delayed and will not be available on Friday as we promised." The best of the best say, "Great news! Our product will be ready on Tuesday!" It's all about the frame you use to describe a problem or situation. With the right frame, you can influence how people choose to see that problem or situation. Put an ugly frame on it and people will see it as an ugly picture.

Babe Ruth chose a very powerful frame when he stepped up to bat. He didn't say to himself, "I hope I hit this one. If I don't, I will not be great, and we won't win." He framed the situation so that he was focusing only on success. "Into which stands do I want to hit this ball?"

We can help people frame their situations in more desirable frames, or we run the risk that they'll start framing their own pictures inadvertently. And often when people do their own framing unconsciously, the frame doesn't always fit. People tend to frame based on their past experiences. They look to their past to outline their present choices. As an example, suppose we ask Cory to make prospecting calls and we also ask him to research marketing conferences. If based on his prior experiences, Cory associates calling potential customers with being rejected, he will likely frame this situation in his mind as "Pick up the phone and get rejected, or research marketing conferences and get appreciation for moving something forward for the team." Inevitably he will procrastinate on the smiling and dialing and choose instead to dive right into the research. So, our past experiences form our beliefs and our beliefs dictate the frame we choose, which then dictates our actions.

But we can help Cory reframe the situation. We can pitch it as a wonderful opportunity to make a huge difference to the whole team by doing some live research by dancing with potential customers over the phone to discover what their current struggles are. Now we have reframed the entire situation for Cory. We have clarified the expectations we have for the calls and explained how Cory can win with this assignment. We have also shared how he can make a difference. Now Cory sees this as a fabulous opportunity instead of a torturous task.

Alternatively, you can reframe the situation for Cory based on his underlying fear of rejection. You can say, "Cory if you don't make these calls, you are going to be embarrassed at the sales meeting on Monday." This will certainly light a fire under his butt, but do you really want to threaten Cory every time you need him to pick up the phone? At some point you need Cory to start the reframing for himself.

In a scene from the 1977 movie *Star Wars,* young Luke Skywalker and the great Jedi Master Yoda are on the planet

Dagoba engaged in Jedi training when Luke crashes his spaceship in the mud. As the spaceship starts to sink, the two characters have the following exchange:

**Skywalker:** We'll never get it out now!

**Yoda:** So certain are you? Always with you, it cannot be done.

**Skywalker:** Master Yoda, moving stones is one thing. This is totally different!

**Yoda (slamming his staff on the ground):** No! No different! Only different in your mind! You must unlearn what you have learned.

**Skywalker:** OK. I'll try.

**Yoda (again slamming his staff on the ground):** No! Try not! Do, or do not. There is no try.

So Skywalker "tries." The ship comes up a bit, but then sinks back down.

**Skywalker:** I can't! It's too big!

**Yoda:** Size matters not. Look at me! Judge me by my size, do you?

Eventually Yoda uses "the Force" to raise the ship and puts it back on dry land.

**Skywalker:** I, I don't believe it.

**Yoda:** That is why you fail.

Yoda was demonstrating the framing effect. Luke's beliefs that he had to be bigger than the ship in order to raise it up framed his mindset that he could not do it. Yoda was demonstrating for the unsuspecting Luke that Luke's beliefs were dictating his actions. Yoda exasperatingly said, "Do, or do not. There is no try." In other words, "do" and "do not" are actions. "Try" is merely a belief.

Right after law school, I found myself pulling out the best-looking frames to land my first job. While studying for the bar exam in Chicago, I had decided in a moxie moment to move to California. I had just graduated from law school and did not have a job to show for my seven years of higher education. So in between bar prep courses I scoured the *Employee Weekly*, a national newspaper for job seekers, looking for any opportunity to use my accounting degree, my CPA, and my law degree. Each week I was reminded in black and white that every employer required a minimum of five to seven years of experience, not just the requisite education.

Because I had become maniacally focused on getting to California, I consciously and flatly ignored their experience requirements. I didn't have time to get five to seven years of experience. I chose instead to frame my situation differently for the potential employers. Every day I mailed letters answering any and all ads for jobs in California that had something to do with accounting, business, or law. I strategically chose words that communicated that I would be a perfect addition to their team. I did not apologize for not having the right experience – that frame was ugly. Nor did I lie. I just did not mention the obvious. I assumed that, in spite of the experience holes in my résumé, I could wow them if they opened the door even a smidgen. So I pitched my degrees and my strengths – not my missing experience.

Not surprisingly, I received a lot of "Thank you, but no thank you" letters in response. I even received a few snide comments such as, "Did you not see our requirements? We're looking for someone with five to seven years of experience." And then I received a call that gave me the chance to change everything.

The recruiting manager at KPMG Peat Marwick, one of the "Big Six" accounting firms (back when there were six), had received my letter. He was coming to Chicago and wanted to meet me for lunch. Bingo! The door had opened. Throughout lunch, I continued to convey my confidence that I had the education, the passion, and the enthusiasm that would make me a perfect addition to the firm, in spite of not having the experience they originally sought. Once off the résumé paper, I let my personality and enthusiasm work in my favor. The recruiting manager pointed out the obvious, that I was not the right person for the five to seven years' experience job; however, my letter had intrigued him, and our lunch had confirmed his prediction. He invited me to California to interview with his office.

The next morning I immediately picked up the phone and called each of the other five "Big Six" accounting firms to let them know I was coming to California to interview with KPMG. I was sure that since I was already going to be out there on someone else's dime that they would want to interview with me as well. Again, the power of my words and the conviction and passion of my voice worked magic. I told them that they just needed to meet me to learn my differentiation from all other graduating candidates. KPMG unlocked the door; I was just brazenly kicking it open from there. With moxie, I landed interviews and eventually an offer from every "Big Six" accounting firm in California.

## Our Beliefs

Tenet #7 says, "We allow our beliefs and thoughts to dictate our ambitions and perseverance." Beliefs are our preconceptions, our biases, our notions, and our fixed ideas. They are our thoughts about a situation, a person, and ourselves that we bring to the table before learning more. For instance, I believe that people on the West Coast are more adventurous than people on the East Coast, while people on the East Coast are more family-committed than people on the West Coast, and that people in the Midwest are nicer than those on either coast. I judge people who dress professionally as smart and people who don't as unambitious. I instantly characterize people who talk on cell phones in the library and kids who text while engaged in conversations with others as rude and disrespectful. I believe that people who complain about work are victims. I judge people with mean kids to be lazy and ineffective parents.

These are just judgments, beliefs, prejudices, and stereotypes I have collected over the years based on my experiences. They are neither right nor wrong. We are all judgmental, and it is rarely our intention. It is just human nature to walk around with a slew of judgments about ourselves and about other people. Even when we are committed to being totally open-minded, we are assaulted by past experiences and the beliefs we have created based on them. (Note: When someone judges people based on things other than their actions and behaviors, such as their race and gender, that person becomes racist and sexist.)

Our beliefs impact our relationships with others. It is more difficult to have compassion for others when we have passed judgment on them without knowing the backstory. We haven't journeyed with people; we don't know what they have been through in their life, let alone their entire day before crossing paths with us in our day. We only see them in one moment and based on the action or behavior in that moment, we make a sweeping judgment about what kind of person they are. It is incredibly limiting to our ability to have transformative relationships with others. We have already passed judgment on them in merely one transaction.

Our beliefs also impact our own ambitions and perseverance. We have collected beliefs about ourselves over our lifetime. The older we are, the more experiences we have had in which we have failed, or in which life has disappointed us. The younger we are, the fewer experiences we have collected, and therefore the less our beliefs get in our way. Our beliefs have one purpose – to protect us. Our beliefs were formed because we were hurt, disappointed, upset, saddened, frustrated, or rejected in the past by some person or experience. That belief was created to protect us from feeling that way again. As a result, our beliefs serve a purpose, but some drive us forward and some stop us altogether.

As an example, I believe that our solutions transform floundering managers into effective leaders. This belief fuels me to pick up the phone and call a new prospect. It drives me forward. However, when a potential client says "No," I have to be vigilant not to allow that "No" to create an overriding belief about something being wrong with me or the company or our solution.

If I do, then that overriding belief will stop me from picking up the phone, lest I feel rejected again. I could instead believe that something is wrong with that person. I could believe that he is a small thinker, not ready to think big. Another belief that will make me feel even better is that he is a jerk and doesn't deserve our great solution. That does indeed feel smugly good in the moment, and it may allow me to pick up the phone again, but in the long run it stops me from considering how my pitch might be improved. Because nothing is wrong with me or my pitch; something is wrong with the guy on the other end of the phone. Regardless, notice how my beliefs have the power to sabotage my actions with this person and other people going forward. I would be better served to stick with my initial belief, suspend my sabotaging beliefs, acknowledge that there is always a backstory, reflect on what I could do better, and take some actions that would have created different beliefs.

Like every person on the planet, I am literally run or stopped by my preconceptions about myself, about others, and about how the world works. My beliefs then create my thoughts and from my thoughts I take action (or in some cases, I don't take action). As a result of my belief that the guy on the other end of the phone was a jerk, I wrote off the entire client and never pitched them again. And then, looking to confirm that belief, I relayed the story to my team members, of course framing it to make me look like the hero. My preconceptions about that guy literally stopped me from engaging with him ever again. Good riddance! I said. And guess what? We never did business with that potential client. As we will see momentarily, filtering experiences to confirm our beliefs creates a self-fulfilling prophecy.

Conversely, I hold beliefs and preconceptions that are far more powerful and support me in moving forward. I believe that people are starved for enthusiasm and attention; I believe that people like to talk about themselves; and I believe that I am an enthusiastic, relentless listener who can easily make conversation with anyone else because I am a master at making people feel like it is all about them. From these beliefs, I carry with me every day the presumption that people will enjoy talking to me. As a result, when I am in new situations, I never hesitate to meet new people. My beliefs create my thoughts, which cause me to take action. I have framed those new situations in a way that makes me eager to connect with others.

In a nutshell, preconceptions are paralyzing when they are grounded in our fears, especially our greatest fear – being rejected. Our fears are just our beliefs dressed up for Halloween. These fear-induced beliefs create fear-provoked thoughts that stop us from taking action or divert our action from our battle cry and our goals.

## Confirmation Bias

Once we have a belief, a preconception influencing our actions, our filters do a great job of locking in those beliefs. We are influenced by a behavioral phenomenon called "confirmation bias." English psychologist Peter Wason originally coined the term, which accurately describes the process in which we take action based on a belief and then we look for evidence to confirm that belief. In other words, as soon as we have established a view about ourselves or others, our brain searches for information that confirms that view, and at the same time it disregards, ignores, and refutes any information that might bring that view into question. Any new information is scrutinized and filtered. If it supports our belief, we embrace it. If it contradicts our belief, we pay no attention to it, discount it, or unequivocally reject it.

Let's go back to the potential client and observe how confirmation bias worked on me. When he said, "No," I embraced the belief that he was a jerk. I then retold the story to my team and they agreed. I filtered what they said as evidence that my initial belief was accurate – there was something wrong with this guy. I even filtered the next call to a potential client through the belief that that guy was a jerk. When they showed interest, I thought, "See, that guy *is* a jerk! Nothing is wrong with me and my pitch doesn't need any improving. Something is wrong with him. I am never going to pitch that company again." That's confirmation bias at work. We literally look for evidence to confirm our beliefs.

Notice that the experience with the guy on the phone did not negate my belief that I am enthusiastic and great at establishing relationships. I scrutinized and filtered his rejection and it didn't support the belief that I am an enthusiastic relationship-starter, so I disregarded the evidence that may have questioned the belief that I am enthusiastic.

### Self-Fulfilling Prophecy

A self-fulfilling prophecy takes the filter of the confirmation bias to the next level to forecast the outcome of events. A self-fulfilling prophecy occurs when people forecast their future and then fulfill that forecast with their actions. They engage in behaviors and take actions that produce results that eventually validate their initial beliefs. Essentially people consciously or unconsciously confirm their beliefs and preconceptions with their actions, and a viscous circle is created. For example, imagine that someone on your team believes she is atrociously weak at rallying troops. We don't think she is, but she does. When we ask her to lead the new project for the team, she can only focus on the fact (it's really just a belief but in her mind it has become a fact) that she is an atrocious troop-rallyer. On the foundation of that belief, she gives the most pathetic kick-off to the project, and *voila!* She successfully validates her belief that she is an atrocious leader. She had literally forecasted her own results based on her preconception about her rallying and leading inabilities. That's a self-fulfilling prophecy at work.

Consider Michael. He is convinced that he is not great at solving problems. His belief was formed years ago and he has been confirming it ever since. He can point to many instances in which he failed to successfully solve a problem. In spite of his own beliefs and preconceptions, Michael continues to find himself in predicaments requiring problem-solving prowess. What usually happens is that Michael procrastinates so long based on his strong beliefs, that his boss or one of his teammates rushes in at the eleventh hour to solve the problem. Just before the entire project implodes, as he is removed as the team lead, he thinks to himself, "See, there it is again! I'm a terrible problem-solver." Michael filters this latest debacle through his restrictive belief to confirm once again that he is in fact a terrible problem-solver. By relying on his own beliefs to frame his actions, Michael satisfied the prediction that he would fail, which then confirmed his belief and strengthened this rickety frame. It's an exasperating vicious cycle that's driving his lack of success. That's confirmation bias and self-fulfilling prophecy at work.

## Commitment Sabotage

Michael's maddening circularity of commitment sabotage confronts even the best of us. People everywhere identify their commitment sabotage, witness it happening again, and then self-flagellate for allowing it to rear its ugly head and sabotage their success. As if they have an out-of-body experience, watching themselves harbor a restrictive belief, take action based on that restrictive belief, and then confirm the veracity of that restrictive belief. They complete the vicious circle with an exclamation, "A-ha! There it is again! It must be true."

To change their results, people focus on changing their beliefs and thoughts. They endeavor to positive-think their way into a new action. They attempt to change their beliefs to change their results. They buy the latest self-help book, hoping to find another way to think. Blaming their weak willpower, they undertake to turn their restrictive beliefs into hopeful, positive beliefs. They try motivation, cheerleading, coaching, and even positive-thinking exercises. As their boss, you muse, why can't they just change their thoughts?

But the entire "positive thinking" movement and the craze over *The Secret* is a bunch of gibberish … in a vacuum. All by itself, thinking positively doesn't change anything because our beliefs and thoughts have roots much deeper than fleeting happy thoughts. However, we don't want to disregard positive thinking altogether. Without it, people are in for a challenge, as negative thinking always tests endurance.

The battle to change thoughts is an uphill one, as the beliefs and preconceptions upon which those thoughts are founded are pretty well engrained and have been for decades. And those well-engrained, restrictive beliefs generate well-engrained, restrictive thoughts which then lead to predictable, restrictive actions and results – the self-fulfilling prophecies. And those predictable, restrictive actions and results work to confirm those restrictive thoughts, which then confirm those restrictive beliefs. And the vicious cycle continues.

No one is immune from this commitment sabotage. Not even you. Everyone risks sabotaging their commitments by looking to their thoughts and beliefs to support them. But everyone also has the ability to combat that sabotage by interrupting the pattern of restrictive belief ➔ restrictive thought ➔ restrictive action by using out-of-the-pattern *actions*. Out-of-the-pattern actions cause a much-needed "Pattern Crush."

## Pattern Crush

The only way to combat the commitment sabotage is to interrupt the cycle of restrictive beliefs ➔ restrictive thoughts ➔ restrictive actions ➔ restrictive thoughts ➔ restrictive beliefs. New thoughts – regardless of how positive and happy they are – will not interrupt the cycle, *only new actions will*. When people ignore the thoughts and start with a new action first, they have an opportunity to create new and different thoughts about themselves. Only through an action-based pattern crush can people actually change their well-engrained beliefs about themselves. Instead of trying to convince themselves to have different beliefs, they look to their new actions and new results to create those new beliefs.

As an example, for a long time I believed that I was not a good public speaker. In fact in the mock trial competition in Mr. Rogina's Business Law 101 class in high school, I formed the belief that I could not think on my feet. So, I memorized my closing statements and as a back-up, wrote every word of my speech on index cards, which I clung to fiercely. I embraced a preconception that I was not a good speaker and this preconception generated many thoughts about not being a good speaker, including being rejected by my classmates and Mr. Rogina. I confirmed those thoughts with my not-a-great-speaker actions. Not only did I confirm my not-a-great-speaker thoughts with my not-a-great-speaker actions, I in fact forecasted that I was not going to be a good speaker during the competition. I was so terrified of failing from my not-a-great-speaker beliefs that I failed – and failed miserably. A self-fulfilling prophecy. I forgot the lines I had memorized, I lost my place in my index cards and fumbled repeatedly and embarrassingly, much to the dismay of my teammates. And as strongly as I wanted to be an attorney, I referenced this belief engrained by this experience when I vowed never to litigate in front of a judge and jury again.

For the next 15 years I harbored these restrictive beliefs, confirmed them regularly, and allowed them to generate restrictive actions. I clung to my beliefs and never spoke in public unless it was a speech that was beautifully crafted by me and that was propped up on a podium behind which I could stand and read, protected by wood from inevitable audience rejection.

When I was transitioning out of the practice of law, I created a new battle cry – to influence people to make change. To influence people effectively, I needed to write and speak. I had to become an influential speaker. But to do this I had to do something about my restrictive beliefs if I expected to stand up and influence more than the lighting in the room. And while positive thinking certainly made me more positive and hopeful about my situation, it didn't make me change my restrictive belief about being a not-so-great speaker.

To change my belief at its core, I needed a Pattern Crush. My Pattern Crush included a variety of out-of-my-pattern actions. I joined *Speaking Circles* to get over my fear of standing in front of people. I joined *Toastmasters* to get over my addiction to using the written word while hiding behind a podium. I became a volunteer director of an entrepreneurial education program at a middle school to force me to speak regularly in front of people. I became an indoor cycling instructor to hone my skill of enthusiastically capturing an audience, guiding them through an experience, and finishing within one hour. Suddenly I was speaking without notes and without melting. Because my experiences were no longer confirming my restrictive beliefs, those beliefs began to fade and be replaced by new beliefs. My actions coupled with my ambitious battle cry were creating new beliefs about myself altogether. Had I suddenly become a great speaker? Hardly. It was years before I could describe my speaking as dancing with the audience from the stage. And it was even longer before I ever earned a standing ovation. But I had successfully crushed the restrictive pattern, and that made all the difference in my ambitions and perseverance.

## Identifying Patterns to Crush

How do you identify restrictive beliefs and the resultant restrictive patterns that are sabotaging people's commitments? Listen to the words they use, watch their body language, and pay attention to the actions they take (or fail to take).

**Words – Say it So it Sticks.** What people say and how they say it impacts their confidence (and others' confidence in them) and therefore their level of ambition and their ability to persevere in those ambitions. Likewise, what people say and how they say it is indicative of their confidence level.

Notice the words that people choose; they offer a window into the beliefs that run them. Observe the use of noncommittal, ambiguous, vague phrases such as "I hope," "I'll try," "I'll cross my fingers," "If I'm lucky," "I'm not sure," "If it works," "We'll see," and my personal favorite, "If it was meant to be." People use these reservation words to frame their lack of commitment and protect themselves from ultimate responsibility. When people inevitably give up or fail, they'll be able to say, "It wasn't in my control. I hoped for it. I tried. I told you I wasn't sure; I said it may or may not work. But I never committed to success."

These words prevent people from making a commitment to succeed no matter what. These words allow people an excuse *in case of* unpredictable circumstances. But we want and need people to commit and execute *in spite of* circumstances; we want them to be relentless and uncompromising; we want them to use their moxie. For words to stick and for a solid commitment created, people must eliminate their spineless language.

When we flag and gut those gutless words, we need to insist the void be filled with commitment words. These include "It's happening." "We'll do it." "I'll be there." "I promise." "I guarantee it." "I will." "I'm going to." "I choose to." "I'll make it happen." The mere act of saying these words out loud works to redefine the preconceived beliefs ➔ thoughts dance. They may not believe they can meet your deadline, but by saying they will, they are essentially snubbing their preconceptions in favor of different actions.

One Saturday morning in the height of the dot-com bubble in Silicon Valley, the leadership team at a technology company had gathered to determine the future of the company. It had become a behemoth by acquiring numerous start-ups, and to stay competitive they were considering many alternatives. It was at this meeting that Alex found himself faced with the biggest challenge of his professional life.

Alex had presented the team with a plan to spin off one of these acquired subsidiaries into a separate company and then to take it public. He had written a business plan and made a pitch to the leaders requesting a $30 million investment to make the subsidiary succeed as a stand-alone company. Essentially, he was asking the behemoth company to act like a venture capitalist and to invest in a start-up company that just happened to be one of its own subsidiaries. The leaders poked and prodded at the plan, but on paper it appeared solid.

When he was done with his inquisition, the CEO placed the challenge at Alex's feet. "We'll give you the $30 million, but if you fail, you're fired." Alex swallowed the fear-induced lump in his throat. He said, "I understand. This new company will not fail." While he had a solid business plan, he had no guarantee it was going to work, but Alex was committed to succeeding no matter what. He was committing his future and the company's future with his actions. He couldn't look to any preconceptions or beliefs to guide him. He had to focus only on his commitment, his battle cry. One year to the day, in spite of a skittish market, 9/11, a looming recession, and other unforeseen circumstances, Alex had successfully led the spin-off of the subsidiary from the behemoth parent company and the filing for a public offering on the NASDAQ. It was one of the last companies in Silicon Valley to IPO before the ubiquitous "dot-com bust." Alex became CEO.

As leaders, you can help people to start changing their beliefs and thoughts by requiring them to use powerful words instead of weak-willed ones.

**Voice – Say it So it's Heard.** The voice is another barometer of confidence. Uncertainty, anxiety, and self-doubt result in uncertain, anxious, and doubt-filled vocal chords. This might be revealed through the tone, the pace, the speed, even the volume. A timid, weak, uncertain voice influences the listener's perception of the speaker. Unquestionably it is an indication that the person whose lips are moving is not confident about themselves or about what they are saying.

**Actions Speak Louder than Words.** People are committed to exactly what they have. If they are overweight, they are committed to being overweight. Conversely, if they were committed to being thin, they would exert the extra effort it takes to regularly work out, eat healthy food, lose weight, and be thin. Likewise, if people smoke, they are committed to smoking. If they were committed to quitting, they would take actions that would have them quit in spite of how hard it would be. Similarly, if people are poor, they are committed to being poor. If they were committed to being wealthy, it would require a whole new paradigm of spending and earning actions, but they would take those actions and make those sacrifices in spite of circumstances. Finally, if people are stuck and unsuccessful, they are committed to being stuck and unsuccessful. If they were committed to being unstuck and successful, we would see them constantly taking actions, reinventing, improving, growing, developing, and changing.

Instead, people have put "change" in a risk-of-failure-and-rejection frame. So they cling to being safe and comfortable and pointing their finger at circumstances. Actions are a good indicator of what people are committed to and as you'll quickly notice, it's usually a commitment to getting (and keeping) exactly what they have.

None of this is meant as a judgment, just a reality check. When people are committed to change, they take different actions than they do when they are committed to the status quo. Just notice it.

**Dress – Look as if You Mean It.** The way people dress also speaks volumes about how confident and committed they feel. Do they look like they just rolled out of bed, or do they look like they are about to enter an important meeting? Are they wearing jeans or are they wearing a suit? When people dress professionally, we take notice. And when they don't, we also take notice. Sometimes we even make a judgment about people based on their dress and conclude that they are either committed or they aren't. Individuals use their daily costume to communicate their beliefs and thoughts to us, sometimes consciously, usually unconsciously.

One Fortune 500 company relies on its call center to connect with thousands of customers each day. In the call center, people sit in a cube for eight hours a day answering customer calls. Most of these call center operators admit that they accepted a job in the call center in hopes that they would be promoted out of the dungeon and into other areas of the company. To their disappointment, however, opportunities to move out rarely come knocking, and most call center managers sabotage any such efforts. As a result, people sit waiting for someone to rescue them from their life of detention in the cubicle walls with a phone glued to their head. Imagine how this perceived trap provokes frustration and resentment year after year.

Their belief that they are resigned to this life is evidenced by their commitment-sabotaging words, their failure to take different actions, and their choice of dress. People who have been in the call center for more than five years eventually resort to wearing sweats to work, some looking as if they just rolled out of bed. Their belief: "What difference does it make what I wear? Customers can't see me and I'm destined to a career in this cubicle and on this phone. Dressing any nicer won't matter."

One man's costume evidenced his battle cry. Preston had been in the cubes for more than five years, but his commitment to the company and to a career that contributes to others never faltered. He came to work every day dressed in the one suit he owned. And without fail, each day, someone would ask him accusatorially, "Why are you dressed up? Do you have an interview?" Aggravated, he shared with me, "I don't understand why they keep questioning my suit. Even my boss looks at me strangely. I just feel better when I'm dressed up. I feel like a professional. I'm determined to give the best service I can to our customers and the best service I can to my career." And then he said the words that really put it all into perspective, "I'm sure no one has ever said to the CEO, 'Why are you dressed up today?'"

## Changing Beliefs with Out-of-the-Pattern Actions

People with high self-efficacy believe they can perform well. Efficacy is an indicator of how someone perceives their ability to navigate the outside world. According to renowned psychologist Albert Bandura, people with high self-efficacy are more likely to view difficult tasks as something to be mastered rather than something to be avoided. These people are less likely to perpetrate commitment sabotage because they already have the requisite I-can-do-it beliefs. These beliefs then drive their success and the commitments they make.

People need high self-efficacy to initiate change for greater success. If they have low self-efficacy, their beliefs cause them to operate out of a smaller frame, so we cannot realistically rely on those beliefs to embrace difficult tasks and challenges. We can, however, help people to reframe their reality. Right now their reality is all based on their own experiences from the past, which have created those low-efficacy beliefs and thoughts that are contaminating their ambitions and their perseverance. Essentially, they are thinking too small because they think they are going to fail otherwise. People are literally destroying their own possibilities – but they don't have to.

If we want people to show up with commitment that is more than a flash in the pan, we must help them reframe and crush patterns with new actions. By doing so, we can influence their intrinsic motivation to operate differently and to persevere in their ambitions and commitments. To help people reframe and crush patterns:

1. Identify patterns to crush

2. Prevent your own preconceptions about people from

sabotaging your commitment to them

3. Show ruthless compassion and uncompromising empathy

4. Focus them on their battle cry

5. Challenge them to take new actions in the face of those restrictive beliefs

First, you must identify patterns to crush, such as procrastination, hedging bets, gutless words, uncertain voice, sloppy dress, empty promises, broken obligations, endless investigation and research, painful engagement of incessant committee reviews. These are all indications that people are searching for evidence to confirm their sabotaging beliefs and to fulfill a prophecy. Commitment sabotage is the symptom *and* the problem. It is causing people to fail but it is also an indication of why people are failing. But you can help them crush their pattern of commitment sabotage. Most people don't change sabotaging behavior because they don't even know they are sabotaging. By catching people in the act, you can help them become cognizant of their sabotaging behavior. Only then you can influence them to choose a new behavior.

Second, you must prevent your own beliefs about people from sabotaging your commitment to them. Through your experiences with certain people you have inevitably created your own restrictive beliefs about them. And isn't it so easy to just write people off? As we have seen previously in Chapter 6, whenever you interact with someone you have a choice. You can contribute to the relationship or you can contaminate it. When you catch people in their patterns, you can write them off with a sweeping judgment, "They're so lazy. I'll work around them." Or you could crush your own pattern about them and stay true to your commitment to their success. (Did I not warn you that you would be applying all of these strategies to yourself while you apply them to others?)

Third, you must show ruthless compassion and uncompromising empathy, for people are saddled with age-old sabotaging beliefs. You do this by kindly echoing back to them their words and mirroring for them their actions. Then you work with them to ascertain the true impact that their words and actions (or lack thereof) are having on their results. Then do what no other leader does. Ask questions and *listen relentlessly.* Step into their shoes. Experience the world from their Cole Haans. Dig deeper to understand their perspective. Listen to them. Listen so hard it hurts your head. Listen so they feel heard. Feel compassion for the fears they harbor, and empathize with those fears. Managers never do this. Only leaders do.

Fourth, focus them on their battle cry. Why are they here? What are their ambitions? What are they passionate about? What are their strengths? What will have them excited to take on new actions in the face of their fears and ferocious preconceptions?

Finally, challenge them to take new actions in spite of their restrictive beliefs and thoughts. Coach them to suggest some actions that are incongruent with their beliefs. Acknowledge that these actions will feel like an affront to their beliefs. Then educate them on the concepts of framing and pattern crushing. End with an authentic commitment to their growth, development, and success, in spite of whatever results from their new actions – success or failure.

My stepson was 11 and did not know how to ride a bike. I had been hearing for the prior three years that he can't, he won't, and he doesn't want to. I had watched him avoid the entire experience while all of his friends, including his younger sister, jumped on their bikes with glee. We tried training wheels but he would not even move the pedals. Clearly the years of not riding had built up the fear in his head so much that it was literally paralyzing him. His belief was that he could not do it, and it was going to take action to change that belief.

After doing some research on teaching older children how to ride bikes, I decided to focus on helping him first discover his balance. I removed the bike pedals, lowered the seat, and drove him to a park with a grassy hill. I reframed the mountain into a mole hill. I told him to forget about riding; we were just going to go out and find his balance. I explained to him that he was going to roll down the small hill at the park and that the grass would slow him down. In addition, his feet could touch the ground allowing him to stop himself at any time.

As we got out of the car, he had a look of panic. He began to cry. Tears were flowing, snot was dripping, and in between sobs he continued to repeat, "I can't. I'm scared." I suddenly realized that his parents and I had spent the last year telling him, "There's nothing to be scared of." Even his younger sister had said these exact words to him. But to him there was everything to be scared of.

I knew I needed to help him feel heard and felt before we could move past this. I gave him a hug and said, "I know you're scared. But the exciting things in life come when we feel fear and we do it anyway." I continued, "I'm scared all the time. I'm scared of driving. I'm scared of flying. I'm scared of speaking in front of people. I'm scared every day. Being scared is normal — when your heart pounds, it just means you're about to do something exciting and important to you. But we cannot allow the fear to stop us from experiencing those exciting and important things." He continued to sob but, starting to show his old soul, this time his words changed slightly. "I'm so conflicted," he said. "I know I can do it but I'm scared." Bingo. He felt heard and felt and he began to approach his out-of-the-pattern action with new words. We had gotten past the word "can't."

I encouraged him to just roll down a very small incline on the hill, and promised to run alongside him. I only needed to support him with that maneuver once. The very next time he wanted to do it by himself. Suddenly he was rolling down the hill and keeping himself up. He had found his balance instantly. He rolled down that hill again and again and again. And each time I cheered for him. Soon he asked for pedals and started rolling with his feet on the pedals. It took exactly one time for him to start pedaling on his own at the bottom of the hill. I cheered. I cried. He not only rode a bike – he overcame his own self-sabotage, using action instead of relying on his beliefs.

On our way home, I said effusively, "You are fabulous! You should be so proud of yourself. You were scared and you did it anyway. That's courage. I'm proud of you. I hope you are proud of yourself!" He leaned over and hugged me. It took an out-of-his-pattern action for him to overcome his preconceived belief that he could not do it.

The only difference between children like my delicious stepson and the people we work with every day is the honesty of the emotions. My stepson cried and openly shared his fears; the rest of us procrastinate, avoid, defend, excuse, and get angry, all to avoid revealing such honest emotions. Adults don't say, "I can't," but they are thinking it, because deep down they believe they cannot.

As middle leaders, we can help people interrupt their belief ➜ thought ➜ action/inaction pattern by creating opportunities for them to first take out-of-*their*-pattern actions grounded in their battle cry, and from there create out-of-*their*-pattern thoughts and beliefs. Some examples: We can ignore our own preconceived notions and beliefs about people and their potential. We can give them new projects and assignments that are out of their comfort zone. We can offer them mentoring to expose them to new ideas and ways of working. We can provide them with new experiences to shake them out of their restrictive beliefs. With a little relentless listening and cheering along the way, we can help them astound themselves.

## Modeling It

People at work take their cues from what they see in the halls, not what they read on the walls. Social cognitive theory argues that people's actions and reactions are influenced by those they observe in others. This means that at work, people are observing and remembering how *you*, their leader, act and react in every situation. Your actions and reactions are shaping their behaviors.

As a middle leader, you have the opportunity to influence people with as little as your own actions. So check yourself in the mirror before walking into the office. From your words to your vocal chords to your actions to your dress, you must model the commitment and confidence that you want to see in others. As Gandhi once said, "Be the change you wish to see in the world." He easily could have said, "Be the change you wish to see in others on your team."

Vince Lombardi drove home the impact of actions with each team he coached. He once chastised a young receiver for his ostentatious display in the end zone after scoring a touchdown. Lombardi reprimanded the hot-dogging with "When you go into the end zone, act like you've been there before." In other words, if you behave like an amateur, people will treat you like an amateur. In addition because of your position, behaving like an amateur will encourage others on your team to act like amateurs. Likewise, if you act like a jerk, you will be treated like a jerk and you will encourage others to act like jerks. Instead, act like a respected professional, be treated as such and model it for others on the team what it means to be a respected professional.

As the founder of Apex Computer Systems, Inc., an IT solutions and technology provider, Philip Chen used his position and his title to model for others what he wanted to see in them. In the process he was also communicating to the company his battle cry as their leader. When he launched the company he gave himself the title Chief Executive Officer but changed the title to Chief Enjoyment Officer to ensure his people and his customers were happy. After a growth spurt followed by a layoff, Philip changed his title to Chief Empowerment Officer because he saw that his role was to empower the company and his people to move forward in spite of any setbacks. He chose the word "empowerment" intentionally because he wanted to give employees the freedom to fail occasionally. He knew that from failures come valuable learning opportunities. After the company rebounded, he changed his title to Chief Enlightenment Officer to enforce a commitment to sharing best practices. Employees were given more power to think creatively and differently about their work. Philip's constantly improving approach became an everyday conversation at now-thriving Apex Systems.

Sometimes leaders fail to realize that people are watching. And more often than not, they do it in a big way – and in front of a lot of people.

One of our early clients in Silicon Valley demonstrated beautifully the impact of social cognitive theory. We had created for this global technology company a community to connect its thousands of employees around the world for mentoring and knowledge exchange opportunities. From our pilot team and all the interviews we conducted with individuals throughout different departments in different corners of the globe, it was clear these people were hungry to start connecting with and learning from each other. So imagine the buzz in the standing-room-only conference room when we were about to launch the program at their headquarters.

Nanette, the head of the Human Resources department, walked on stage to introduce me and the program, and in one breath she managed to kill the potential of the entire program by modeling trepidation. We had designed the community to require people to complete a profile, like an online résumé, which other people could use to search and then connect with each other for quick knowledge-exchange conversations or more intense mentoring relationships. But it was entirely dependent on people entering the community and sharing information about themselves.

During the kick-off, someone from the audience asked Nanette if she was going to join the community. A worried look swept across her face. She responded, "Uh, sure. I'm looking forward to getting involved. However, I will be participating with an alias." And then she looked over at me on the side of the stage and in front of the entire audience, meekly asked, "That's possible, right, Ann? You can set me up with an alias for my profile?" She should have just said, "I'll be in the community but I don't want anyone to know so I'll use a different name. Then no one can really see, connect with, or learn from me. And of course, I have nothing to learn from any of you, so an alias will work just fine."

I must have had the most dumbfounded look on my face. I couldn't believe it. I wanted to push the pause button, walk over to her, slap her, and shriek, "What don't you understand about the word 'community'?! You are the leader, act like it."

With one word, "alias," she echoed the fear that already permeated the mindsets at this company and cemented the abyss between leaders and individual contributors. By asking for an alias, she was sending a message to everyone that she was so important she could not be exposed in the community. In addition, she was saying that she did not want to connect with her people in this way. Shame on me for not asking her ahead of time if she would be participating in her own community and for not vetting her before putting her on stage. I had just assumed that as the head of a department, she understood that people were watching her.

As a result of Nanette's dim-witted, leaderless comment, people in the audience started raising their hands, requesting the same. Could they have an alias, too? The guillotine dropped and the community died before it ever launched.

Unlike Nanette, Kansas City Royals pitcher, Gilbert Allen "Gil" Meche, demonstrated what it means to model with actions. In 2007 Meche left Seattle to sign a five-year, $55 million deal with the Royals. But in 2010 with one year left on his contract, he was injured and was going to be out the entire 2011 season. For merely warming the bench, Meche was going to take home $12 million. At the beginning of the 2011 season, he announced his retirement, giving up the $12 million due on the last year of his deal. As commented in *The New York Times*, Meche has always been known for his integrity, but this action was astonishing. According to Meche, he realized he wasn't going to be earning his money and did not feel like he deserved it. So he retired, no longer a pitcher, just a leader.

## Putting It Into Action

- Practice reframing a choice for people when you want to influence their choice or deliver bad news in a less damaging way.

- Identify your preconceptions and judgments about the people on your team.

- Observe where your own beliefs are stopping you from taking chances or stepping outside the box.

- Identify how people sabotage their commitment with words and actions. Then share with them the impact of their words and actions and ask them what new words and actions they can use instead.

- Create out-of-their-pattern actions for people that will contribute to them creating new beliefs about themselves instead of them relying on their patterned beliefs.

- Model the behavior you want to see in others.

# Chapter 8

## Label Intentionally

. . . . . . . . . . . . . . . . . .

I was getting settled in my seat for a flight from New York to
Ohio when Larry Kellner, now former Chairman and CEO of
Continental Airlines, caught my attention. His face appeared on
the safety video that is protocol before every flight, but it was his
words that made me listen. He launched the video by saying that
he has "the privilege of working with 40,000 of the best men and
women in the industry." I was struck by the pride and sincerity
in his voice and the words he used so effortlessly. *Privilege?* What
CEO talks about what a privilege it is to work with people?

I then flipped open the airline's complimentary magazine to
peruse the articles and was greeted once more by Larry Kellner,
this time in print. In his welcome message, Larry again talked
about providing me with the best service in the industry. In
fact, he said that when it comes to providing quality service,
his co-workers (and yes, he used this word; he never mentioned
"my employees") are second to none. He then bragged about the
many awards they ("they" - not "him" - "they" - his co-workers!)
had received that prove how fabulous they were, including "Best
Airline" and "Best Flight Attendants." He went on with pride about
how his co-workers also show their commitment to service by
giving back to their communities. Again, his pride and sincerity
jumped off the page.

As the doors closed and we were about to take off, the pilot
then welcomed us on board. He talked about the flight, the

forthcoming atmospheric conditions, and when we should expect to arrive. He then finished his genuine welcome message with "Now, sit back and enjoy our world-class service." I stopped. What pilot sings the praises of the service with such confidence?

They had my attention. I was eager to experience the flight attendants' service to see if they were going to provide the level of service that the CEO and the pilot had promised. Without fail, they did. They were enthusiastic, patient, professional, efficient, and classy. They treated every passenger like a client. I wondered what came first, their great service or the world-class-service messages from the CEO and the pilots?

## The Power of the Label

The Continental flight attendants were labeled "world-class." When we get labeled, our brain molds and shapes our behaviors to fit that label. In psychology the term for this phenomenon is "diagnosis bias." Essentially, once someone diagnoses us, our brain filters information seeking evidence to confirm that diagnosis. The power of labeling is so influential that it literally causes us to distort or ignore data that contradicts the label. Diagnosis bias works similarly to the confirmation bias we explored in the last chapter, but the confirmation bias begins internally with our own beliefs, whereas the diagnosis bias begins externally with other people's beliefs about us.

Psychologist Franz Epting is credited for discovering the influence of the label. Through various experiments, Franz concluded that once we get labeled it's easy to start acting out that label through our behavior and decisions. And once we start acting out a label, we self-perpetuate that label as we continue to reinforce and reaffirm it with more behavior and decisions. We literally confirm the diagnosis.

Once the Continental flight attendants were labeled as "world class," they began to mold their behavior to fit that label. The minute they took on the behavior and actions of "world-class flight attendants" the label was reinforced by each other, their supervisors, the pilots, and their CEO. "World-class service" became a self-perpetuating diagnosis that started with the leader declaring that he had the privilege of working with the best women and men in the industry. They were labeled publicly and repeatedly by someone influential – their boss – with a label that was buttressed with admiration and respect. It's no wonder the flight attendants stepped into those shoes.

Green Bay Packers coach Mike McCarthy similarly leveraged the diagnosis bias to influence champion behavior in his team when they needed it most. The night before the Super Bowl, Coach McCarthy had each player and coach fitted for a Super Bowl championship ring. The next day the Green Bay Packers won Super Bowl XLV over the Pittsburgh Steelers 31-25. Did Coach McCarthy predict the win or just influence it? Was it simply presumptuous and brazen or incredibly strategic?

While other coaches are busy navigating football superstitions and enabling "one day at a time" mindsets, McCarthy's moxie was a breath of fresh air. By putting those Super Bowl rings on his guys' fingers, Coach McCarthy was leveraging a few of the cognitive biases that we have been exploring that influence every human being. In doing so, he evolved from a manager of a football team to a leader of people.

*1. Diagnosis Bias.* As we are exploring in this chapter, we listen to what other people say about us, especially people we admire, respect, and value. When other people diagnose us and we the one making the diagnosis, we tend to mold our behavior to match their diagnosis, which then confirms that diagnosis and makes it our own.

By fitting the players with Super Bowl rings, the Coach was diagnosing his players as winners before they even walked on to the field. The players respected and admired their coach, so they listened to what he had to say about them. The players then molded their behavior to be that of Super Bowl champions. Green Bay Packers guard Daryn Colledge said of the ring-fitting exercise, "It just set that mental mindset that you've got to go out there and you've got something to accomplish."

*2. Framing Effect.* As we saw in the last chapter, people approach the same situation differently depending on how that situation is presented. In effect, people will make inconsistent decisions when presented with the same situation just framed differently.

Coach McCarthy could have said, "The game is going to be tough. Just go out there and do your best. Whatever happens, I'm proud of you." But more likely he said, "You guys are champions! In fact, let's go try on your rings so when you win tomorrow, you are ready to wear them." Linebacker A.J. Hawk said of the coach's brazen move, "It made things real for us." Of course it did. Coach McCarthy was framing the situation for his players.

*3. Spotlight Effect.* A cousin of the diagnosis bias, the Spotlight Effect occurs when we think that people are closely watching us to see what we do. And when we think people are fixated on us, we conform to what we think those people expect of us. (The reality – and the irony – is that they're actually not paying attention to us at all because they're too busy thinking that *we* are closely watching *them*.)

By putting those Super Bowl rings on their fingers, Coach McCarthy was ingeniously reinforcing for the players that millions of people would be paying close attention to them at the game the next day and that those people expected the players to win. Coach McCarthy was also communicating his expectations. "We respect the Pittsburgh Steelers and the way they play. But we fully expected to win this game. This is our time."

After reading this section of the book, my mom experimented with the concepts immediately. Because of her ruthless commitment to serving people as the manager of a successful real estate office, she is well respected, admired, and appreciated. So it was no surprise that she attended an awards ceremony honoring successful real estate agents in offices throughout the firm. When the event had ended and people were exiting the banquet hall, she invited one of her up-and-coming agents to walk across the stage and envision receiving an award the following year. She wanted the agent to taste success and know what it will feel like when it's the agent's turn to be up there. My mom grabbed the perfect opportunity to influence her agent's behavior by labeling her a winner with the walk-across-the-stage exercise.

## Pygmalion Effect

When we brand people with a label and those people respect and admire us, they will embrace that label and then mirror the expectations we have for them. They literally take on the characteristics of the brand. The Green Bay Packers took on the expectations of champions, the Continental flight attendants took on the expectations that the pilots, the CEO, and the passengers had for world-class flight attendants, and my mom's real estate agent will take on the expectations that she has of successful realtors.

The impact of the label was proven by two psychologists, Robert Rosenthal and Lenore Jacobson, in an experiment in the Chicago public school system in 1968. A group of teachers were brought together and apprised of great news: because of their stellar teaching abilities, they had been handpicked to work with a group of gifted students for the year. The school communicated its high expectation that stellar teachers always work magic with gifted students, which is why these particular teachers were chosen. The teachers in turn had high expectations for these gifted students. They expected that at the end of the year their gifted students would outperform all other students in the school district. Neither the teachers nor the students disappointed.

Each performed above and beyond expectations. However, unbeknownst to the teachers, the students were not gifted, nor were the teachers chosen for their stellar teaching abilities. Everyone was chosen at random.

What happened in the Chicago school system is now called the "Pygmalion Effect." The school labeled the teachers "stellar" and the school regarded them as stellar. These teachers were responsible for the district's most prized possession – its gifted students. The teachers respected the school and therefore they assumed characteristics of stellar teachers, the ones who are so effective that they can teach gifted students. As a result, they performed as stellar teachers should – brilliantly.

The school then labeled the students "gifted," and the school and the teachers regarded the students as gifted. The students were responsible for exhibiting gifted academic results. The students respected their teachers and the school and therefore they assumed characteristics of academically gifted students. As a result, the students performed as gifted students should – magnificently.

The teachers assumed the positive traits assigned by the school and the school district, and the students assumed the positive traits assigned by the teachers. Everyone was impacted by the power of labels. In essence, the Pygmalion Effect created a form of self-fulfilling prophecy in which the expectations of others influenced reality.

## The Golem Effect

The Golem Effect is Pygmalion's dark side. In this behavioral phenomenon, the power of labels works to influence reality but with a negative focus. As a result, low expectations encourage and create negative performance.

Henry's story is a great example of the influence of the Golem Effect. Henry loves his job in large part because of his huge admiration and respect for his boss. But Henry's boss keeps calling Henry "introverted." She said it to Henry, she said it publicly to the team, and she even wrote it on his performance review. She was not intentionally trying to be mean. She was merely organizing her team out loud to better ensure that she has placed extroverted team members in front of clients and introverted ones on other assignments. What she didn't realize is that the more she labeled Henry as introverted, the more she cemented that diagnosis. Unconsciously, Henry looked for evidence that proved he was introverted and discounted evidence that suggested the opposite.

Henry assumed the expectations that his boss and society have for "introverted people."

Henry started acting and behaving as an introverted person would – shy, timid, withdrawn, and reserved. His molded actions and behaviors then confirmed the introverted diagnosis to Henry and to his boss. Soon Henry also saw himself as introverted. He stopped expressing his opinions and ideas in meetings. He became reticent to take on new challenges and opportunities. He took on characteristics of being introverted and after each experience he would say to himself, "See, there it is again! I *am* introverted." Henry even interpreted his emotions through the filter of the diagnosis, which then reinforced and reaffirmed the diagnosis of being introverted.

Similarly, a friend of mine proves the Golem Effect every time she calls her son "learning disabled." Some expert in kindergarten once suggested that my friend's son, Daniel, might be a little slower developing than his peers. Daniel is now 19 and a savvy, outgoing, personable, ambitious young man. However, there is not a day that we don't hear about Daniel's learning challenges, not from Daniel, but from his mother. She practically introduces Daniel as "This is my son, Daniel. He has a learning disability." Daniel's mom keeps pointing out instances where Daniel would have done better but the school did not help him with a special testing room to accommodate his learning challenges. Over the years, Daniel would come home from school with a C instead of an A and my friend would declare, "See? It was the learning disability that caused the C." No one suggested that maybe Daniel just needed to study differently or harder or eliminate the video games and excessive television time. While my friend is busy protecting herself from any criticism about her parenting skills, Daniel is busy taking on characteristics of someone who is learning disabled – and affirming his diagnosis.

To be clear, I am not suggesting that Henry is not introverted and that Daniel does not have a learning disability, or that introversion and learning disabilities don't really exist. I'm suggesting that Henry's boss took a class on personality styles and put Henry in the box called "introverted." And I'm suggesting that Daniel's mom heard a diagnosis when he was in kindergarten and has been perpetuating it ever since. What a disservice they both did with their quick labels. Who knows what would have happened if, in spite of a learning disability, Daniel's mom spent the past 19 years telling Daniel how brilliant he is instead of reminding him of his limitations. And who knows what would have happened if, in spite of Henry's telltale signs of introversion, his boss spent the year telling Henry how bold he is instead of reminding him of his proclivity to cower.

## Pygmalion and Golem Go to Work

Psychologists at the State University of New York in Albany proved that the diagnostic effects of Pygmalion and Golem operate in the workplace. They concluded that people rise to meet the high expectations set by their supervisor. And conversely people shrink to the low expectations set by their supervisor, even when those low expectations are conveyed through subtle messages.

The influence of the Pygmalion effect at work was demonstrated by Pete, a trained architect at a very prestigious company. The CEO approached Pete with a new opportunity. He was launching the firm's diversity department and wanted Pete to own the initiative. He approached Pete with the opportunity, and not surprisingly, it took some convincing for Pete to see beyond his own perceptions. In Pete's mind, he was just an architect, not a leader of a ground-breaking initiative. The CEO, however, clearly saw a leader in Pete; he perceived potential and promise, not lack of experience or an uncalculated risk. Pete chose to believe the CEO's perceptions instead of his own, accepted the challenge, and rose to meet the high expectations. Two decades and three companies later, Pete is now leading all diversity initiatives for a multinational company – without any regrets. His whole world changed because a boss saw more in Pete than Pete saw in himself.

Conversely, the Golem Effect was perfectly demonstrated in a small commercial construction company owned and controlled by Anthony for 15 years. Over those years Anthony mastered the art of demoralizing everyone who worked for him. He screamed at them when they made mistakes and micromanaged them daily. He expected people to screw up without him. Soon his people came to expect that as well. When they did something right, Anthony would say, "Guess you're not as dumb as I thought you were."

As a result of Anthony's own need to feel important and make the world revolve around him, he successfully created a team that could not survive without him. Worse than that, his team didn't even believe they could think on their own. Zapped of all enthusiasm and commitment, they just did what Anthony told them to do. Anthony didn't trust them to make any decisions without him, and neither did they. When Anthony died suddenly of a heart attack (are we surprised?), his team literally fell apart (are we surprised?). Anthony's low expectations had influenced the reality of their abilities. He had conditioned them to believe that they could not function on their own. Anthony held low expectations for them, and he proved himself right, even from his grave.

The dichotomy of both the Pygmalion and Golem Effects is perfectly demonstrated by the true story of the flailing basketball team highlighted in the praise-winning movie *Coach Carter*. Actor

Samuel L. Jackson portrayed Coach Carter, head of the basketball program for a high school in an impoverished area of Oakland, California. Coach Carter expected his players to work effortlessly, both on the court and in the classroom. He insisted that their futures rested not just on basketball, but on also their brain power. He christened each of them "high potential students," while the rest of the school, including their teachers and parents, had less-than-flattering descriptions for their classroom capabilities. They only expected these boys to perform on the basketball court and to stay alive long enough to graduate from high school. Even their parents did not expect them to attend college.

When Coach Carter refused to let the boys play basketball until they took their school work seriously, the parents and the school board were furious. Their restrictive beliefs about these boys' capabilities created restrictive actions, which led them to protest Coach Carter's stunt. But Coach Carter was determined to crush the patterns by which these boys were operating. He was committed to their success in life, not just on the court. He was so committed, in fact, that he risked his job. Coach Carter literally padlocked the door to the basketball court, threatening to keep it closed until the boys started taking their studies seriously. The basketball players' respect and admiration for Coach Carter and his commitment to them had cemented over the basketball season. Accordingly, the players rose to his challenge and met his high expectations, to the shock and awe of the entire school – including the parents.

### Naysayers

"Your ideas for compensating people won't work," Benjamin said to Helen, his top sales manager. Helen insisted that the company's compensation plan was driving the wrong behavior. She wanted to tweak the plan to make it easier for salespeople to understand how they make money. But Helen's boss, ever the politician at their Fortune 1000 company, wished Helen would stop trying to rock the boat. Soon, however, the CEO got wind of Helen's stance and asked for a meeting with Helen to learn more. As she was preparing for her presentation, Benjamin dispatched her with a warning, "Your ideas for compensating people won't work. I suggest you keep them to yourself."

Corporate America reeks of naysayers like Benjamin. These are the people who deem it their job to tell others why an idea won't work or why the sky is falling. They walk through the halls of the office like Eeyore from *Winnie the Pooh.* In their mind, the glass is half empty and the sooner they inform everyone else, the better. When people like Helen move forward in spite of the warnings and predictions, the naysayers just wait in anticipation, bursting at the seams to scream, "Told you so!" when the ideas and plans don't come to fruition exactly as desired.

## The Root of Naysaying

People naysay for a few cognitive reasons, which we have already explored. First and foremost, it usually occurs, and often unconsciously, because the naysayer has lost sight of his own reason to show up. He is running into battle without a battle cry. Floundering, he realizes that he is no longer moving forward. He is clearly stuck and in need of justifying his stuckness.

In addition to lacking a battle cry, naysayers often have adopted certain restrictive beliefs and have engrained certain patterns that support that stuck-ness. When a yaysayer emerges excited to shake things up with her new approach, the naysayer begins to question his own decisions, justifications, and beliefs. At that point, he must decide one of two things: (1) there is nothing wrong with his approach, decisions, justifications, or beliefs. This, of course, means there must be something wrong with the yaysayer's approach, because it flies in the face of his beliefs; or (2) the yaysayer's approach is correct and the naysayer's approach is off the mark. But nobody likes to be wrong, because being wrong is a forerunner to being rejected. In addition, being wrong will require a change in approach. People dread being rejected and loathe the idea of changing. So, when a yaysayer materializes with her new idea or approach, which questions the naysayer's modus operandi, the naysayer chooses to cling violently to his approach and the decisions and justifications that got him there, instead of contemplating that he might be wrong. The naysayer discovers that it is far easier to make the yaysayer wrong than to deal with his own fears and patterns.

Notice that whenever anyone changes jobs or cities, they go out of their way to verbally justify their move to anyone who will listen. They wax on about the interesting company, the fabulous commute, the innovative products, the great employee benefits, the personable colleagues and neighbors, the intriguing work, the better pay, and the future growth opportunities for their career. Then they start comparing their old job to their new one, continuing the verbal validating. There's nothing wrong with this whatsoever. Clearly they are doing it to make themselves feel better about their decision to change. But sometimes their actions alone inadvertently reject another's decision not to act. The act teeters on the brink of unconscious naysaying. And when people feel they are being naysayed and rejected, their first instinct is to defensively reject back.

Fred's story is an example of inadvertent naysaying. Having moved across the country, Fred left behind friends and family who wouldn't dare leave the old neighborhood. They've lived in the same town – some of them in the same house – their entire lives. They see no reason to leave. But Fred, an adventurous soul, is starting a new life with new adventures in Miami, and Fred is overjoyed with his moxie move. But his change inconspicuously questions some people's decision not to change. Fred's decision to move away from this town inadvertently and unintentionally communicates to his friends and family that something is wrong with their decision to stay put. If these people interpret Fred's communication that way, then Fred would be right and they would be wrong. People hate being wrong, and even more than being wrong, people hate admitting that they are wrong. It's uncomfortable and dissonant, and it allows for rejection to follow. So instead, they're going to advise Fred that his decision to move is a mistake. Naysaying Fred will make them feel better about their decision to stay. This is ultimately at the crux of naysaying. It has nothing to do with Fred; it has everything to do with the naysayers' discordance.

Like Statler and Waldorf, the ornery, disagreeable, cantankerous Muppets who sat in the balcony of every show, naysayers continue to pass judgment on other people's decisions and choices. When Fred moved, his family and friends were ruthless behind his back. Fortunately, he was not there to hear them. At first he struggled to find a job and they smugly commented, "See? He never should have moved." When Fred's car was broken into, they all righteously remarked, "See? He never should have moved."

Some people cave in the wake of naysayers. Others exert as much energy as the naysayers to prove them wrong. Fred did the latter.

Let's observe how naysaying plays out in a typical workplace scenario. Imagine I've been working at Company PDQ for the past decade. I have my established routines. And while I may not see myself as stuck, there are certain things that I won't try or don't do because, well, they just are not done. I have a belief that it would be political suicide to do those certain things so I do not do them. Then along comes a newly baked college graduate who brings her fresh ideas for running my team better. To me, her approach feels off-putting and disrespectful. Doesn't she know that I have been running this team effectively for 10 years? Who does she think she is coming in and trying to make changes? Immediately I don't like her. Obviously there are reasons why I haven't made changes to the team and she should know that. By suggesting that we do things differently, she is indirectly questioning the way I have been doing my job. My immediate response is to reject her ideas and her approach because I am starting to feel rejected. My ego and my reputation are at stake. Instead of considering her fresh ideas, I highlight what's wrong with them. I contradict, refute, oppose, and naysay until she cowers under defeat. It was close, but I killed her ideas before I had to make any changes or admit I've been doing anything wrong for the past 10 years.

This is how naysaying is born and then breeds, like a cancer in every organization.

## Learned Helplessness

Where does all of this clinging to our decisions at the expense of our goals come from? Learned helplessness. People are not born helpless, they learn to become helpless over time through different disappointing and disillusioning experiences. As a result, they learn to stop trying. They then justify the fact that they stopped trying by justifying their current situation and rejecting anything that suggests that they have the power to change their situation. Let's look at where this "helpless" mentality originates, so we can better understand the cause of naysaying.

In 1967 psychologist Martin Seligman's experiments on dogs identified where this stuck feeling came from and its enduring effects on people's experience of the world. Marty placed in a pen a group of dogs wearing collars that delivered electric shocks. A few of the dogs discovered that they had the power to stop the shocks by jumping over a short partition in the pen. For a second group of dogs, nothing they tried would turn off the electric shocks they received. After a while the dogs in the second group stopped trying altogether – their fate of receiving endless electric shocks was sealed. They finally lied down and took the shocks. They had literally become helpless to affect their situation. In their minds, they had learned that they had no power or control to change their situation. They formed restrictive, limiting beliefs that there was nothing to do but stop trying. Notice if your office is chocked full of electric-shocked dogs.

When people say, "I'm stuck," or act as such, it is just a sign that learned helplessness has invaded. They believe that no matter how hard they try, they won't succeed, so they give up altogether. But not wanting to feel rejected, they reject anything and anyone who questions their decision to give up. People become victims of their circumstances then righteously justify those circumstances.

Whether they feel stuck in a project, their job, a home, a relationship, or in any situation, people have learned their stuckness. They have learned to be helpless. They believe they are helpless and then they confirm that helplessness through their own helpless actions. People who believe they are helpless act as if they have no power or control to change the situation, when in fact they always have the power to change a situation, even if the change might be complicated, uncomfortable, painful, and thorny. So their stuckness is just a *perceived* lack of control over the outcome of a situation.

This phenomenon has been proven in many research studies similar to Marty Seligman's dog experiments. For example, put jumping fleas in a mason jar and close the lid. The fleas will work incessantly to jump out of the jar, but only for a while. After smashing their bodies against the lid numerous times, the fleas finally give up. Soon they jump only as high as the lid will allow, ensuring that they no longer smash their bodies on the lid. After a while, we can take the lid off the jar and the fleas will continue jumping, but only as high as the top of the jar. They will not jump out of the jar because they have conditioned themselves to believe that there is a lid that will stop them if they jump too high. That is learned helplessness in action. Many people we work with are just like the jumping fleas.

The walking zombies we see in the halls of our offices are victims of their own mason jar. Their continued focus on their failed attempts has caused them to shrink their world to a small circle of safety. They have given up on making changes. In their restrictive, limiting beliefs, they have no power to do anything but what they already know. They have learned to be victims instead of victors.

When faced with naysayers, "stuck" beliefs, jumping fleas, electric-shocked dogs, and other learned helplessness, you have two choices: (1) revive them, or (2) douse them.

Let's start with door number two – douse them, like extinguishing a flame. One totally acceptable option is to let someone go because *fixing* people is never your responsibility. In addition, the impact of their helplessness on others is precarious, incalculable, and intolerable. If your legal and HR departments won't allow you to extinguish the flame, look at reassigning these naysayers, or shifting their responsibilities to dilute their impact on colleagues and customers. Whatever the circumstances, just be vigilant of their impact and do whatever you can to protect others from their naysaying and toxicity.

Alternatively, you can choose door number one – revive people by helping them to unlearn their learned helplessness.

When faced with the desire but not the luxury of rebuilding her entire team, Deanna chose to eliminate the creeping helplessness. She instituted this shift in conversation with a new rule that applied to everyone who worked for her (even her boss), "No complaints, only observations with solutions." Deanna said it so many times that it became the team's mantra. It took a few weeks and a lot of reiteration to break their banal habits. "Is that a complaint?" Deanna would ask. But soon her team began to recognize situations where they complained but took no action, or where they griped but offered or attempted no solution. Once they renamed a problem "an observation," and identified a solution, Deanna required her people to take some action, some step in the direction of the solution. She outwardly rebuffed requests from those who only griped and she stopped supporting people who did not take any action. As a result, Deanna had reframed the problems into challenges and opportunities. This forced people to stop complaining and start solving. Her people moved from victims to warriors, and the entire sales team immediately saw the impact in their first quarter numbers.

Similarly, Rodney Morris, Chief People Officer at Romano's Macaroni Grill, regularly asks people, "What is the obstacle?" and "What are you going to do about it?" I particularly like these questions because they are blunt without being callous. Rodney doesn't even fill in the blanks to qualify the obstacle. He doesn't ask, "What is the obstacle that is standing in your way?" "What is the obstacle that is preventing you from moving forward?" or "What is the obstacle to our success?" He simply asks, "What is the obstacle?" Then he places responsibility for addressing that obstacle squarely on the other person. He doesn't say, "What are *we* going to do about it?" That would indicate shared responsibility and Rodney doesn't want to share in the responsibility, nor be responsible for holding anyone accountable. He wants people to own their own solutions. He wants to prod them to success without having to join them on the journey.

It takes a while for people to learn their helplessness; it will therefore, naturally take a new conversation for them to unlearn it. But taking any sort of action – regardless of how small – is the first step for people to combat their learned helplessness. It is our job to remind them that short of having a boulder roll over them, they are never stuck.

Most people complain about getting old. Not my septuagenarian friend Norm Webber, who has been swimming almost a mile every day for 30 years. He says, "When you stop moving, they throw dirt on you." Growing old mentally is being helpless to the aging process. Staying young through physical activity like Norm is combating learned helplessness.

## Our Own Learned Helplessness Toward People

When we diagnose ourselves with limiting labels, we limit our potential. Similarly diagnosing others with limiting labels limits their potential. But we have labels for everyone in our lives because labeling others makes it much easier to survive from moment to moment. Our brain has already deciphered this person from our previous encounters and has placed a label on them for future reference. Then when we cross paths with one of them, our brain doesn't have to work so hard to figure them out again. It just refers to their label. We know what to expect without working too hard. For example, if we have labeled Jill "whiny and negative," then when Jill shows up in our world, we are on guard, ready for her whining and negativity—we expect it and we look for it. If, on the other hand, we labeled Tyler as someone who is fun and vivacious, then we perk up when Tyler shows up in our world because our expectation is that it will be a fun and vivacious interaction. Our labels tell us what to expect from each of them and our behavior shifts according to the labels we have put on Jill and Tyler.

We use our preconceived beliefs about people to file them into easy-to-predict buckets. Tulsi is bright but not funny. Sam is tactical but not strategic. John is strategic but not tactical. Warren is personable but disorganized. Lynda is organized but not very bright. Our confirmation bias then goes to work immediately in each interaction with these labeled people. We literally look for evidence that confirms those buckets. We roll our eyes and say, "There it is again. She is so ... and he is so ... Nothing ever changes."

Suppose Sally is someone on our team. Every interaction with Sally is frustrating and annoying. She talks in circles and makes more work than is ever needed. It's always exhausting. We've labeled Sally "annoying and trying of our patience." We have a belief that Sally is annoying and it's such a strong belief that to us we hold that belief like it's the truth, as opposed to just our opinion. When Sally walks into our office, we internally cringe.

We think to ourselves, "OK, brace yourself! This conversation is going to be annoying, frustrating, and a waste of time." We take a deep breath and say with a voice laced with annoyance, "Hi Sally. What can I do for you?" Sally starts in with one of her nonsensical, absurd monologues laden with gibberish. We feign interest, but we are thinking, "Jeez. Here we go again. It's always the same with Sally. Couldn't she tell from my voice that I'm annoyed?" Our confirmation bias immediately points to the evidence in front of us and confirms our belief. Bam! We cement her label once again.

Here's where we do a disservice to people. We treat everyone on our team and in our workforce the same way we treat Sally. We label each one of them as good or bad, smart or stupid, conscientious or lazy, enthusiastic or apathetic. We limit people's contributions because we think we have them all figured out already. No matter what they do or say, we take it as evidence that confirms our preconceived beliefs about them. If they actually surprise us, our confirmation bias flatly rejects it as evidence to the contrary and thus we make up some excuse, such as "They were just lucky. They must have cheated. Someone must have done the work for them. The project was easy."

The perilous part of the label is that no matter what Sally says, we have already filtered it, labeled it, and discounted its value. We haven't even listened to her because we walked into the conversation ready for useless garbage. Sally may have some great ideas and significant contributions, but we wouldn't know. Our confirmation bias has filtered out any value.

We have learned to be helpless as it relates Sally and other people. Our beliefs, judgments, and limiting labels are causing us to act helpless. We nail the coffin closed when we consciously and unconsciously communicate those limiting labels and that learned helplessness through all of our everyday interactions with others.

## Un-Learning Our Own Learned Helplessness

If you are going to choose to revive the helpless instead of extinguish them, then you need to first address your own learned helplessness about that person. The difference between you and a mediocre manager is that the latter never recognizes the need nor deems it his responsibility to revive people.

When it comes to labels, mediocre managers rely heavily on their preconceived notions about people. Inevitably their own naysaying taints people's potential. Influential leaders, on the other hand, also have preconceived notions, but suspend those notions and instead remain curious. Mediocre managers allow their egos to engulf the situation, and as a result, they are constantly looking for evidence to prove their labels correct. Influential leaders don't check in with their egos, instead considering that they may be wrong about their beliefs and labels. Mediocre managers so dread the thought of being wrong and rejected for it that they will make others wrong and reject them before risking rejection.

I've noticed how people routinely and conveniently slap limiting labels on kids. I once smugly declared at family movie night that the waitress in the movie *Grease* was actually John Travolta's mother. Jack, my stepson said, "No, it's his sister." A limiting label sprung to my mind about Jack being too young to know such things. I strongly disagreed and scoffed, "No, it's not." Because I hate being wrong, I filtered his contribution through this limiting label and then leveraged the 30 years I have over him to intimidate him into thinking he was wrong and I was right. A few breaths later, I went onto Google to confirm the truth. I then retracted my declaration for a new one, "Jack, I'm sorry. You were right and I was wrong. It is John Travolta's sister." Dumping my mediocre manager suit for my influential leader outfit, I didn't even make an excuse as to why I had the wrong information. I just admitted to being wrong and apologized for not recognizing that he was right.

We evolve into influential leaders when we start placing bold, audacious labels on people instead of relying on our own learned helplessness labels. With my stepson, I have decided to label him precocious instead of naïve. Bold, audacious labels like this allows all of us to influence with the Pygmalion effect instead of the Golem effect. When we suspend beliefs, judgments, and resultant labels, we risk being astounded by what people will do instead of risk being rejected by their success over ours. And what do we have to lose by giving people big, brazen, audacious, juicy labels (other than our own naysaying)? Let's let people surprise, delight, shock, and astound us – and them.

As managers, when you don't halt your people-judging, filtering, and discounting, you literally fail to lead. This failure to lead was never clearer than in my interactions with Steve, a manager who worked for one of our clients. We were strategizing the rollout of an enterprise-wide mentoring solution to his people across hundreds of offices. Because we are cognizant that people support that which they help create (see Chapter 4), we relentlessly incorporate ways for people to get involved in the creation, support, and execution of any of our people effectiveness programs. To that end, we strongly recommended to Steve that we create a champion team to support the rollout of the mentoring program, a team of people recruited across functional lines and called a "Mentoring Champion Team."

It was at this recommendation that Manager Steve said, "Ann, we don't need any more champions at the company. These are just individual contributors. We don't want them thinking they have any power when they really don't. Let's think of another title." I had to work hard not to scoff. Yes, let's not have too many people at the company enthused to lead a people-development program.

What Steve was really showing me through his comment was the filter he had for people below him based on his sweeping belief that they were all incompetent, powerless, and essentially futile to him. Through this filter, he was discounting the potential of any individual contributor and constantly finding evidence to prove his beliefs about them. Bam! He managed to kill off these people and their ability to contribute. He was also showing me that while he may have been a manager, he was no leader.

In response to his insipid comment, I suggested we call this team of program champions "Mentor Leaders." And just when I thought the lunacy had already been voiced, he continued.

Like a scene out of an episode of *The Office*, this bungling manager announced the reason we could no longer use the word "leader" to rally people to support a people-development program. I was trying to hide my furrowed brows and the sneer of insolence as he declared, "We don't like to refer to people at the company as leaders when they're really not." Unfortunately, he continued, "We like to reserve the title 'leader' for people who really are leaders – our supervisors and managers. If we refer to this group as 'leaders,' they may think they are when they aren't. And then they'll want to act like leaders, but they're not leaders. We just cannot dilute the term 'leader.'"

Huh?!?

"Ann, I don't want these individual contributors to get confused and think they are true leaders in this company."

Of course not. We certainly don't need people feeling and acting like leaders when they shouldn't be. We must wait until someone declares them to be leaders before we allow them to act like leaders. That makes sense.

I had to fight to suspend my *own* belief that was forming about this louse from discounting what he was saying. My experience with this manager continued to prove that he had a propensity for saying very little while spewing a lot of corporate jargon. He brilliantly manipulated every conversation, thwarted anyone's efforts, and confused every issue. And he consistently revealed this in each interaction we had. At least that's the evidence I was collecting through my own filter.

Warily I said, "Well, Steve, what do you suggest we call them?" Without missing a beat, he responded, "Coordinators." Really. Now that's exciting. I can see how a group of people would rally around being called a "Coordinator." But he didn't want to enthuse, empower, or excite them. He wanted to keep them in their place.

Manager Steve is not a leader. He discounts people with his arrogant, haughty, condescending manner. He clings to his commitment to being right about people. Influential leaders, on the other hand, focus on being related, not about being right.

If Manager Steve was the embodiment of the broken leader, Marina was the pillar of championing for people. Marina was a partner at Pillsbury Madison & Sutro, my first law firm experience. We watched Marina as she approached each person on her team with curiosity, optimism, and anticipation. Even with associates the rest of us had killed off with our labels and filters, Marina paid the utmost respect. Once in a while someone would do Marina a favor and let her know the truth about someone in the firm. Marina listened but never allowed the other person's judgments to influence her own. She continued with an open mind and suspended judgment. To Marina, everyone had potential to contribute and succeed. As a result, people did just that – contributed and succeeded. Because she is a quintessential people leader, people continued to follow her. Marina become the Managing Partner of the first woman-led law firm in the United States. Not surprisingly, she left Pillsbury years later to become the CEO of the Girl Scouts of Northern California, an organization founded on the principle of girls' potential.

## Yaysaying

We could label people "yaysayers" and "naysayers," but those are just more labels that limit people's potential to surprise us. Instead, let's specifically address the act of labeling and the act of naysaying and let's do so with the act of yaysaying.

When Ed Whitacre, the retired chairman of AT&T who then became the chairman of General Motors, joined the bankruptcy-threatened, cash-hemorrhaging company, he pronounced that General Motors would rise to prominence and preeminence again. He said this in spite of a slew of evidence proving otherwise and in spite of past experiences with people and situations that justified a different stance. He pronounced this without knowing exactly how it was going to be done.

When Gailene Cowger won the award for the "Most Positive Manager" at her real estate firm instead of an award for her office's revenue results, she responded with, "I'm positive that our office will be number one next year." She continues to declare this battle cry in spite of a lot of evidence and experiences otherwise. She declares this in the face of unknowns.

Larry Ellison once said, "When you innovate, you've got to be prepared for everyone telling you you're nuts." In other words, be prepared for the world of naysaying to attack, but naysayers never succeed in innovation. Larry is also celebrated for saying, "I have had all the disadvantages required for success." It takes a true yaysayer to say that publicly.

Does it mean that Ed, Gailene, and Larry never succumb to labeling, learned helplessness, or naysaying? Not at all. It's human nature to label people, to learn our helplessness, and to naysay as a means of warding off rejection. What these leaders do differently, however, is to realize that people are already engulfed in labeling, helplessness, and naysaying – they're own and everyone else's. They don't need more of it. They need another perspective. They need a different approach. They need to balance the naysaying with yaysaying.

Notice that each of these people has created a battle cry. And action-inducing battle cries demand yaysaying – in fact, they are dependent on yaysaying. Naysaying never generates a battle cry; it only puts bullets in the battle cry.

Yaysaying occurs when we encourage others in spite of past experiences we've had with them or with similar situations. When we respond to ideas with, "Interesting, tell me more," we are yaysaying. When we approach others with possibility instead of with doubt, we are yaysaying. When we silence the need to tell someone why something will or won't work, we are yaysaying. It even occurs when we put aside our fears that another person's success will mean our failure.

Yaysaying happens when we suspend our labels and judgments about others, ignoring our own learned helplessness. In so doing we remain curious and committed, expecting to learn something out of every effort. Yaysaying happens when we support people's exploration and growth instead of labeling them "one-trick ponies" and limiting their development of more tricks, as many dreadful managers do.

Yaysaying is easily identified in people who remain interested and curious, always asking the Second Question. I could say, "I am considering raising llamas in the backyard," and a yaysaying person would instinctually exclaim, "Wow. How interesting. How did you decide on llamas?" People who naysay scowl, "Have you thought about that? I'm not sure that's such a great idea. It will probably cause a ruckus with your neighbors and the town, not to mention the costs of maintaining those kinds of animals." People who yaysay suspend their judgment and leave it up to me to discover if raising llamas in the backyard is a viable or ridiculous idea. They know that I will quickly figure it out on my own, and that I may even surprise them. People who yaysay are cognizant that they gain nothing by spoiling my discovery process. Their ego is never in the way, hungry to grab the spotlight. They look forward to exploring the idea with me. Their commitment rests in being a leader, not in being right. (Of course, as you leverage yaysaying, how much leash you allow for interesting ideas certainly depends on your battle cry.)

Yaysaying also occurs when we hold out for the high potential in every person we hire, instead of labeling some people "high potential" and letting the others to guess at their potential. The former president of In-N-Out Burger demonstrated this concept regularly. When Rich Snyder took over the chain from his parents at the age of 24, he remained steadfast in his commitment to everyone's ability to contribute, from part-time summer burger flippers to store managers to executives. He instilled a sense of ownership in each person from the way he talked to them to the way he trained them to the way he compensated them. As a result, about 80 percent of store managers started their careers picking up trash at an In-N-Out restaurant. The company boasts one of the lowest turnover rates in the business and per-store sales that trump those of Burger King and rival McDonald's. Industry-wide, only 50 percent of fast-food workers last for more than one year. At In-N-Out, the typical tenure for a manager is 14 years and the average for part-time associates is two years. Rich knew the power of being a yaysayer for his people and it has manifested in an impact on the bottom line, which continues today, more than 15 years after Rich's death.

One of my favorite examples of yaysaying was described in a vignette that John Medina shared about his mom in his fantastic book, *Brain Rules*. John's mom yaysayed John every step of his ever-changing interests throughout his childhood and into adulthood. When John was 3, he was obsessed with dinosaurs, so his mom decorated his room with dinosaurs and bought John dinosaur books and cooked "dinosaur food." When John's fascination changed to spaceships, rockets, and galaxies, she transformed his room and the theme throughout the house from big dinosaurs to Big Bang. When his obsessions turned from outer space to Greek mythology to geometry to rocks to airplanes, John's mom transformed the house and her conversations with him to fuel his passions. Even when he declared that he had become an atheist, John's mom, a devoutly religious woman, bought him a copy of Friedrich Nietzsche's book *Twilight of the Idols* and said, "If you are going to be an atheist, be the best one out there." John Medina's mom gives us a rich example of yaysaying in action. It was not her place to inform John which obsession of his was good and which ones were ridiculous or futile. It was only her job to support him in his exploration. In doing so, John's mom taught John what it meant to surround himself with people who support him relentlessly.

### The Cure for the Common Naysayer

Naysaying is as pervasive in organizations as the common cold. It manifests in a number of ways, from snide comments to rejected ideas to corporate policies that communicate the "We-don't-believe-in-our-people-to-make-smart-decisions" message. Often people naysay with comments such as "I don't think that's a good idea," or "We've tried that and it doesn't work," or "We'll never get approval for that." Sometimes naysaying transpires as a furrowed brow, a snicker, or a roll of the eyes. A little more subtle, naysaying even occurs when people check their BlackBerry in the middle of a conversation. That small act of looking elsewhere communicates "I am not interested in this conversation," or "I don't believe in what you're saying." Naysaying at its extreme occurs when people sabotage projects or efforts with incorrect data, rumors, or hidden information.

Why do people do it? Why do they naysay? A number of reasons. They have lost sight of their battle cry. They don't feel important or appreciated. Their dreadful fear of rejection is causing them to do the rejecting first before being rejected. They are allowing their own beliefs about themselves or a situation to dictate their ambition and perseverance, and those beliefs have generated their own learned helplessness.

Like it or not, you can influence a cure for the common naysayer. This role may seem daunting when you discover how insidious naysaying is in the mindsets of people all around you. The longer people exist in corporate America, the more they believe they cannot make change, the more they feel helpless, the more they become resigned. If you look around, naysaying is so pervasive, it feels like a pandemic.

The good and the bad news is that people are conditioned to naysay – it's just learned helplessness in action. As the influential leader, you can condition people to yaysay instead. You do this by being extremely powerful, ubiquitous, and relentless in yaysaying and intentional labeling. First you need to be vigilant of its existence and its influence on you. Not only must you identify it creeping into the room, but you must not allow it to creep into your own mindset, becoming weak to it, like Superman was to kryptonite. Instead, be the unrelenting voice for another perspective. You don't need to be Sister Mary Sunshine, but you can simply say in the face of a negative, gossipy comment, "I don't know. There are always three sides to every story and I don't know the other two sides or the backstory. Who knows what really happened?" In other words, that's not my business nor am I going to be swayed to pass judgment, engage in gossip, or fall into learned helplessness mode.

As example, Gerald is constantly attempting to convince Caroline that she could not possibly like everyone she does in the office. Gerald saunters into Caroline's office and asks, with a roll of his eyes, if she has met, say, Romulus yet. Caroline nods enthusiastically and Gerald exclaims, "Isn't he such a narcissistic bore?" Taken aback, Caroline responds, "I don't know. He's nice to me." That is her rote response to every characterization that Gerald makes about someone. Gerald's labels and perceptions are not Caroline's, nor is she going to allow them to become hers. In refuting Gerald's naysaying, she is reframing the situation without rejecting Gerald. A powerful way to protect her own perspective.

Another tactic for addressing naysaying is to point it out. Literally let people know by making an observation about their naysaying. Most of the time people don't know they are naysaying. They get caught up in regularly drama-sharing with others, moaning, groaning, complaining, or griping. Or they are so focused on bad news or failed attempts that they cannot pull away from it, like rubber-necking past a car wreck on the highway. That's when we need to pull people aside (because as influential leaders we praise in public and observe in an office) and share our observations about their naysaying.

As we've seen already, an observation in a vacuum is not as powerful as an observation coupled with some advice. And observation coupled with advice is exponentially more powerful when the observee generates their own advice because they will own that advice as opposed to resent it. It could sound like, "I couldn't help noticing that you have commented numerous times today that someone's idea won't work. Are you aware that you are doing that? Also, have you noticed the impact you have on others when they hear your comments? It's not serving you or your battle cry. How can I support you in quickly eliminating this outlook?"

By confronting naysaying head-on and with ruthless compassion, you will do two things. One, you are reframing the situation for them, showing them another way to see it. In addition, you are leveraging the Spotlight Effect that Coach Mike McCarthy from the Green Bay Packers used to influence his team to see themselves as champions before they were officially crowned champions. By addressing someone's naysaying using the approach outlined above, you are confirming for them that you are watching them while also communicating your expectations that you do not want to observe them naysaying any longer. And when people think someone is fixated on them and they respect that person, they conform to what they think that person expects of them.

## Turn Naysaying into a Challenge

Charles found himself deep in the "Land of No" when he worked at Verizon. He was working on the largest Citibank deal in the history of the company when one of his executives attempted to infect the deal with his naysaying. Mr. Executive was so consumed with learned helplessness that he actually bet Charles that Verizon would never structure an agreement that Mr. Executive would agree to and that Citibank would actually sign. Essentially he did not believe the deal would ever happen – his learned helplessness – nor did it seem that he even wanted the deal to happen. If we peel back the layers of protected ego, we would probably have seen that Charles' success was about to question Mr. Executive's inability to ever create or lead such a deal himself. So Charles was forced to battle with executives at his own company and at Citibank's. But Charles was too focused on his battle cry to allow their beliefs to dictate his own ambitions and perseverance. If anything, Mr. Executive's bet energized him to prove the naysaying executive wrong. By approaching the naysaying as a challenge, Charles won the bet when he negotiated an $84 million, seven-year agreement with Citibank, the first of its kind in the industry.

Jan, like Charles from Verizon, used her colleague's naysaying as fuel to challenge her great career. When Jan started as a meter reader for the state's public utility company in 1975, it was an atypical career path for women, and some men did not approve. During her first week, one man sneered at her, "Women should be home, barefoot and pregnant, not reading meters." Since she did not value, respect, or admire this man, Jan was not influenced by a diagnosis bias or a confirmation bias. Incensed by his naysaying and his rudeness, Jan chose to reframe it as a challenge to prove him wrong. She recently retired from the same utility company after 35 years of service and vibrant career success. Along the way, she often laughed at the absurdity of his comment, glad that she did not allow his naysaying to infect her.

One of the best defenses you have to others' learned helplessness, Golem-inspired labels, and negative diagnoses is to reframe the naysaying into a challenge. Do it enough times and others will start modeling your behavior. As we explored in Chapter 7, people's actions and reactions are influenced by observing and remembering *your* actions and reactions. Your actions and reactions are literally shaping how they choose to behave.

Don't miss the opportunity to teach people to reframe naysaying as a challenge, not a roadblock. Help people understand that the act of naysaying has nothing to do with the receiver and everything to do with the naysayer. More importantly, when they comprehend the impact of naysaying and its ability to taint their perspective, they'll become more vigilant to protect themselves from listening to it.

## Some Yaysaying Ideas

When the workplace is intoxicated with naysaying, your challenge to defend against it is huge. If you don't do something, it has the power to poison the beliefs of others. People rely on their beliefs to determine their ambitions and perseverance. Consequently, you are also reliant on those beliefs. So it is essential that we must do what we can to prevent others' tainted beliefs and learned helplessness from tainting those beliefs upon which everyone is relying to persevere. You cannot afford not to help people keep perspective on naysaying, stay vigilant to the dangers of it, eliminate it from their own beliefs, reframe naysaying as a "challenge," create yaysaying environments, and support yaysaying relationships.

Following are some ideas you can use to encourage people to keep their perspective and create yaysaying environments and relationships:

1. Create a Toastmasters Chapter

2. Start a Mastermind Group

3. Encourage Communities

4. Launch a Mentoring Program

5. Enroll Coaches

6. Put Naysaying into Perspective to Reframe It as a
   Challenge

*1. Create a Toastmasters Chapter.* Toastmasters is a global organization that supports people in becoming better speakers through a structured meeting focused on opportunities for everyone in the meeting to practice speaking. Engrained into each chapter meeting is a ritual whereby everyone in the meeting claps for any person who stands up to speak regardless of how long they spoke and how well they did (or did not do). Members praise each other for incremental success, they mentor each other for improvement opportunities, and they celebrate each other constantly. Naysaying is never tolerated in Toastmasters. (www.toastmasters.org)

*2. Start a Mastermind Group.* Napoleon Hill first introduced the concept of the Mastermind Group in his timeless classic, *Think and Grow Rich.* He surmised that when two or more people come together to work toward a definite purpose, they create a third, invisible intangible force – a third mind. In other words, the brain power of two or more people working together is exponentially more powerful than the sum of the each individual's brain power. Essentially, people working together can accomplish more than they can on their own. There is no room for naysaying in Mastermind groups.

*3. Encourage Communities.* Communities are created when people share values, beliefs, and meaning. Toastmasters is a community. Many officers sponsor employee resource groups or other associations to bring together people of like gender, race, or circumstances to support each other in the corporate experience. These associations create structures of yaysaying that are necessary to combat the inevitable naysaying when those particular individuals venture into the corporate environment alone.

*4. Enroll Coaches.* A coach helps people see beyond their own limitations and self-sabotage by probing with questioning, reframing, challenging, spotlighting, and diagnosing. By their nature, coaching is grounded in yaysaying, not naysaying.

*5. Launch a Mentoring Program.* Participants who volunteer to participate in mentoring programs do so because they are committed to contributing to their peers' success. While there may be a few exceptions, people do not participate in such a program for the purpose of devaluing others. They sign up in order to help others succeed.

*6. Put Naysaying into Perspective to Reframe It.* While helping others put naysaying into perspective, we are simultaneously helping to reframe the toxic naysaying from an obstacle to a challenge. Do this by recounting some of the thousands of victors who have persevered when someone said it could not be done. Let's look at a few historical examples:

- Ben Hogan, one of the world's greatest golfers, was told he would never walk again after a head-on collision with a Greyhound bus in February 1949 left him at 36 with a double-fracture of the pelvis, a fractured collar bone, a left ankle fracture, a chipped rib, and near-fatal blood clots. Four years later, Hogan won five of the year's six golf tournaments and the year's first three major championships. The feat became known as the "Hogan Slam."

- Bethany Hamilton became a champion surfer at eight years old. At 13 while surfing one morning in October 2003, a tiger shark attacked her, ripping off her left arm just below the shoulder. She lost almost 60 percent of her blood and was told she would never surf again. Less than one month later she got back on a board, and in 2005, she took first place in the NSSA National Championships.

- Lucille Ball, award-winning comedian and actress, began attending the American Academy of Dramatic Arts in hopes of becoming an actress. After one month, Lucille's mom received a letter from the school, "Don't put any more money into this. This girl will never make it."

- Even Bob Hope's older brother declared, "He'll never amount to anything," after hearing Bob perform. Bob Hope went on to become one of Paramount Studios' biggest stars.

- When Matt Long, a NYFD firefighter, a 9/11 survivor, and an Ironman triathlete, was training one morning on his bicycle, a bus making an illegal turn ran him over. Within inches of death, Matt underwent over 40 surgeries and more than 5 months in the hospital. He not only lived to inspire others about it, he got back on his bike and became an Ironman triathlete once again.

## Putting It Into Action

- Identify the labels you have placed on each person on your team.

- Create new, bold, audacious labels for people to influence how they think of themselves.

- Identify the naysayers on your team. Observe how they are infecting others. Catch naysaying in the act.

- Practice yaysaying by simply suspending your judgment and instead saying, "How interesting! Tell me more."

- Ask people to write a list of their yaysayers and naysayers.

- Have them generate a list of responses to naysaying.

- Encourage people to join groups like Toastmasters and other employee resource groups where yaysaying thrives.

- Encourage people to create and use Mastermind groups.

- Enroll coaches to get people out of their self-inflicted labels.

- Start a mentoring program, initiative, or rotation.

# Chapter 9

## Deliberately Spoil Sabotage

. . . . . . . . . . . . . . . . .

When he first met Steve Jobs and Steve Wozniak, Ron Wayne was chief draftsman at Atari. Jobs and Wozniak had already fashioned the idea of a personal computer, but their headstrong personalities were threatening their success. After appealing to Wayne's sense of reason on numerous occasions, Jobs and Wozniak asked Wayne to join them as the adult-in-chief, the tiebreaker who would balance the free-spirited Wozniak and the spendthrift Jobs. They proposed that Jobs and Wozniak would each get 45 percent, while Wayne would get 10 percent. Wayne agreed, drafted the company's partnership agreement, and on April Fool's Day, 1976, he filed the paperwork with the registrar's office in Santa Clara County to officially launch Apple Computer.

Wayne was instrumental at the start of Apple. He designed the company's original logo, wrote the Apple I computer manual, and mediated disputes between the obstinate partners. But he started getting nervous when he couldn't contain the uncontrollable partners. Jobs and Wozniak were off and running, committing to orders they could not fulfill, borrowing money to make products, and learning as they were going, the entire time hanging off the cliff. Wayne was wary of the unknown. Twelve days after filing the corporate formation documents with the county, Wayne renounced his role in the company. He wanted out. He sold his 10 percent back to Jobs and Wozniak for $800.

Today, a 10 percent ownership in Apple is worth about $22 billion.

So what stopped Ron Wayne from persevering with the partnership? What stopped him from taking the risk with his original investment that could have made him a billionaire?

## Blockades to Change

What stopped Ron Wayne stops all of us from making or sticking with any sort of change in our behavior or our situation. Blockades to change. When faced with the opportunity or the obligation to make a change, we are met with one of only two types of blockades to change: internal blockades and external blockades. The barrier is either us or the rest of the world.

Let's start with the rest of the world since that one is easy to identify. With this type of obstruction, there is something on the outside of our brain that is making it difficult – not impossible, just difficult – for us to change our behavior or embrace a change in our circumstances. External factors include things like the weather, the economy, government regulations, geography, company policy, and the natural laws of gravity. These are things over which we do not have control and yet they do pose blockades. Sometimes those blockades stop us. For example, humans cannot fly and so a goal to take flight without the help of machinery and fly to the next state would be blockaded by the natural laws of gravity. And sometimes those blockades just pose barriers and obstacles that force us to resourcefully find other ways to accomplish our objective. For example, if our goal is to attend a conference in another state and fly there, then natural laws of gravity would merely pose an obstacle but because we are so committed to getting there, we do so in a plane or using a rocket-propelled backpack, if need be.

Everything else that is deemed a "blockade" is merely a blockade in our own mind. We create the blockade. We perceive a situation, a person, a circumstance, or ourselves, and we create a story in our head as to why the situation cannot change, the person cannot change, the circumstance is the way it is, or we are just that way. For example, "My boss looked at me funny when I told him about leading a new project for another team. He doesn't approve and he will stop me from growing and developing my career. This is just like the time he rejected my request to take the executive management training. He does not want me to develop. He is such a jerk."

While the boss is outside of us, the blockade to developing our career is an internal one. The boss is annoying and a hindrance to our goal, but he is not the reason we are not developing ourselves. *We* are the reason we are not developing ourselves. That makes this an internal blockade, not an external one. In Chapter 8, we called this helpless stance "learned helplessness" because we have learned to be helpless in certain situations, with certain people, and in certain circumstances. That learned helplessness is an internal blockade to change.

## Fear

Ultimately, it all boils down to one thing: fear. When people are their own barrier, it's because they fear something. Only by understanding the fears that run people will we be able to serve people as a change agent.

What do people fear? It might be easier to answer the opposite question: What *don't* people fear? People fear everything from the unknown to the known, from being wrong to being right, from failing to succeeding. Sometimes these fears are christened "limiting beliefs." Let's refer to them instead as "victim beliefs" because they don't just limit people, they cause people to act like victims instead of victors. Recall Influencing Tenet #9, which states that people allow their beliefs to dictate their ambitions and perseverance. If people's beliefs are victim beliefs, their ambitions will be undermined and their perseverance diluted.

Victim beliefs cause people to "act" like victims. I intentionally use the word "act" because many other people presented with similar circumstances will respond differently based on their individual beliefs – their own stories that they have made up in their head. And their varying responses will predict whether they move forward or recede. Think about the people on a team. Each one of them responds differently when presented with the same circumstances. Some are enthusiastic when faced with a challenge, some cower, some cringe, some become paralyzed, and others resourceful. They each make up different stories in their heads about whether they can persevere in their ambitions to succeed, and each story is dictated by their own individual beliefs and fears.

As an example, recall my experience with Matt at Whole Foods from Chapter 4. Matt could perceive his job to be merely stocking shelves in the dairy section, but instead he believes that his job is to make a difference for customers. He certainly did that for me when he brought back my Cherry Vanilla Brown Cow yogurt. Compare my experience with Matt with my experience with Tom at FoodCity, a local grocery chain. I was unsuccessful in locating the chili sauce I needed to make my family's favorite meatballs. So I approached a young man who was wearing a FoodCity shirt and asked him where I might find Heinz chili sauce. He sneered, "I don't know. I don't shop here." Not only was he rude, but whatever disrespect he had for his company, he unloaded it on me. Two guys, same job, opposing beliefs – one a victim, the other a victor.

**Fearing the unknown** is somewhat understandable. People don't know what is around the corner and they wonder if they can handle it or if they will be rejected for trying and failing. So they demonstrate the ostrich effect, in which they tend to bury their head in the proverbial sand in hopes that it all goes away. In their minds, they have just figured out how to handle their work as it is without being rejected, and they are not sure if they have it in them to handle anything more challenging, nor are they sure they want to risk rejection.

The employees in the accounting department at Enron adopted the ostrich position for a few years before the ground in which they buried their heads erupted. Enron, an American energy company based in Houston, led the world in electricity, natural gas, and paper and pulp. In 2001, Enron reported revenues of nearly $101 billion. At the end of the same year, the Enron scandal unraveled, exposing the reality that their revenues were the product of institutionalized, systemic, and creatively planned accounting fraud. They intentionally did not report in their financial statements many of their debts and losses. When it appeared that the stock would fall, Enron executives who knew about the hidden losses began selling their shares in the months prior to the disclosure. As much as everyone likes to point fingers and place blame on the officers of the company, CEO Kenneth Lay, CFO Andrew Fastow, and COO Jeffrey Skilling, there were many people who suspected and others who knew firsthand that something was wrong with the financial statements and inflated stock price, but did nothing to pursue it. Their fear of the unknown paralyzed them into hoping the situation would just go away.

**The fear of the known** is equally logical. People know how hard the new frontier will be and frankly they do not want to do the work, they do not think they will like it, or they do not think they will succeed. To avoid the known, they do not make any changes or try anything new. Of course, they only *think* they know what the new frontier will be like, but they have made up that story as well. Who really knows how situations will turn out? We only really know when we are on the other side of the situation and our hindsight is 20/20.

Ron Wayne, the trepid Apple founder, suffered from both the fear of the unknown as well as the fear of the known. He thought he knew what it was going to be like to work with Jobs and Wozniak, and in his mind the risk was not worth it. On the other hand, he had no idea what was going to happen working with these two and that scared him as well.

**The fear of being wrong** is reasonable although maddening. People hate to be wrong. They think it's a character flaw instead of merely a flaw in their most recent attempt. As we've explored, being wrong is the first step in being rejected, a state every one of us dreads. When faced a challenge, people disregard every other success they've ever had, instead placing enormous pressure on their next move to define them as a success or failure in the world, as if it were Judgment Day. People fear being wrong because they fear being rejected if they are.

Ernie has this annoying habit of saying, "I know, I know," every time someone offers him some new idea, some coaching, or some suggestion. People are gifting him with information and feedback, and instead of thanking them for the gift, he mutters, "I know, I know," as if there was something wrong with not knowing. In his mind, there is. If he accepts the suggestion or new approach, it is an acknowledgement that he doesn't know. Underlying the "I know" is just a fear of being rejected for not knowing.

**The fear of being right** is like the fear of the known. People are afraid that they will be right about their suspicions of a person, a boss, the company, the client, or themselves, and they would rather not face the truth. So, they avoid being right by not progressing. But similar to the fear of the known, people have no idea if they are right. How can they know that they are right about a person or a situation? They don't. They just made up that story in their head. Ron Wayne made up the story about what would happen if he continued down the entrepreneurial path with Jobs and Wozniak. His fear of being right cost him billions of dollars.

**The fear of failing** is the fear that seems most familiar. People fear failure. Like being wrong, no one wants to fail because it's just a precursor to being rejected. When people fail they make it mean something about them personally when it really means nothing other than they tried and it didn't work that time.

As a result of this fear, people procrastinate instead of trying, paralyzed to make any move out of a fear of making the wrong one.

If you have ever been frustrated by someone's tendency to procrastinate, you can bet that a fear of failure is gnawing somewhere beneath the surface.

**The fear of success** requires a little more mind-bending to fully grasp. People are concerned that if they succeed, others will come to expect them to repeat that success. What if they can't? What if their success was a fluke? What if they were just lucky and they cannot repeat the same success?

When people succeed, there's a part of them that feels a bit like an imposter. They don't believe that they really belong in the winner's circle. With all of that doubt swirling around in their head, they begin to fear success for the added pressure it will inevitably bring to succeed again. Consequently, they will unconsciously sabotage their efforts to avoid success and the accompanying pressure altogether. Sabotage manifests when people refuse (or "don't have time") to practice, study, follow up, pick up the phone, exercise, stay organized, research, or block out time in the calendar to execute on a commitment. Then they can say, "I would have succeeded but let me tell you how busy I was! I just had no time so that's why I didn't succeed." People don't want to succeed but they also don't want failure to be their fault. The result? Procrastinating, excusing, and justifying the status quo – people know how to operate really well with exactly what they already have.

Each of these fears is paralyzing the people we work with. They are petrified. It's fear that fuels the proclivity to cling to mediocrity. What is everyone really afraid of? As stated before, it's being rejected. Rejection is at the heart of all fears. People everywhere fear that their failure in the face of the unknown, the known, being right, being wrong, failing, and succeeding, will equate to rejection.

## Cementing the Fear: Confirmation Bias

As if the myriad of fears is not enough, confirmation bias is at work cementing those fears. People make up stories and then look for evidence that their story is correct. Once convinced of the way the world works, they point to their story as the truth for why they did not take action, change, or succeed. Their story is the reason the world should not reject them.

See? There it is again – evidence that my boss does not want me to succeed. It's not my fault, so don't reject me.

These mind games people play create the internal blockades to their growth, development, and change.

As we explored in Chapter 7, the confirmation bias has a powerful influence on people. The confirmation bias works to reinforce diagnoses or labels. When it comes to fears, however, the confirmation bias reinforces the justification for the fears.

The confirmation bias works as follows. People perceive something and that perception fuels one of their fears. They then look around for evidence to confirm that fear, and once confirmed, they engage in self-sabotage. For example, imagine that Morgan perceives that her projects always fail and that in fact she is downright unlucky. When Morgan's boss presents her with a new challenge, she hesitates because she is convinced that she knows exactly how it will work out – it won't. Her perception fuels her fear of the known. She then looks for evidence to confirm that fear and her decision to not take any action. Funding is cut on a project she has been working on and she tells herself, "See, there it is again! My projects always fail." So she refuses the challenge offered by her boss with an excuse about being too busy, and she congratulates herself for dodging that bullet and averting predictable disaster once again. That's the confirmation bias at work locking in fears and obstructing change.

## We Hate to Lose

Fueled by our fear of rejection is our aversion to loss. We hate to lose. We each like to think of ourselves as a winner, not a loser. In fact, there is a phenomenon behavioral economists call "loss aversion" and it is ubiquitous in internal blockades. In essence, we hate to lose twice as much as we love to win. And when we perceive that we are about to lose, we get irrational. For example, Abe pulled out a rusty old bike for the garage sale and put a sticker on it for $80. A young man came by and offered him $50 for the bike and Abe adamantly refused, so the young man walked away without the bike. The truth of the matter is that Abe would never have paid $80 for this rusty old bike, let alone $50. Nevertheless, the thought of losing the $30 was so strong that it caused Abe to vehemently and foolishly walk away from the $50 and to keep his rusty old bike for another year, instead of gaining $50 and space in his garage.

Loss aversion was responsible for a lot of despondent souls at Riverstone Networks when I led the legal department in early 2000s. We took the company public in one of the last IPOs of 2001 before the tech bubble burst. The IPO price was $12 per share and after six months, employees were allowed to start selling their shares. We had each received options to purchase the stock at prices significantly less than $12 per share. Some of the early employees were granted the right to purchase stock at $2 per share, others at $5, $6, or $7 per share. As the stock price rose and hovered around $24, the halls were abuzz with promises to sell as soon as the stock hit $25. Some early employees were positioned to earn $1 million if they had sold their shares. Others like myself were counting on $250,000 to pay off mortgages.

Well, the stock did hit $25, but only for a minute and then it immediately dropped. It continued dropping over the following year from a high of $25 to a low of $3.82 per share as a result of impending lawsuits and an economy that was recalibrating on the backs of start-up companies everywhere. We held tight, willing the stock price to increase to recoup the "loss" we felt from not selling when it was at its high of $25 per share, even $24 per share. Most of us sold a few shares, but held on to the rest hoping it would come back. We could have sold our stock at $15 per share and made money, but it was not the amount of money that we had tasted previously.

All of us spent hours mourning our "losses" even though we didn't really lose anything. We were not required to purchase our shares until the moment we wanted to sell them, so we weren't even out of pocket any cash. We just lost on paper. Oh, we bemoaned, what we could have done with all of that money!

Ironically, most people didn't sell their shares to make even a little money; they just watched the stock drop and drop and drop, thinking maybe just maybe it would go back up. Soon the stock was worth less than the price at which we had the right to buy it. We all promised ourselves that we would sell our shares as soon as the stock went back up. But we were so focused on what we lost out on by not selling at $24 per share that we forgot to focus on what we would gain by selling at any price above what we could buy it for. In essence, we hated to lose twice as much as we would have loved to "win" the money. If we loved winning more than we hated losing, we would have sold a set number of shares every month as long as the price was above what we could buy it for. That way, we would have always taken advantage of some decent price, instead of gambling for the best price. In the investment world, this is called dollar cost averaging.

Now let's apply this to choices people have to make every day in their jobs. If they hate to lose twice as much as they love to win, they will irrationally make decisions to avoid the risk of losing. And when they sense they are losing, they will irrationally justify, protect, and defend to avoid that loss. The train wrecks at Enron, WorldCom, and Lehman Brothers can be traced back to loss aversion. If we cover up this error in judgment just a little while longer, the market will rebound and we will recoup what we lost.

## Fears Manifested

It is merciless not to feel some compassion for people right about now. The fears, the different perceptions, the made-up stories, the irrationality caused by loss aversion, and the eventual mind games are all working 24/7 to sabotage success. We can identify when these fears are toiling on people simply by the behaviors they exhibit. Fears manifest in three main behaviors: (1) procrastinating, (2) excusing, and (3) hiding.

*1. Procrastinating.* People procrastinate when they don't know how to do something, don't know what to do, don't want to do it (usually because they don't know how), or they don't know why they are doing it. Of course, we now understand that all of these reasons for procrastinating are just masking some fear – fear of the known, unknown, being right, being wrong, failing, or succeeding.

The way people procrastinate runs the gamut. I've seen procrastination result in over researching, excessive planning, inordinate number of committee meetings, Facebook updates, and even clean offices. When we see people engage in procrastinating behaviors, know they are being run by fear, and that fear is standing in the way of their progress.

One procrastination technique is dictated by a phenomenon called "information bias." People have a proclivity to seek more and more information before they decide on something – even when they know that the new information cannot affect the decision. But because they are afraid of making a mistake (and losing), they believe more information is needed before making a move. How many times has your boss delayed making a decision on your recommendation because she wanted more information, facts, expertise, data, and research? How many times have you done this to people you work with? How many times have they done this to you? What have we all lost in terms of productivity, time, and opportunity as we procrastinate on a decision because our fear of making the wrong one warrants more and more information?

Another procrastination technique is over-planning, which can be explained by a behavioral influence called "optimism bias." This bias describes the propensity to be overly optimistic about the outcome of planned events versus spontaneous events. People over-plan because they believe that it will produce a better result, when in reality extra planning does not guarantee a better outcome. It only allows people to procrastinate.

Over-planning does nothing but waste time and gratify our loss aversion. I represented hundreds of entrepreneurs in my legal career and most of them slaved for months over their business plans. They could not get started until the plan was complete. Invariably every single business plan was outdated by day two in business. No matter how much these ambitious entrepreneurs had planned, it was impossible to plan for every single variance. The ones who got a jump-start over their competition considered their business plan a living document, launching the business with a simple plan and updating it as their knowledge and experience about their business and the industry grew.

*2. Excusing.* People make excuses to justify when they have been blocked from change. They make excuses to justify the status quo. They make excuses to justify why they didn't do what they said they were going to do. "I didn't have time." This is one of my favorites. I used to pull all-nighters when I practiced law. We would never dare tell a client we didn't have time. We could always sleep less, watch less TV, waste less time. There is always enough time. The reality is that we didn't *make* the time, not that we didn't *have* the time.

People make excuses to justify the fact that they didn't prioritize their commitment. They didn't prioritize success. As their manager, you can always help people manage their time better. But as their leader, you have an opportunity (and a responsibility) to dig beneath the excuse to discover what fear is really creating their reality.

One popular excuse that people fling is the status quo. People justify what they have (and know) and argue fervently against anything new or different. This behavioral influence is called "status quo bias" and it occurs when people justify the status quo out of an irrational fear of their inability to succeed in anything other than what they already know. Their gut-wrenching fear of the unknown causes people to cling to the status quo.

Wall Street clung to the status quo when in 1973 Dr. Jerome Swartz brought investors a revolutionary idea that would transform business processes. Holding the patent for the handheld laser-based bar code scanner, Dr. Swartz founded Symbol Technologies to manufacture mobile technology solutions. When he sought funding on Wall Street, investors told Dr. Swartz that the bar code would never catch on. Thirty-five years later, Symbol Technologies was acquired by Motorola for $3.9 billion. The Wall Street investors pulled a Ron Wayne and provided us with an excellent example of clinging to the status quo out of fear of the unknown – and then missing out.

*3. Hiding.* Finally, we can identify fear when it manifests as hiding out. People hide out when they cancel meetings, consistently show up late, decline to offer their ideas or opinions, and dodge opportunities to volunteer. When you are so busy trying to manage people instead of lead them, it can be easy for people to blend in, fly under the radar, and coast through their days. But hiding out is just another manifestation of fear. It's learned helplessness that causes people to believe that they have no power to change, and that if they just hide out then no one will ask them to try to change that which they think they cannot change.

## Stop the Madness of Sabotage

Procrastinating, excusing, over-researching, hiding, over-planning, justifying, and clutching to the status quo are sabotaging people's success. As you can imagine, people expend inordinate amounts of time and energy avoiding rejection and averting loss. In the end it materializes as "trying to figure it all out" or "paralysis by analysis."

You are similarly tested by these fears and biases. If you merely manage, you will sabotage your success, while managing others who are sabotaging their own. If you lead, however, you can deliberately spoil sabotage with your understanding of these influences. Not addressing the sabotage will result in thwarted battle cries, blocked commitments, and halted ambitions and perseverance. You and the people you work with cannot afford to be deviated by what-ifs, opinion-shopping, committee meetings, over-planning, and excessive research.

At this point you may feel like pointing a finger at your own leader, who may be engaging in sabotaging behavior or doing nothing to thwart it. Now that you know what is really going on, you will notice when people circumvent change or when they procrastinate in taking action where action needs to be taken. Have compassion and know that they too are being run by their fears.

But never allow *their* sabotage to contaminate *your* success. As a manager, you are merely a victim of it. As a leader, you can be a victor in spite of it. Let's look at 10 ways you can spoil sabotaging ways.

## Ten Strategies for Spoiling Sabotage

There are 10 strategies you can use to spoil other people's sabotage:

1. Discover the reason for sabotage

2. Focus on the battle cry

3. Celebrate effort, not just success

4. Advocate for discovery over proficiency

5. Reframe for a "say yes first, figure it out later" approach

6. Mitigate the risks

7. Break mountains into molehills

8. Leverage mentoring

9. Dance with counterfactual thinking

10. Pilot

*1. Discover the reason for sabotage.* Everyone does it. Not everyone knows why. You now have some great insight into the why. Discover through inquiry the reason behind the sabotage and you can help people address the reason in order to move past it. Managers focus on the sabotaging behavior, while leaders address the reasons behind the sabotage.

*2. Focus on the battle cry.* People get married without knowing how to succeed in marriage. People raise children without knowing how to succeed as parents. People apply for jobs without knowing exactly what that job entails and how to be successful. They take these actions not without fear but in the face of their fears and biases. Why? Because their focus on their battle cry is stronger than their focus on their fears. Let a focus on the battle cry work its magic for you as well.

When people see that the risk of not pursuing their battle cry is greater than the risk of failing, they will take action. Focus people on that risk of missing out and you will help to minimize the risk of not succeeding. Ask, "What is more important? Staying safe or pursuing your own battle cry?" When people care more about their own goals than they do about what others think of them, they'll take action. If we continue to get pushback, it just may be because they have not defined a compelling battle cry.

*3. Celebrate effort, not just success.* It's easy to cheer for success, but what do you do when someone on your team fails? Do you berate, chastise, ridicule, ignore them, or worse yet, just do it yourself next time? Do you react or do you respond? Realize that your reaction to their failure is being triggered by your own fears outlined in this chapter. When you can step around those fears to applaud and celebrate their attempts, not just their success, you will be making an investment in the long-term growth and development of people.

*4. Advocate for discovery over proficiency.* As we will explore in Chapter 10, a discovery mindset is essential to thwart the kryptonite-like power of fears and biases. If people know that failure is merely part of the discovery process, and that failure does not result in character assassination, they will more easily take action in the face of those fears. A discovery mindset over a proficiency mindset is also essential to innovation and progress, as we'll explore in Chapter 12.

People do not ask because of their fear of rejection. People fear that you will say "No," and there is no greater evidence of rejection than the word "No." In addition, people fear the judgment of others for not knowing and needing to ask. People fear that others will think they are dumb, greedy, naïve, incompetent, or inexperienced. Most people don't ask because they are convinced that everyone else knows the answer and they'll look foolish for even asking. We need people to ask, but people are not good at it. You need to model the art of asking, including the attitude that not knowing is completely acceptable.

*5. Reframe for a "say yes first" approach.* While planning should not be abandoned altogether, we need to free people from the notion that they need to know all the details before they can say "Yes!" Just like the successful entrepreneurs who regard their business plans as a living document, you are better served when people say "yes" and figure out the how as they go, knowing that they will course-correct along the way. Help people reframe the situation from one of needing to know before they begin to one of learning how after they begin. Say-yes-first frees people to move forward.

*6. Mitigate the risks.* There is no denying that there are risks in business and in life. Ron Wayne may have felt an excessive amount of risk dancing with Steve Jobs and Steve Wozniak, but there were many ways he could have mitigated the risk without running for the hills. As a former corporate attorney, my job was to mitigate risk for entrepreneurs using contracts. But I also felt a responsibility to help my clients balance those identified (and unidentified) risks with a reality check on probability and with the potential of losing the deal. In so doing, I found other ways for my clients to mitigate risk rather than building in 75 pages to a contract, which only delayed the deal, increased the frustration level of all the parties, and risked the completion of the deal. Mitigation included such activities as purchasing more insurance, forming a corporation to protect personal assets, creatively structuring the deal to shift risk to other parties, and clearly communicating and documenting expectations.

When someone is sabotaging success as a result of a huge burden of risk, your job is to help them mitigate that risk. You're never going to eliminate risk no matter how long your contract is or how much insurance you purchase, but you can get creative to mitigate the risk.

*7. Break mountains into molehills.* When confronted with an enormous challenge, people are at greater risk of being influenced by their fears and biases. As an example, when I was preparing to ride my bicycle across the country, 3,700 miles seemed overwhelming and insurmountable. But when I embarked on a series of 10-mile rides with eating opportunities in between, suddenly it felt attainable. Saving $100,000 for a down payment on a house is overwhelming, whereas saving $1,667 a month for five years seems possible. Writing a thesis seems unattainable, while writing a page a week seems achievable.

People just want to know how to win. They don't want to lose. So help them break huge, mountainous goals into mini-achievable molehills and watch them take that first step.

*8. Leverage mentoring.* Mentoring is an amazing solution for exchanging institutional knowledge, addressing fears, and drawing on various approaches. When people are sabotaging their success with fear-based behaviors, you can engage the wisdom of someone else to share their been-there-done-that advice. Yoda did it for Luke Skywalker. Anyone in your organization can mentor someone on your team to move beyond their fear with advice, guidance, and lessons-learned wisdom. In addition, mentors will be great role models for people to see that no one melts from unsuccessful efforts or from discovering a better way by attempting a not-so-great way.

*9. Dance with counterfactual thinking.* Counterfactual thinking describes the human tendency to imagine how things could have turned out differently. It's "what if" hindsight. People regularly wonder "what if?" When we ask them to do it intentionally, it has the power to infuse meaning into their role and responsibility, thereby influencing their actions. What if this challenge did not exist? What if their job did not exist? What if the company did not exist? What would their life be like then? People imbue more meaning into what they do have when they are asked to think about what their world would be like if they did not have the challenge, the job, or the company in front of them.

We can use counterfactual thinking to drive even greater impact by using it with foresight by asking, "What is the worst that can happen if we do take action?" Someone should have asked this of Ron Wayne about his $800 investment in Apple.

*10. Pilot.* The word "pilot" is amazing. With one word, we can give people permission to experiment without repercussion. We'll cover more of this in Chapter 12, but for now know that when you allow people to engage in a pilot, you are encouraging them to discover instead of forcing them to have all the answers. This one word alone has the power to cut down on approvals, committee meetings, research, data-gathering, and planning.

One of our large corporate clients strategically plays with the word "pilot" to avoid bureaucratic red tape. The Director of People Development at a large corporation hired us to create a mentoring program to identify and develop future leaders. As part of the program, we crafted the requisite communications for recruiting participants and management support. The Director was cognizant that their corporate communications department would unnecessarily delay the program while completely changing the message of the communications and the program. She also knew that if we called the program a "pilot," the communications group would not get involved at all. As a result, the strategic Director has been calling it a "Pilot Mentoring Program" for three years now.

## Becoming a Change Agent

Any or all of these ideas for spoiling sabotage may cause you to recoil even a little, as you imagine your own managers walking you to the proverbial guillotine. They won't. They are starved for successful, enthusiastic, committed leaders like you to drive discovery, learning, and progress. It's just your preconceived fear and past experiences that are causing you to want to jump back into your comfort zone. But consider how long you have allowed your own fears to foster fear-driven mindsets in others instead of discovery mindsets. People are watching you. It's time to lead the change.

How did "change" become such a burdened word, loaded with visions of torture, pain, and suffering? To avoid the pain and suffering, we choose to avoid change and the requisite decisions that accompany it. But not making a decision *is* making a decision. Inaction is a choice in the spectrum of change, albeit not a powerful one. Change is not optional, in spite of such intentional inaction. As Rob, our NYNEX sales superhero often says, "Change is inevitable. It's the pain and suffering that are optional."

A battle cry depends on progress to succeed, and progress requires change. Change can be as small as confronting someone who is not acting in the best interest of the company and as big as overhauling a product line. Standing still, however, should never be an option – for you or for your people.

You have a choice. You can manage change or you can lead it. Managing change requires you to direct it, supervise it, and control it. Leading change demands you to guide people through their own change. In leading it you will become their change agent, welcoming the progress – and the setbacks and lessons learned – that comes with it.

One way to powerfully guide people through change is to use the GROW Model.

## The GROW Model

The GROW Model was developed by Graham Alexander, Alan Fine, and Sir John Whitmore to solve problems and set goals in the executive coaching world.

It is an influential tool for you to use as you effectively lead people through any sort of change. By asking people strategic questions, they will arrive at their own prognosis as well as an action plan that they own. The model involves asking questions in four buckets: Goal questions, Reality Check questions, Obstacles and Options questions, and Way Forward questions. Through the use of questions in each category, you can lead people in defining an objective they want to reach, clarifying the current situation instead of their subjective impressions of that situation, developing several courses of action, and creating concrete action steps that they own.

Some examples:

### Goal Questions

- What result would make this conversation a great success?
- What outcome would make this year a great success?
- What result would you like to achieve from our time together now?
- What result would you like from our time together this year?
- How can we measure that we achieved this result?

### Reality Check Questions

- When was the last time you achieved a result like that?
- What have you actually accomplished on this result so far?
- What else have you tried already?
- Who else is involved in this situation and how?

### Obstacles and Options Questions

- What obstacles have you/are you facing right now?
- Are these obstacles external or internal?
- What could you do about those obstacles?
- What other courses of action can you think of here?
- Who could help you?
- What other resources could you draw on to address this?
- If you had unlimited resources and knew you could not fail, what would you try?

### Way Forward Questions

- Which option do you want to pursue?

- How can you turn that into an action step?

- What will you do, by when?

- What step could you take this week that would move you closer to your goal?

- On a scale of 1-10 how likely is it that this step will get done in the time frame you have set?

- How could you alter that step and change a 6 to an 8?

*Be the one.* A change agent is a driving force for change. When you champion change, the ripple effect will impact more than just your team. Invariably you may feel frustrated about your own leaders' lack of ability to change or worse yet, their sabotage of your efforts to effect change. Remember that they are run by their own fears; stay committed to your battle cry. Championing change is not dependent on the paralyzed. Stewarding in an enthusiastic, on-fire, moxie mindset is never dependent on status quo militants. You can instigate change in spite of them. Remember, if not you, then whom? And if not this, then what? And if not now, then when?

Ruthless compassion is your secret ingredient for leader moxie. Ruthless compassion means you are hardnosed and merciless in the pursuit of a battle cry and yet compassionate that people are faced with their overwhelming, paralyzing fears. Being a champion for change requires that you maintain a balance of ruthless compassion and calculated risk. Calculated risk means you take deliberate risks. To spoil sabotage while effecting change, you must relentlessly listen to fears so you truly understand their predispositions, while at the same time pushing people to jump in spite of those fears. If you are sincerely committed to the success of others, you need to foster an environment in which taking risks is expected in order to move on the one thing that is of utmost importance: the battle cry. When people lose sight of the reason they show up every day, they cling to comfort and status quo, and they forgo risk. But with your ruthless compassion, people will quickly realize that battle cries suffocate in the comfort zone and that progress happens only when we are uncomfortable.

## Putting It Into Action

- Find someone who is notorious for procrastinating and identify the root of it.
- Notice how over-planning is sabotaging success on a project instead of ensuring it.
- Notice what excuses people are throwing at you.
- Employ the 10 strategies for spoiling sabotage:

  1. Discover the reason for sabotage

  2. Focus on the battle cry

  3. Celebrate effort, not just success

  4. Advocate for discovery over proficiency

  5. Reframe for a "say yes first" approach

  6. Mitigate the risks

  7. Break mountains into molehills

  8. Leverage mentoring

  9. Dance with counterfactual thinking

  10. Pilot

- Practice using the GROW Model to guide people through initiating their own change.

# Chapter 10

## Advocate for Discovery
## over Proficiency

In the late 1950s the Eastern Bloc countries discovered that in spite of rigorous training routines, their athletes were stagnating. At first befuddled, they soon named the phenomenon "General Adaptation Syndrome" or "GAS." They determined that when an athlete's body is exposed to a new stress, their muscles initially go into alarm. The body gets weaker. But after continued exposure to the stress, the muscles begin to adapt. This is known as the adaptation stage, in which the body supercompensates for the stress in order to better deal with it. However, if the body is continually exposed to the same stress for too long, it begins to exhaust. In the exhaustion stage, its adaptation may actually decline and stagnation sets in. For example, introducing the quadriceps muscle to a squat with a heavy weight will shock and weaken the muscle at first. With continued exposure to the squat and weight level, the quadriceps muscle adapts and becomes stronger in order to supercompensate to the new position and weight. After successive workouts with the same squat and weight, however, the quadriceps muscle becomes exhausted and may actually lose some of its strength gained during the adaptation stage. In other words, athletic trainers discovered that doing the same thing all the time does *not* in fact lead to improvement.

In response to GAS, the Eastern Bloc countries developed a program based on the concept of "periodization," in which athletes are exposed to systematically manipulated training variables over a period of time. Exposing athletes to different training phases optimizes their adaptations to resistance training. For example, in cycling, athletes who practice periodization engage in microcycles, or short duration cycles of different training phases, including base training, strength training, interval training, and high intensity, peak performance training.

## GAS and Work Muscles

Let's apply General Adaptation Syndrome to the people at work. When people are new to their positions, they are stressed. They work hard. They often stay late while they are figuring out their new responsibilities. They adapt to the stress and get stronger. Then as the months and years roll by, they enter autopilot. Their excitement fatigues, their progress stagnates, and their strength declines. They can practically do their job with their eyes closed, and often they do just that. They have internalized the steps to do their job, and there are no new variables to force them out of their adapted stage. Active, conscious thought is no longer required.

In this adaptation stage of autopilot, people stop growing. And when people stop growing, their intrinsic drive weakens. They are out of motivation and energy. To maintain their high effort and enthusiasm, people need continuous opportunities to grow and develop. They need to be challenged. But challenging people does not mean more of the same work. It means challenging them to think differently. Just like the quadriceps muscle exposed to the same stress for too long exhausts, people similarly exhaust. And as we saw with the athletes, during the exhaustion stage, people get weaker, not stronger with more of the same stress. Stagnation ultimately sets in. And when people stagnate, they stop growing, they stop caring, and their effectiveness plummets.

Even offering new training classes simply compounds the situation. Once people pass the learning curve and they're in the adaptation stage, they no longer question the logic or the common sense behind a task. They merely mutter, "That's how we've always done it." Training just adds to what they already know, but does not force them to think beyond that or question why they even do things that way. As evidenced by some of the people who act like sheep and those who walk the halls like zombies, doing the same thing all the time does not lead to improvement.

Now imagine applying the concept of periodization to this person whose work muscles, as a result of being thrust into the exhausted stage, are now declining in strength and stagnating. If we challenge those work muscles by exposing them to systematically manipulated opportunities over a period of time, we can optimize their adaptation in which those work muscles are supercompensating to the stress without exhausting the muscles. This would require that we engage in microcycles of work, or short duration cycles of different assignments, tasks, challenges, projects, and opportunities.

As a corporate attorney in Silicon Valley during the height of the dot-com bubble, I regularly stayed at the office until 10:00 every night. Once a week for over a year, I pulled an all-nighter, working around the clock just to tackle the piles of contracts that seemed to spawn in my office. At the beginning it was exciting. I felt so important. Then I became good at my job of drafting and negotiating venture-backed financing deals. I adapted to the life of a lawyer. But there was no end in sight to the deals. And they were always the same. While I was a good attorney and loved the firm and my clients, I noticed my excitement for the next incorporation and Series A financing waning and my work muscles declining. I didn't need more training; I didn't need a sabbatical; I needed some periodization—challenging new tasks, assignments, projects, and opportunities in which my muscles would need to learn to adapt by supercompensating.

## Forget about Retention; Create Microcycles

Retention denotes stalemate and stagnation. Keeping people in the same job for years *is* the problem. Their work muscles just exhaust, decline in strength, and stagnate. We don't want exhausted, weak, stagnated contributors. We want fresh, new, productive, excited individuals. Losing people is merely a sign that we ignored them, like a plant we forgot to water. They stopped growing. So, forget about retaining people and instead focus on periodization.

With periodization, the key is to create microcycles so muscles never have an opportunity to exhaust, decline, and stagnate. If people are most effective at the beginning of a new challenge when their work muscles are adapting in the learning curve, focus on presenting them with new challenges as soon as their muscles have adapted to the old challege. "New challenges" does not require a whole new job. It means finding challenges within the current job.

Let's look at the many ways you can create microcycles. Sometimes it's as simple as asking people to apply their knowledge and perspective to address a totally new challenge. Just like the Eastern Bloc trainers, you can systematically manipulate the training variables of the people you work with to optimize their adaptations. Your objective is to assign people to new responsibilities, expose them to fresh perspectives, compel them to experience their own efficacy, and apply their work muscles to a new project. By doing so, you are challenging them to employ their experience and knowledge – their work muscles – in a new way, thereby creating microcycles. Here are the top three ways to create microcycles:

1. Task Forces

2. Rotations

3. New Assignments

## Task Forces

Task forces oblige people to think creatively and differently about their work. In short, a group of people who are not familiar with an issue gather together for the purpose of sharing their perspectives and ideas to solve a problem and address that particular issue. When we assign people to a task force, they are challenged to apply their experience and knowledge to solve a problem that they were not previously asked to solve. In addition, they are exposed to new issues and perspectives from others on the task force.

At Apex Computer Systems, CEO Philip Chen used a task force to change the way the company bid on new contracts. In the past the bidding department answered a request for proposal (RFP) using the limited information they had. Philip changed the process by forming a task force to incorporate into the RFP the viewpoints and ideas from accounting, business development, and delivery. He looked to the task force to decide whether the project was doable, to understand the customer's perspective. This allowed the bidding department to more effectively respond to the RFPs by outlining how the customer could achieve their goals by hiring Apex. As a result of the buy-in process around the RFP, more and more task forces began to emerge throughout the company bringing together people from different departments to address various business needs and identify solutions.

Similarly, mobile technology giant Motorola Solutions creates "Work-Out Teams," cross-functional teams formed to solve various business problems. For instance, when the mergers and acquisitions group is considering entry into a new segment of the mobile technology industry, it forms a Work-Out Team and invites individuals from different functions of the business to share their various perspectives. Invariably the members of the team are grateful for the opportunity to contribute their ideas to the company's decision while simultaneously learning the perspectives of others in the company. As a result of the Work-Out Team, the mergers and acquisitions folks acquired a glimpse into the world of sales and the sales folks gleaned a new perspective that impacted their day-to-day interactions with Motorola's clients.

## Rotations

By rotating people to new challenges, opportunities, assignments, and roles, you can keep things fresh. In sales, you can move them to new clients and new accounts. In marketing, you can give them a new product to market. In business development, you can give them new projects. In finance, you can assign them a new report.

Creating some sort of rotation in their work is critical for exposing people to new functions and issues that impact the company. As a Vice President at a welding supply company, Brian convinced the three other Vice Presidents to institute their own rotation to gain such exposure to people in the field. Brian and the other leaders spent one year rotating among the company's four field locations, spending one quarter at each location. They went with the intention of exposing the employees in each location to one of the company's leaders. What they didn't anticipate was the enormous value of being exposed to the functions and issues in each of these offices. This exposure greatly impacted their ability to lead from the home office.

When I was practicing corporate securities law at a large law firm, my only exposure to a client's business was through the eyes of their CEO. I was charged with negotiating and closing their venture capital funding, but I never saw the impact of the financing on the company's viability, nor did I understand the impact of the financing process on the CEO and the others at the company. In fact, I naively considered the financing more important than anything else the CEO could possibly be working on. I was convinced that my client's world revolved around me and my ability to get their financing closed – a little self-delusion goes a long way with attorneys.

Eventually when I was recruited by one of my entrepreneurial clients to join his company as in-house corporate counsel, I quickly discovered how executives truly regarded lawyers – a necessary evil. Suddenly I was privy to the trials and tribulations of entrepreneurs from the in-house perspective. The legal stuff was just one small part of running a business. Years later when I launched my own law firm representing small businesses, I was a much more effective attorney and partner to my entrepreneurial clients for having directly experienced their world. I had inadvertently created my own rotation, and as a result, I was better able to serve my clients.

Nationwide Insurance has a rotational program that similarly creates learn-by-exposure opportunities for its employees. Connie had been working at the company for a few years when she was presented with an opportunity to leave her role as a project manager and take part in a rotation as a coach. She jumped at the chance to learn new skills and explore new areas of the company. During the rotation, Connie learned ways to coach people through problems, a skill she had never thought about previously. When the rotation ended, she returned to managing projects, but did so with a whole new approach, making her extremely effective.

People benefit similarly from exposure to different departments, functions, and issues that depend on and impact their role in the company. Apprenticeships, internships, and cross-functional mentoring each operate from this premise, providing people with much-needed exposure to other people's roles.

## New Assignments

Assigning people to new projects is like pushing them off the high dive. When we place people on new projects without training, we force their work muscles to learn by doing. This jolts those muscles out of adaptation and the comfort of autopilot and activates their conscious thinking. By forcing people to learn by fire, we leverage the benefits of periodization.

Learning-through-doing is an engrained custom at Capital One, where people intentionally develop their careers by taking on new assignments. Because they know they will be supported in the learning process, Capital One employees frequently seek out lateral moves in order to embrace new challenges and discover new skills. The benefit for the company is twofold. While people maintain their high effort and enthusiasm required to adapt to the new challenge, the company's leaders are concurrently laying the groundwork for succession planning.

Contrast Capital One's fresh approach with that at another major corporation where employees are strongly dissuaded from applying for a new role at the company unless they have the expertise for the role already established. As a result, employees don't apply, feeling trapped in their positions, nowhere to go until their boss retires. Imagine the dense stagnation in the air as work muscles everywhere not only decline but atrophy.

Moving people into new positions forces them out of their autopilot mode and into a fresh perspective. At General Electric, leaders regularly rearrange employees to form teams of people with varying approaches to tackle a new project. Even medical school programs require residents to rotate from one type of practice to another to expose them to different doctors and issues. In addition to the exposure, the rotations keep the residents' minds active during the peak of intensity in their medical training.

One manager at a high-tech company requires everyone on his team to create a "Passion Project" that must be started and completed within the year. A Passion Project, as defined by this manager, is a project that is not part of their job responsibilities but contributes to their development and/or contributes to the team, and that the individual who owns it is excited to undertake it. For example, one man on the team really wanted to launch a customer advisory board. This was not part of his job but he knew it would benefit the team and he was eager to work on it. Of course he was! He created it. As we saw in Chapter 4, people support that which they help create. This manager used his leader moxie and took it one step further. He recruited a mentor to support each person in the execution of their Passion Project.

## The Role of Mentoring

No matter what the assignment, the rotation, the task force, or the Passion Project, mentoring is your secret weapon. It is the way that institutional knowledge is exchanged among people. The stuff that isn't written down anywhere. The unique insight that organizing meetings after the boss's lunchtime yoga session increases the odds of the boss's approval. The person in procurement to engage and the ones to avoid. The switch to flip before turning on the motor. The inside scoop to navigating a career at the company. The who and what to know. How to get things done. With mentoring, *your* people are developing *your* people. It doesn't get any sweeter and simpler than that.

After Brian Dunn's first day selling VCRs for Best Buy in 1985, his store manager inquired about Brian's initial day on the job. Brian confessed to his store manager that it had been a lousy experience. The store manager invited Brian to come in on Saturday morning and he would personally teach Brian about how he had operated on the sales floor when he was in Brian's position. The store manager's persistence and his commitment to Brian's success made all the difference in Brian's experience and ultimately his performance. The store manager mentored Brian, clearing the way for Brian to be not only good at his job, but to love his job. Twenty-one years later, Brian became president and COO of Best Buy.

The challenge with "mentoring" is that the word alone is laden with expectation. Therefore you must dispel the myth that Obi Wan Kenobi is coming to save them. With tempered expectations, you can embrace a very broad definition of "mentoring," which can then support people in all of their microcycles. When you include mentoring in periodization, you can strategically help people to develop their effectiveness for projects today and their readiness for challenges and opportunities tomorrow.

At its essence, mentoring occurs whenever one person contributes to another person's growth or development. That's it. By sharing inside information, a strategy, a tactic, a piece of advice, a tip, or a lesson learned, one person is mentoring another. The shared information does not have to be life-altering, and the relationship does not have to be career-lasting. With this expansive definition, we can see that mentoring is occurring all around us every day – intentionally, unintentionally, formally, and informally.

Imagine that Connor is on our team and he's struggling with the company's new computer system. Mary has been using it for a few weeks and has become very proficient with the system. When she sees Connor struggling, she offers her insights to help end his frustration. While their interaction is short, the tips Mary shares allow Connor to end the struggle and increase his productivity instantly. Mary mentored Connor in that moment. Obviously, it was not intentional, formal mentoring relationship that developed Connor through his next career move. But it was an exchange of knowledge that accelerated Connor through some moment of being stuck. And you didn't have to be there at all and you didn't have to hire an outside training firm to train Connor on the computer system again. It was a mentoring conversation that contributed in a small way to Connor's growth and development.

Now let's look at our assumptions about Connor and Mary. Did you assume that Mary is older than Connor? Did you assume that Mary is higher on the pay scale than Connor? Imagine instead that Mary is the new kid on the block and Connor is the CEO. Mentoring is blind to rank. It just implores people to contribute to each other, and assumes that everyone has something to contribute to someone else.

Mentoring triggers two behavioral influences that cause people to rise to the occasion. First, mentoring has an element of accountability that influences people to perform differently because they know that someone is watching them. This is the Hawthorne Effect in action. Based on the Hawthorne experiments described in Chapter 2, we have a tendency to perform differently when others are watching us. We step up our game when we no longer rely on our own thoughts and willpower, and rely instead on the fact that someone else cares about our performance.

In addition to the Hawthorne Effect, mentoring also triggers the Spotlight Effect that we saw Green Bay Packers coach Mike McCarthy leverage in Chapter 8. According to this influence, when people think others are fixated on them, they conform to what they think those other people expect of them. As an example, when Mentee Lulu believes that Mentor Diego has a spotlight on her, Mentee Lulu will conform to what she thinks Mentor Diego expects of her.

While mentoring is one of your most powerful, cost-effective tools available to develop people, there are a few influencing tenets that are competing for attention that may sabotage the potential of mentoring and professional development in general.

## Competing Influences at Play

Let's explore the competing influences so you know what is underlying people's desire to move, grow, learn, develop, and be challenged, and underlying their desire to avoid growth and development altogether.

*1. People desire to understand and influence their environment.* Intrinsically, we each are constantly seeking to make sense of the world in which we live. We have a natural curiosity that is at the core of society's advancement and innovation. It is this curiosity that leads to a desire to explain various phenomena we experience. Apply this to work and naturally we want to understand and influence our environment.

*2. People desire to become everything that one is capable of becoming.* According to Abraham Maslow and his hierarchy of needs, self-actualization is the acme of needs. It encompasses our desire to become more and more of what we are, to become everything we are capable of becoming. Apply this to our careers and we can see how we are inclined to move forward on a career path instead of wandering in a career adventure or getting off the path altogether.

*3. People want to feel important and make a difference.* When we invite individuals to participate in a rotation, a special assignment, a task force, a new challenge, or a Passion Project, we are singling them out and making the world revolve around them. They are no longer lumped together with a group of people called "employees." They are special. They are important. They are needed to help a team or a project succeed. Their work is making a difference. These are hugely powerful influences on intrinsic motivation.

Now let's understand the competing influences that are causing people to avoid those challenges, rotations, and passion projects.

*1. People fear rejection.* As we have seen consistently throughout this book, we all fear being rejected. If I am given a new assignment, I start to wonder if I can do it and more importantly, if I will be rejected for failing to do it. If I think there is a chance I will be rejected for trying something new, then rest assured, I'm not as eager to try.

*2. People want to win, not lose.* We want to win. We don't want to lose. And if we are given a new assignment, we want to understand what it will take to win. Because of our fear of rejection, we tend to avoid challenges where we risk losing and being rejected for it. If I don't know how to win or if I don't feel like I have the freedom to figure out how to win, then the potential to lose is high, and I will hesitate even trying rather than risk rejection from losing.

*3. People don't think there is anything to develop.* People inherently believe that they are better than the average Joe walking down the street. This is called, conveniently enough, the "Better-than-Average Effect" or the "Illusory Superiority Bias." We don't like to admit that there is anything wrong with us, for that's just a slippery slope to rejection. At the core of all of our actions and inactions, however, is our fear of rejection. We take on the illusion of superiority to prevent others from seeing our weaknesses and rejecting us for them.

So what does all of this mean in terms of your role as the manager-turned-middle-leader who is committed to elevating the importance of people development? It means you have to keep these influences in mind as you introduce any type of microcycle. You can't present development to people like something is wrong with them and expect them to embrace it. You can't throw out a new challenge and then lace it with "you better succeed or else" and not expect them to be paralyzed with fear. And even if you'd never use those words, don't let your body language and voice betray your words and thus corrupt your commitment.

Instead, advocate for a discovery mindset in which people are constantly learning by discovering themselves and the world around them. Implore people to discover their way to growth.

## The Case for a Discovery Mindset

Foster a discovery mindset because you want warriors, not victims. Warriors are still growing. Victims are broken. Warriors extol and accept responsibility. Victims blame and vilify.

Warriors discover a new way. Victims stand in the way. Warriors are constantly working on themselves to grow, develop, and succeed. Victims blame their lack of success on their leaders, their company, and the economy, but never on themselves. Your success and your organization's success are contingent upon having a group of warriors who are always discovering, not a group of victims who are always blaming.

To instill a discovery mindset, you need to let people discover independently, not come to you for the answers. Espouse, don't enable. Granted, it's so much easier just to solve their problems, answer their questions, fix their dilemmas, and move on. But it is a disservice to you and to them. First, you are creating a dependency that will keep you in "manager" mode and prevent you from leading. Second, you are enabling them to not learn, discover, and figure it out. Enabling people this way never contributes to their growth and development. Finally, when you require someone to address their own problems and create their own solutions, you are forcing them to own that solution. By creating their own solutions, people will own them and go to great lengths to make them work or risk being wrong for their own solution. No one likes to be wrong – it's just a precursor to rejection.

Meg has been feeling rather desperate in the economic climate of late, and desperate times call for desperate measures. Her company increased her target revenue number by $20 million and decreased her team by five members. With 22 years of sales experience, Meg was finding herself instinctually solving client problems for the people on her team, especially with an additional $20 million on the line. But Meg quickly discovered that she had created a team of people who called on her for every answer. They were acting as if they were entitled to her leadership, and the answers they knew she had.

Only after frustration nearly buckled her, Meg decided to start enabling her people instead of fueling their entitlement. Instead of handing out answers each time someone approached her with a client issue, she started asking, "What do *you* suggest we do?" It took a bit of training on the part of Meg and her people, but soon they were bringing her challenges *and* proposed solutions. Meg had empowered her people, saved her own sanity, and surpassed the whopping sales number. She had evolved from a boss to a leader.

Keep people focused on the battle cries and let *them* figure out how to win the battle in the process. Only then do you even have a chance of working with people who are empowered to succeed instead of entitled to succeed.

## Celebrating Attempts, Not Just Successes

Recall the influences that stand in the way of people engaging in discovery. They fear rejection. They fear losing because they fear rejection. And they don't believe there is anything to develop because if they did they would be a loser on the verge of rejection. So if you want people to attempt new things, eliminate their fear of being rejected for not winning and for not already knowing how to win. You can do this by constantly celebrating attempts, not just successes. Thomas Edison was notorious for running Edison General Electric like a laboratory. He attempted more than 2,000 experiments before he successfully created the first light bulb. He reputedly said, "I now know 2,000 ways not to do something."

Leaders at Indian companies similarly run their workforces as laboratories. The leaders at automaker Maruti Udyog, for example, throw issues to their people and let them examine and beat up on those problems with trial-and-error approaches until they come back with solutions. As we'll explore in Chapter 12, innovative companies like Maruti Udyog constantly engage in a ritual of celebrating attempts – they are relentlessly curious about what worked and what didn't.

## Discovering Their Strengths

Knowing what we now know about how people are constantly assaulted by their fear of rejection, biased to see their limitations, unremittingly working to feed their esteem needs, responsive to self-delusion, and sensitive to self-deflation, you can understand how undermining it is to focus on people's weaknesses. They're already focused on their limitations, drawbacks, liabilities, and weaknesses, and when we focus on those weaknesses, as we explored in Chapter 4, we just add fuel to their self-deflation fire. Everyone performs better under the self-delusion that they are great and that the world revolves around them. When we encourage people to discover their strengths, we continue to fuel that essential self-delusion.

In Silicon Valley, the name Jorge is like the name Oprah or Madonna. No last name required. Jorge built the thriving start-up practice at Pillsbury Madison & Sutro LLP (now Pillsbury Winthrop Shaw Pittman LLP). Most people don't know, however, that Jorge started his career as a litigation attorney. He was drawn to practicing law, likely with strengths around analyzing, strategizing, and negotiating. He learned skills, acquired knowledge, and practiced. His strengths became stronger. But in the process of that career path, he discovered additional strengths around entrepreneurship, deal-making, and growing the firm's Silicon Valley office. He convinced the partnership to allow him to hone this newly discovered strength by working with partners in the corporate side of the firm to learn new skills, acquire new knowledge, and practice. Eventually he transitioned from a full-time litigation practice to a full-time corporate practice. The partners at Pillsbury encouraged Jorge to develop his strengths in corporate law; they didn't focus on any weaknesses he may have exhibited in his litigation practice. Jorge has now been with Pillsbury since 1982, and a partner since 1990, spearheading one of the most successful start-up practices in Silicon Valley.

Unfortunately, people are so afraid of failing that if they are not immediately proficient at something, they dub it one of their weaknesses instead of considering that it may be one of their strengths that just needs some skills, knowledge, and practice to improve. Jorge was not proficient in practicing corporate law on day one, but he was energized by it – and the rest he developed.

Because the word "weakness" is immensely burdened with condemnation, let's stop using it in spite of any HR demands to the contrary. Instead, acknowledge the reality that people have a myriad of traits – some are strengths and some are not. Some traits contribute to people's performance, while others don't.

How do people discover their strengths? Strengths questionnaires and self-assessment. I recommend using both because people will identify trends. There are a multitude of questionnaires on the market, some free, some not.

While self-assessments are quick and easy, there is nothing on the market that allows me to experience me other than a self-assessment. You are already creating opportunities for people to experience themselves under new circumstances and in fresh situations by creating microcycles – task forces, new assignments, rotations. Now encourage them to pay attention. What were they drawn to? Which ones gave them energy and buzz? Where did they shine, regardless of whether they needed to hone or add skills, knowledge, and practice?

Once they discover their strengths, you need to help them rearrange their work to incorporate those strengths. This does not mean give them a brand new job instantly; it means consider how you can incorporate into their current job some opportunities and experiences that call on those strengths. Dr. Mihaly Csikszentmihalyi, the author of *Flow*, reveals that people perform at their peak when their strengths are aligned with their tasks. People develop capabilities when they focus on their strengths. They handicap those capabilities when they focus (or are forced to focus) on traits that are not their strengths – their weaknesses.

Why am I insisting that *you* encourage them to rearrange their work to incorporate opportunities for them to use those strengths? Because we've already explored the influence and the result of the alternative: self-deflation and mediocrity. It's what riddles every workforce. A once- or twice-a-year performance evaluation followed by a plan to correct identified weaknesses. It's deflating, debilitating, flagellating, suffocating, and unnecessary. Especially when the alternative is so easy, so much more fun, and will reap enormous benefits.

I discovered one of my strengths during my junior year in high school in Mr. Rogina's Business Law 101 class. I devoured every assignment. I could not get enough of it. Following graduation, I headed to college and law school with the intention of becoming a business lawyer. Clearly I needed the skills, knowledge, experiences, and practice to hone the capabilities and develop into a great business attorney. But it was obvious to anyone who knew me that I was drawn to studying and analyzing anything related to business law. When I finally became a corporate lawyer, I fell in love with my job. Much to my friends' bewilderment, I regularly took home Series A Financing documents to study them after work. I wanted to learn term sheets more than I wanted to hang out with my friends.

It was while I was practicing law that I discovered another strength – the ability to influence people to succeed. This is not a strength often associated with the word "attorney," so I understand why it was obscured for so many years. I entered Silicon Valley at the height of the dot-com boom, when there was more work than warm bodies. I also joined Jorge's thriving start-up practice at Pillsbury and had the great experience of learn-by-fire. Unlike law firms in Chicago or New York, I didn't hide behind contracts and legal volumes for years before working with clients. I was thrust in front of clients during my first month on the job. This allowed me to discover additional strengths rather quickly. I found myself energized by helping entrepreneurs succeed. I was drawn to educating my clients about the financing process, the contracts they were signing, and the issues I was negotiating on their behalf. I couldn't wait to teach them about the term sheets that I had spent weeks learning.

The identification of this newly discovered strength was exciting, but I did not need to change my job to incorporate it into my work. I merely rearranged my work to ensure that I made time to educate my clients and help them succeed through their incorporation, contract negotiations, and financing process. This gave me great joy and a renewed sense of responsibility around my job. I was making a difference in many ways. And my clients appreciated working with me because I fed their need for esteem. By educating them and helping them succeed, I appreciated, valued, and recognized them. I also incorporated into my job various opportunities to help new associates succeed in acclimating to the firm and to the corporate securities practice. It was not long before I was promoted to Senior Associate and became responsible for overseeing the work of three other attorneys. All of this fed *my* need for esteem and fueled *my* self-delusion.

Not once did any one of my bosses ever focus on my "weaknesses." They only encouraged me to strengthen my strengths – my passion for negotiating financing deals and for helping others succeed. As a result, I loved my career as a lawyer. Many former lawyers do not share that sentiment. What a missed opportunity that their managers could have influenced otherwise.

## The Case Against Proficiency

Society seems obsessed with proficiency. We are glued to the television to see who wins the gold for ice skating in the Olympics; we couldn't care less about the silver or the bronze medalist. We place bets on who will win the Super Bowl, which horse will come in first at the Kentucky Derby, which driver will win NASCAR, which pitcher can throw a "perfect game." We then transfer this obsession to our kids. We want to see A's on the report card, while the B has become the new C. We then allow this obsession with expertise to dictate Wall Street and the stock market. We don't care what you, Mr. CEO, learned last quarter that will make you a wildly successful company in five years; you missed your projection by $0.01 and therefore you will pay for it in your stock price and in your job.

The problem with our obsession with proficiency is that it leaves little room for discovery. And without discovery, there is no learning, growth, or development. When we expect people to be proficient, talented, skilled, competent, and capable, there is no room for error, mistakes, or failure. And when there is no room for failure, rejection looms. This alone paralyzes people from taking any action, discovering anything new, or growing in any direction.

And when people don't try anything new out of the threat of failure and rejection, they continue to do the same thing they've always done in the same way they've always done it. This leads to exhaustion and eventually to a decline in strength of those work muscles. That dumps us into stagnation. A mediocre, but safe place.

## A Transaction or a Transformation?

Mary Anne Walsh, an amazing executive coach, is credited with distinguishing for me the difference between a transactional relationship and a transformational relationship. I go to the ATM for a transaction. I put my debit card into a machine, which then gives me money. That's a transaction, a deal I made with the bank. I want to withdraw money at any time and the bank has agreed to give me money provided there is a balance in my account. I exchanged information with a machine, but nothing about me was transformed in the process. The only thing transformed when I use an ATM is the amount of money in my account.

A transformation, on the other hand, is an alteration, a change, a shift, an adaptation. Our muscles are transformed as a result of lifting weights or working with a trainer. Our muscles adapt and change to compensate for the stress we are putting on them. We saw this with the General Adaptation Syndrome at the beginning of the chapter.

In your interactions with others, you have a choice. You can allow them to be purely transactional – I need this report by Thursday at 3:00 pm. Transactional interactions are sometimes a one-way communication, other times a simple exchange of information. Transactions are our default position.

Alternatively, your interactions can be transformational. How best can I support you in succeeding? What have you discovered from that new assignment I gave you? What Passion Project would you like to take on this year? Granted, not every exchange can, nor will, be transformational. We don't have time for that. We have deadlines. But acknowledge that people under your purview can and will only grow, adapt, discover, and strengthen when you interweave transformational interactions.

A commitment to people requires your ongoing commitment to contribute to their transformation, to their evolution and progression. It's not a once-a-year agenda item in a performance review or a competency generated by HR or the Leadership Development group. It's a regular conversation. However, the reality is that because every organization is driven by deadlines and bottom lines, we get stuck in transactional, not transformational, interactions. Then once a year we are reminded to "develop people" when performance review time comes around like tax season.

People are so busy with transactions that they rarely make time to reflect upon their learning or think about improving, let alone transforming themselves. And managers are in the same boat with barely enough time to remember transformation, let alone encourage the requisite discovery. People everywhere are manically focused on surviving today, instead of developing for tomorrow. But that's just accepting mediocrity.

The solution is to build it into the structure of your team, like contributions to your 401(K). Invite and encourage your people to request such transformational conversations. Make it an agenda item at a weekly or monthly meeting with your people. Configure transformational questions into your transactional Weekly Snapshot or ask transformational questions after reviewing it. Create off-site meetings to transact and to transform. And never stop working on the relationships, not just in them.

When challenged with this, ineffective managers rebut, "What if we develop people and they leave?" Such mediocre thinking. Effective leaders, on the other hand, worry, "What if I *don't* develop people and they *stay?*"

## Putting It Into Action

- Create a mini-mentoring program among your team members.

- Recruit people from other departments to speak to your team on a monthly basis.

- Assign people to teach each other about an area of their expertise.

- Carve out time during each team meeting to share lessons learned from the week.

- Share "worst practices" and "best practices" discovered that week from trial-by-error.

- Create task forces to solve problems.

- Create rotational assignments to push people out of their comfort zone and learn something new.

- Require people to take on a Passion Project to explore an area or an issue about which they are passionate.

- Ask daily: What can we learn here? What will we do better or differently next time? What worked? What didn't?

- Use the word "pilot" when launching something new.

- Clarify for people that you do not expect perfection, that you instead expect best efforts and wisdom gained from each project.

- When anyone asks you for a solution to a problem, put it back on them to come up with a solution. Ask, "What do you think we should do?" "What are our options?"

- Celebrate attempts, not just successes.

- Talk about capabilities instead of disabilities. Focus on what people can do, not what they cannot do.

- Leverage the Weekly Snapshot to keep apprised while reinforcing your commitment to a discovery environment.

# Chapter 11

## Teach the Art of Bouncing

The access road to the Polihale State Park on Hawaii's Kauai Island was destroyed in the winter flood of December 2008. The park is a favorite spot for locals and a hub for tourists, and without tourist access, the businesses in the park were in jeopardy of closing. The road is the lifeline for these businesses. The Department of Land and Natural Resources estimated that it would take two years and $4 million to repair the damage. But the department did not have the money, nor did it know when it would see any additional funds from the federal government. So it shrugged its collective shoulders in response to the island residents and business owners.

After a spell of complaining about state and federal bureaucracy, the residents decided to take matters into their own hands. They gathered as a community, brought together donated machinery, materials, and manpower, and three months after the flood, on March 23, 2009, they initiated the repairs themselves. Eight days later they were done.

The island residents had had a choice. They could have sat back and waited until the government found the funds and fixed the road. Their resentment would have mounted, and they would have suffocated in their frustration and despair. They could have watched their businesses fail from lack of tourists. Then they would have righteously blamed the government for the failure, and everyone would have said they were justified in blaming the government. They may even have taken it to court to hold the government responsible for the failure of their businesses. Instead, they took responsibility for their own future. They chose to do something about the situation. The residents responded – instead of just reacting.

What drove the residents to take action instead of point fingers? Their commitment to their livelihood. Their steadfast focus on their goals – their battle cry. Their feisty and resourceful approach to the situation, which had them ask, "What can *we* do about it?" instead of "What is someone else going to do about it?" Their refusal to let obstacles and setbacks stop them from what they needed for their businesses to thrive. Their enthusiasm, perseverance, and determination in spite of the circumstances. Their moxie.

Most people fling excuses instead of effort. Most people complain and criticize instead of champion. Most people point fingers instead of holding themselves accountable for their own happiness. Most people cling to resentment and rancor instead of offering forgiveness and acceptance. These residents are not "most people."

## Responding, not Just Reacting

The workplace halls are teeming with people who react. You need people who respond. The art of bouncing, which we are about to discover, requires a response, not just a reaction.

Reacting is a human tendency based on our aversion to loss, our fear of rejection, and our inclination to think of ourselves as winners. When we react, we scream and yell, cry and pout, pound our fists and stomp our feet, get defensive and point fingers, and blame and reject others. It is unrealistic to think that we can switch off that part of people. It's a natural part of being human. So reacting in the moment is understandable, but not moving past the reaction and into a response is unacceptable. People need to go beyond reacting and ask, "What are we going to do next?"

Undoubtedly the residents of Hawaii were disgusted, frustrated, angry, and exhausted. Certainly they criticized the government's red tape for jeopardizing their businesses. Understandably they yelled at a few government employees at some point. But what separates the residents of Hawaii from *most people* is what they did when they were done reacting. They responded by taking action. The operative word is "respond." It demands action in the face of all that would justify a perpetual complaint. The Hawaiian residents bounced back.

A FedEx driver in Manhattan demonstrated how to bounce when her truck broke down in the middle of her delivery route one afternoon. When the replacement van was running late, she could have shrugged her shoulders and demonstrated a not-my-problem reaction while pointing fingers at everyone from the mechanics to the vehicle manufacturer to the driver of the replacement van. Not this resilient, resourceful, responding driver. She took action. She began jogging around the city delivering the remaining packages *on foot.*

When she realized that her progress was too slow and some customers would not get their packages on time, she could have shrugged her shoulders and copped an oh-well-I-tried-to-be-a-hero-but-it-didn't-work-out-and-it's-not-my-fault reaction. But she didn't. The FedEx battle cry is "We live to deliver" and so she did just that. She flagged down a competitor's delivery van and won him over with her resilience, resourcefulness, and moxie. She convinced him to take her on her last few deliveries. That's what a bounce looks like.

So what does it take for us to foster this formula of attitude and action in people? Why do *most people* get stuck in the reaction and never find their way across the chasm to the response? How do we move people from entitled-to-react to committed-to-respond?

## Brain Conflict Wreaks Havoc

People are hardwired to defend their actions and inactions. In fact, defending and reacting are as innate as breathing. As we've seen with the influences of loss aversion and fear of rejection, we are programmed to react with excuses instead of respond out of perseverance. At the crux of this programming is a bias that is influencing each of us to react instead of respond, to be lackluster instead of resourceful, to be resigned instead of resilient: cognitive dissonance.

Our brain — the cognitive part — is in conflict — the dissonance part. Let's refer to this phenomenon as "brain conflict." Being our ultimate champion, our brain is relentlessly working for us to win. It tells us constantly that we are smart, successful, and accomplished. According to our brain, we are winners, not losers.

But when we make a mistake or fail to follow through, our brain is met with dissonance. Conflicted, the brain attempts to understand how a smart, successful, and accomplished person would make a mistake, neglect to follow through on a commitment, or otherwise fail. To relieve the conflict (and the obvious headache this discord is causing), our brain makes an excuse as to why we got stopped on our way to accomplishing a goal or following through on a commitment.

Psychologists invented a great word for the fabrication of these excuses: "confabulation." People rarely acknowledge that they just stopped. They are always finding an excuse and identifying something or someone else as the reason they got stopped — confabulating. It is nearly impossible for people to admit that they just stopped for no reason, because smart, successful, accomplished people don't just stop. They are stopped by something. And the sooner they identify what it is that stopped them, the sooner they can alleviate their brain conflict.

Brain conflict and confabulation can quickly cause a downward spiral from success to failure. People hate being wrong. As Influencing Tenet #4 states, we each like to think of ourselves as winners, not losers. We would much rather make an excuse than accept responsibility for not winning. As a result, when cognitive dissonance is working its magic, the brain conflict causes brain fog. And when we're in brain fog, it is nearly impossible to learn anything from a mistake or a situation; we are more prone to gain excuses than lessons.

One of our clients saw firsthand how brain conflict cost a salesman his job. Ryan was hired because of his track record as a champion soccer player in college. When his future boss learned about Ryan's record-setting foray into sports, he was confident Ryan's fire in the belly would translate to a record-setting sales career. He was sure that fire would make him a star salesman on his team. But Ryan's flame had petered out.

Ryan spent his three years at the company complaining, griping, grumbling, whining, and nagging. He complained about his accounts. Why didn't the boss give him better accounts? He griped about his sales number. How could the boss expect him to make that number with such limited accounts? He grumbled about his colleagues. Didn't the boss see how unfair it was that the other guys on the team had better accounts and sales numbers? He whined incessantly about company policy. He nagged his boss to fix every situation.

The irony is that in spite of his grumbling and protesting, Ryan made his number every year. What he didn't make were any allies. His colleagues didn't want to support him. His boss was exhausted from coaching him to approach work differently, only to be met with confused, blank stares and righteous, indignant eye-rolling. After a while, even Ryan's customers requested a different account rep be assigned to serve them. They were tired of dealing with his bad attitude and lack of action on their behalf.

When Ryan's boss was required to select one person from his team to be laid off during the company's workforce reduction, he gladly picked Ryan. None of Ryan's accounts wanted to work with him, none of his colleagues wanted to support him, and his boss was done with Ryan's energy-sucking ways – energy his boss needed to support the rest of the team. So, in spite of Ryan making his number three years in a row, he was being fired.

Ryan's brain conflict went into overdrive. It was clearly not Ryan's fault that he got fired – he made his number every year. Why was he – a smart, successful, and accomplished person – being fired? Since it was not *his* fault for being fired, it must be someone else's fault. He pointed the biggest finger at his boss. His boss was unfair. His boss had favorites, and obviously Ryan was not one of them. His boss had it out for him to fail. Ryan's objective was too high, his account list too limited, his boss' support too weak.

In the two weeks following the announcement, Ryan sent hourly e-mails to his boss badgering him for an explanation. Ryan's boss offered to sit down with him to discuss his decision. But then Ryan threatened to appeal the decision and file a lawsuit. On advice from the company's legal department, the boss stopped communicating with Ryan altogether. This incensed him even more. People hate to be ignored; it feeds their self-deflation that the world doesn't revolve around them.

After a few weeks, Ryan calmed down and signed the settlement agreement in exchange for a severance package. He then sent an e-mail to his boss requesting a conversation. Thinking more clearly now, he acknowledged that while he did not agree with his boss's decision, he never wanted to be in that position again so he needed to understand what had happened. Perhaps the hours of coaching made its way through the fog after all. Only after Ryan stopped reacting did he have the wherewithal to respond.

Upon learning about Ryan, I shook my head in disbelief. How could he not see it? It seems obvious that he was responsible for being fired. But knowing how his mind (and everyone's mind) works will give us some insight into Ryan's situation – and some tools for navigating the hardwiring that similarly holds your people back.

## Serotonin — the Vigilant Grandmother

Our brain, the champion, relies on the naturally occurring chemicals in the emotional system to constantly seek out pleasure, respond to rewards, and avoid harm. There are synaptic neurotransmitters in our brain that create these chemicals: dopamine, norepinephrine, and serotonin. These chemicals cause us to drive toward certain goals and avoid others.

Consider serotonin like our worried grandmother – one of its jobs is harm avoidance. It remains vigilant, ready to warn us of harm and help us avoid it. Because rejection is one form of harm, serotonin is on guard for anything that appears like rejection or creates the risk of us being rejected. When we make a mistake or are at fault, we are at risk of being rejected by others. Serotonin's job is to quickly identify other reasons for that mistake and obviate our own responsibility for it. This protects us from the vulnerability of rejection.

Serotonin is also responsible for the behavioral influence called "self-serving bias." This bias describes our predisposition to claim more responsibility for successes than failures. Our harm-avoiding, confabulating mind perceives that we are responsible for desirable outcomes but not responsible for undesirable outcomes. But of course! Smart, successful, accomplished people are always responsible for desirable outcomes but never responsible for undesirable outcomes. Can you blame the brain? We consider ourselves winners, not losers. We want to win, not lose. Therefore, we want credit for the good results but we don't want to admit when we fall short in any area. Kids are constantly demonstrating the influence of the self-serving bias. They beam with pride when their parents gush about their victories but they quickly point the finger at their siblings in response to any reprimand or criticism.

When our serotonin is high, the worried grandmother's guard is down, so we are happy, socially confident, engaged, and motivated. We are not highly sensitive to rejection or easily deflated by events that should just roll off our back. We feel confident and less vulnerable to slights or injuries. But when our serotonin is low, the worried grandmother's guard is on overdrive. As a result, we react strongly to small personal slights and disappointing news. We are more defensive and less willing to take risks. Thus, we go out of our way to avoid situations in which we might be rejected. This hinders our ability to take risks, even when those risks might make us more successful at work or in other aspects of our lives.

In addition to being a vigilante, serotonin helps regulate our emotions and moods. The level of serotonin in our brain fluctuates based on several things, including how much physical activity we get. We can increase serotonin a number of ways. The easiest is with the anti-depressant drug Prozac. The not-so-easy ways include exercise, mediation, and generating success.

When Jeff's tax practice was expanding, he hired Eric, a fantastic practitioner in another state, but soon discovered that Eric needed a boost of serotonin every morning or he was not that fantastic. If Eric did not get out of bed and exercise, he would not get out of bed. Days would go by without any work produced. Jeff didn't want to lose Eric, but also couldn't run a successful business hoping Eric would get out of bed. So, Jeff and Eric created an agreement. Each morning Jeff calls Eric to wake him up and get him off to the gym. Jeff agreed not to request any work from Eric until Eric has completed his workout. As soon as Eric is through exercising, his serotonin kicks in and he is like a brand new person for Jeff. This is not the solution for everyone, but based on Jeff's observation, inquiry, and commitment to Eric, it became the solution that works beautifully for both of them.

Based on this X-ray into the brain regulators, now consider Ryan's situation. When was he at his all-time best? When he was playing soccer in college and winning. The requisite physical activity to play at that level naturally caused his serotonin levels to be high, which caused his confidence and his willingness to take risks to be high. He was less likely to be vulnerable and defensive when he made mistakes, and more willing to learn from them. Upon entering the working world, he stopped playing soccer altogether. In fact, as he got married and had children, he stopped all physical activity. His serotonin levels plummeted.

## Kick Up the Serotonin to Kick Up the Bounce

So how do we help the Ryans in our world kick up their serotonin and bounce back after any setback, obstacle, mistake, error, failure, or oversight? Short of forcing them to take Prozac and meditate, how do we kick up the serotonin before their rejection sensitivity kicks them in the butt? We help people bounce.

Here are five strategies to kick up the serotonin to kick up the bounce:

1. Advocate for discovery over proficiency

2. Create an environment of accountability

3. Identify lessons learned

4. Reframe the focus from feelings to commitments

5. Model it

### Serotonin-Kicking Strategy #1: Advocate for Discover Over Proficiency

Tom Watson Sr., founder of IBM, and its leader for more than four decades, consistently demonstrated the discovery mindset. As a 1960s legend has it, a talented junior executive of IBM was responsible for the loss of $10 million (approximately $70 million in today's dollars) from engaging the company in a risky venture that turned out to be a debacle. When Watson summoned the anxious executive into his office to discuss the situation, the young man bemoaned, "I guess you want my resignation."

Watson said, "You can't be serious. We've just spent $10 million educating you!"

The key to kicking up the serotonin is to foster a discovery environment instead of a proficiency environment. As we explored in Chapter 10, in a discovery environment, we give people permission to discover how to be world-class instead of expecting them to be so at any cost, which is what a proficiency environment demands. With the permission to discover, people anticipate obstacles, setbacks, mistakes, and errors, and setting expectations calms the worried grandmother – serotonin.

You can foster a discovery environment by cultivating a mindset in which a setback is just an indication of something they have not yet learned. Once people are calm about the setback we can help them see the bigger picture, their journey to becoming a world-class performer. Their failure has nothing to do with their capabilities or lack thereof. It is merely a failed attempt. They are still on their way.

Responding to failed attempts requires the world-class-performer-in-training to identify what it is they need to learn next. Reacting, on the other hand, inevitably keeps people stuck in their reactions.

When proficiency-minded people do not succeed, they see themselves – not just their attempts – as personal failures. They attribute success to already possessing the ability and the knowledge. But if they fail then that is confirmation that they do not have the ability or knowledge, and therefore learning it is not even an option. Proficiency-minded people think in terms of black and white. They either have it or they don't. Consequently, they have one of two reactions to a setback. They either offer an excuse in order not to have to accept responsibility for the setback; or they accept the reality that they don't have it, which causes them to get stuck wondering what to do with the realization that they don't have it. When they admit to not having the ability and knowledge required to be successful, their motivation plummets.

Accordingly, most proficiency-minded people work assiduously to demonstrate the ability and the knowledge they do have, and work diligently to prevent anyone from finding out what ability and knowledge they lack. Essentially, the proficiency mode is unproductive, inefficient, and ineffective.

When we cultivate a discovery environment, we are adamant that people learn from every successful and unsuccessful attempt. We require them to respond, which eliminates the finger-pointing, excuse-making, sabotaging reactions. This approach reframes for people their failures, thereby allowing them to win, which triggers the serotonin they need.

As a middle leader, you have the power to set people up for success. You can do this by advocating for discovery and by teaching people how to bounce out of their reactions and into a response. You also have the responsibility to acknowledge and address proficiency mindsets that are infecting the discovery process. How to do all of his? By engaging in discovery yourself. By observing and then sharing those observations. By acknowledging that you are in discovery mode with regard to your people. By following serotonin-kicking strategies #2 - 5 below.

### Serotonin-Kicking Strategy #2: Create an Environment of Accountability

N. Wayne Hale Jr. was NASA's launch integration manager in 2003 when the space shuttle *Columbia* exploded killing all seven astronauts aboard. He took full responsibility for the disaster in a public e-mail to his colleagues on the space shuttle team:

> I had the opportunity and the information and I failed to make use of it. I don't know what an inquest or a court of law would say, but I stand condemned in the court of my own conscience to be guilty of not preventing the Columbia disaster. We could discuss the particulars: inattention, incompetence, distraction, lack of conviction, lack of understanding, a lack of backbone,

laziness. The bottom line is that I failed to understand what I was being told; I failed to stand up and be counted. Therefore look no further; I am guilty of allowing Columbia to crash.

In spite of admitting to egregious errors and accepting ultimate responsibility for the deaths of seven astronauts, Hale went on to a long and fulfilling career at NASA. His integrity strengthened, his leadership solidified, his passion bolstered.

In stark contrast to the integrity of Wayne Hale Jr., the 1980s band Aerosmith demonstrated what it means to lack accountability when they cancelled their sold-out show on Maui in September 2007. They released a statement with an excuse that they were unable to get their gear in time to Hawaii from a show they had played a few days earlier in Chicago. But somehow that same night their gear magically made it to Oahu, a neighboring island, in time for Aerosmith to play a private show for a group of Toyota car dealers. The dealers paid $1 million for their concert, far more than the 8,300 Maui fans had paid. Aerosmith fans were outraged. They filed a class-action lawsuit and won. The judge required Aerosmith to reimburse all ticket holders for their out-of-pocket travel expenses. In addition, everyone who bought a ticket received a free ticket to a rescheduled concert on Maui.

The marketing team at a Fortune 100 company could have learned some lessons in the area of accountability from our NASA launch manager and Aerosmith. At this company, a typical cover-your-butt (CYB) mindset dictates every move. As one of the top performers on the sales team, Jane is always searching for ways to reach new customers and stay competitive in her industry. She recently discovered a virtual conference, in which all of her competitors would be attending, but surprisingly not her own company. Considering that perhaps the marketing team had not known about the conference or had other reasons for not participating, she quickly sent them the information and inquired why the company was not participating. With a typical CYB reaction, the marketing team did not thank Jane for identifying another opportunity for the company to showcase and compete. The small-minded marketing minions shot back an eight-paragraph e-mail to Jane copying the entire marketing team, including the department's Senior VP, confabulating five reasons why they were not participating in the event. In addition, they attached a *200-page* marketing plan document to assure Jane that the marketing team had all of its bases covered. In response, Jane sent a one-line e-mail back also copying the entire team that said: "Thanks for the document. Again, help me understand. Why are we not participating in this conference along with our competitors?" No response.

Why didn't the Senior VP send an e-mail back to Jane thanking her for her contribution, acknowledging that they did not know about the event, and committing to researching it? Typical CYB grounded in fear, loss, and brain conflict, instead of remarkable accountability founded on a battle cry.

It is the marketing department's job to research, identify, and explore opportunities. If people outside of the marketing department contribute to that effort, why defend and deflect? Why not be grateful and encourage others to continue to assist in the effort? If the marketing team could get out of their own way, they would see that the sales team can be a great ally. Sales people have their finger on the pulse of opportunities even more than the marketing team, and working together, they could attack these opportunities. Instead, the marketing team and their CYB mindset are ensuring that the marketing and sales teams will continue to work in their silos separated by an abyss.

We are so used to witnessing individuals who are not held accountable for success – their own and the company's – that it's become second-nature to blame corporate policy, the customers, or the economy for failure. As a result, people do not go above and beyond because we do not expect them to, and worse yet, we do not ask them to. In the void that's left from not trusting people arises the threat of consequences from failure. And when people are too busy protecting themselves from fault or blame – that is, avoiding harm and rejection – they're covering their butt instead of finding ways to accomplish their battle cry.

Too often, ineffective managers get sucked in to excuses, confabulation, distractions, and diversions. Leaders, on the other hand, hold people responsible for that success in the face of circumstances. "I've observed that ..." "I've noticed that ..." "So I'm curious, how are we going to succeed in spite of this situation?" "What are we going to do next?"

### Serotonin-Kicking Strategy #3: Identify Lessons Learned

Venture capitalists in Silicon Valley love working with leaders who have a failed start-up somewhere on their résumé. It communicates a commitment to lead and learn. If these leaders operated from a proficiency mode instead of a discovery mode, their failed start-up would evidence their failure as a CEO, thereby precluding that person from bouncing into the next adventure. Instead, the CEOs who come back for more are not dictated by the feeling that they lack the requisite ability and knowledge. They are run by their commitment to become world-class, and that includes stomaching a bombed start-up along the way.

"So what have we learned?" This single question asked again and again and again will compel people to bounce out of their reactions and into a response.

In the early 1800s, Charles Goodyear spent a decade working on a battle cry of making rubber the material of the future. While his family and friends contributed funds, potential investors laughed at him, and creditors threw in him jail numerous times. But he continued his experimenting – even from his jail cell. When he accidentally spilled a concoction of rubber and other materials on a hot stove, he discovered the mixture that could stand up to extreme temperatures – the requisite mixture to make a tire. But had he not engaged in a decade of failed experiments, he never would have recognized the mixture as the one that he required in order to be victorious in the battle cry.

Whether we call it failure, a mistake, a glitch, a slip-up, an error of judgment, a breakdown, an obstacle, a setback, or a disappointment, people avoid it. They fear embarrassment from the perception that the mistake is a reflection of their intelligence, taste, or competence. But the problem with constantly working to avoid the slightest mistake is that people feel trapped about making a move unless success is guaranteed. Consequently, they don't make any discovery moves, thereby guaranteeing their status quo.

But what if we give people the permission to fail or make a mistake by reframing the conversation from mistakes made to lessons learned? If we take off the pressure to constantly be right, then we could help people discover success through experiments like those of Thomas Edison and Charles Goodyear.

Goodyear persevered based on his battle cry: to make rubber the material of the future. His relentless experimenting was in pursuit of winning that battle cry. The challenge we are witnessing in proficiency-minded people is that their big goal has become to not make a mistake, get laughed at, reprimanded, or fired. That's not a battle cry, that's a desperate cry. And when there's no battle cry, there's no progress.

For leaders who have been versed in the rigidity of Six Sigma error-elimination process, welcoming failure may seem sacrilegious. And for leaders who are forced to answer to the demands of Wall Street, the boardroom, the shareholders, and the investors for higher stock prices, there will be little room to tolerate failure. Unfortunately, this enables people to talk about innovation and progress but in reality stomach them only if success is guaranteed. Consequently, the only thing guaranteed is more of the same – status quo and mediocrity.

Based in Mountain View, California, the start-up mecca, the leaders at Intuit, Inc. know their success lies in keeping people in discovery mode. In 2005 in front of 200 Intuit marketers, Chairman Scott Cook presented an award to the team that created an adventurous but failed marketing campaign to marry tax-filing drudgery with hip-hop style. The campaign flopped, but as Scott said, "It's only a failure if we fail to get the learning." In that discovery-mode spirit, the team engaged in a postmortem process to document its insights before moving on to new risks. In addition to postmortems, Intuit has begun focus-on-failure sessions during which participants recount stories of failures and resultant lessons learned. Jana Eggers, head of Intuit's Innovation Lab, plans to distribute booklets about failed projects so that people can share the pain felt by others – and benefit from their learning and discoveries.

Give people the permission to let go of being right in every move they make. First, encourage their experimentation without repercussions. Second, with any failure or mistake, force people to answer the questions "What did we learn?" and "What are we going to try next in pursuit of our battle cry?"

By answering these very questions, Canada's cough syrup company, Buckley's, has become number one in its industry. Buckley's battle cry is to "deliver the most effective product to its customers." In the pursuit of that battle cry, the engineers at the company worked tirelessly to make its cough syrup palatable. But no matter how they worked and reworked the formula, they failed. The medicine just tastes horrible. Leaders at the company lamented over their failure while answering the two bounce questions, and decided instead to capitalize on the failure. They began an advertising campaign with the motto "It tastes awful. And it works." In advertisements they cited the unique herbal ingredients that taste nasty but make the product so effective. Leaders at the company even launched a Bad Taste Tour, a contest to discover the customer with the best grossed-out expression, and an advertisement with the company's CEO wisecracking, "I wake up with nightmares that someone gives me a taste of my own medicine" and "I came by my bad taste honestly – I inherited it from my father." Following the campaign, the company's market share increased by 10 percent.

Embrace mistakes and failures, for they are the windows to our opportunities to learn. Share with people the stories of Buckley's, Goodyear, Intuit, and others where leaders have embraced failure and have accelerated their journey to becoming world-class performers as a result. Encourage people to identify their own lessons learned from stories of failures each month at a "What Did We Learn Celebration."

### Serotonin-Kicking Strategy #4: Reframe the Focus from Feelings to Commitments

It is critical that we compel people to follow their commitments and ignore their "I-don't-want-to" feelings. In *The Oz Principles,* one of the best books on accountability I have ever read, authors Roger Connors, Tom Smith, and Craig Hickman advocate asking relentlessly one key question to establish accountability: "What do we need to do to get the results we want?" In other words, thanks for your excuse, I get it, I empathize, but what are you going to do next *in spite of* that excuse?

When people don't follow through on their commitments, they are busy answering to their feelings. "I'll see how I feel in the morning." They don't *feel* like working that hard or risking failure. They don't *feel* like taking a risk and getting their ideas rejected. They don't *feel* like getting up early to work out. They *feel* like eating junk food. They *feel* disappointed when a better offer or an easier route comes along and so they break an earlier commitment to ensure they don't miss out. They give up too quickly. They *feel* fear that any success will require them to work even harder to sustain the success, so they choose laziness. They *feel* like any success will result from mere luck, and thus be undeserved. So they sabotage their success by answering to those feelings – not their commitments.

Influencing Tenet #9 states that we allow our beliefs and thoughts to dictate our ambitions and perseverance. Feelings are just an expression of those beliefs and thoughts, and they are bullying people's ambition and perseverance. From there the confirmation bias goes to work to confirm and reinforce those feelings and foundational beliefs. When it comes to fears that manifest as procrastination and excuses, the confirmation bias reinforces those excuses and justifies the fears. When people offer up an excuse as to why they got stopped instead of making an effort to try again, it is a guaranteed sign that they have lost sight of their battle cry and are now merely a victim of their feelings. Only when they crush the pattern of allowing those feelings to dictate their actions will they stop being a victim to those circumstances and start following through in spite of them.

No one likes to admit that they did not follow through on a commitment. But most people don't have much experience with taking responsibility for a promise. People operate as if they will melt if they admit ultimate responsibility for an unfavorable outcome. In reality they are just operating in proficiency mode, and as we've seen, admitting responsibility for a failed outcome is admitting to a personal failure instead of merely to a failed attempt. So they argue that a force outside themselves has done it to them.

Ginger sat and stared at the phone. She needed to do her daily recruiting calls, to recruit new agents to her practice. But Ginger loathed this part of her job, so naturally she procrastinated, and inevitably she chastised herself for procrastinating. We discerned that at the heart of her procrastination was a fear of being rejected. She kept focusing on her competition in the community and the incentives they were using to successfully recruit agents. She believed she couldn't compete and this belief created the fear of rejection. And that fear of rejection was bullying her commitment.

When Ginger reframed the situation from a focus on the fear to a focus on her battle cry — to be the number one office in the industry by serving her agents, the community, and the company — she was able to reframe the recruiting calls altogether. In fact, she stopped labeling them "recruiting calls" and renamed them "serving the community" calls. She adopted a mantra from Lynne Twist, non-profit fundraising guru: "It is a disservice not to let people know how they can donate their money." Ginger decided it was a disservice to the community not to let them know about her office and the opportunities that awaited them with her serving as their leader. Ginger now looks forward to her "serving the community" calls and continues to successfully recruit agents every week. And when a competing firm closed its doors, agents called *Ginger* ready to join her office, confident Ginger would serve their success.

Instead of getting caught in the trap of people's excuses and stories, you must hold people to their promises. Shake them from their victim mentality by reframing the situation to focus on their battle cry and on the commitments they made in pursuit of that battle cry, and away from whatever meaning they have made up about their setback. Focusing on the "what's next" promotes the discovery mode. Ask people, "What are you going to do about it?" And of course, when you force people to create their own solution to this question, they'll own that solution and go to great lengths to make it work, lest having to admit to being wrong once again.

Paul Chadwick and Katie Hemming reframed their own situation and saved a million-dollar real estate listing. They had pitched their services as the realtor team of choice to a retiring couple wanting to sell their 10-acre farmland. They knew the competition was stiff, but they had prepared meticulously and delivered an outstanding presentation. On top of which they had connected personally with the couple and left confident they would be doing business together. The couple said they would follow up with Paul and Katie in a few days. But a few days came and went, and Paul and Katie heard nothing. They waited and waited but no phone call and no e-mail. They were very disappointed.

After a week had passed, Paul and Katie were attending a networking breakfast when they overheard that another real estate company had won the listing. Paul and Katie were stunned. They immediately called the couple. They were sick to their stomach when they learned the reality. The couple had e-mailed Paul and Katie congratulating them on winning the listing, but when they never heard back from Paul or Katie, they had assumed that the duo was no longer interested in the business. Mortified, Paul ran to his computer and found the e-mail in his spam folder, apparently dumped there on the basis of the couple's spam-like subject line: "Congratulations! You won!"

Paul and Katie's first instinct was to whine about how unfair it all was, but then they asked themselves, "So what are we going to do about it?" They decided to respond like the world-class realtors they initially presented themselves to be. They immediately called the couple and asked for a follow-up meeting. They printed the webpage showing the spam folder with the couple's e-mail in it and headed to the house with their best pitch in hand. They showed the couple the print-out of the spam folder, took responsibility for not following up with a phone call and an e-mail, apologized profusely, and committed to delivering world-class service, including daily contact with the couple should they grant the team another chance. The couple had wanted to work with Paul and Katie all along and appreciated their response and zealous commitment, so they awarded them the business.

Paul and Katie's contract to list the couple's farm was set to expire on May 15. Even in one of the worst real estate economies they've experienced in their careers, Paul and Katie confirmed the couple's great choice by selling their 10-acre farmland on May 1.

Questioning excuses and reactions is the most pointed way to move people from reaction to response. When people run to you with a problem, whine with a sob story, or react with an excuse, show ruthless compassion and unyielding empathy. Then respond to them with only one question: "What are you going to do about it?" Engage in relentless listening, acknowledge their story or their excuse, empathize with how they must be feeling, and then repeat the question. "I got it. You must be so frustrated that John did that. What are you going to do about it?" They may look dumbfounded. They may try repeating the story, but if you do a great job of relentless listening, they won't.

People are not used to being held responsible for an outcome, let alone invited to make a decision, so logically, they may be appear dazed. Ask them to reframe the situation in terms of their battle cry. Wait for it. Then repeat the acknowledgement and question, "Again, I understand how frustrating it must be that John did that. What are you going to do about it?"

### Serotonin-Kicking Strategy #5: Model It

Monkey see, monkey do. We've been learning to behave using this methodology since we were babies. As we explored in Chapter 7, social cognitive theory argues that people take cues from their leaders for how to react and respond. They are influenced by observing *you* reacting and responding. Your actions, reactions, and responses are shaping theirs.

Bosses whose cognitive dissonance is on overdrive do not have the capacity to respond. They only have room for reactions, resulting in excuses, procrastinating, accusations, finger-pointing, and hiding behind company policies. Ironically, these are the same bosses who look shocked when their people behave similarly. On the flip side, leaders who hold themselves accountable are refreshing and inspire the same in others.

I witnessed the power of modeling a respond-don't-just-react mindset on a United Airlines flight from Newark to San Francisco. On my way to the airport, I became engulfed in unexplainable gridlock and called the airline to find out what my choices were in the likely event that I would miss my flight. When I finally made it to the airport, I was relieved that my flight had been delayed. I rushed to the gate and made it to my seat in plenty of time. As the doors closed, the captain's voice greeted us over the intercom. He said, "As the captain of this flight, it is my responsibility to be here on time. While I could blame the traffic jam on the New Jersey Turnpike that many of you found yourself in, the rest of you made it on time and I didn't. I apologize for being late and commit to not allowing that to happen again in the future. I will get us to San Francisco as quickly and safely as I can."

I recall how stunned all the passengers were listening to this. First of all, for a leader to admit responsibility unabashedly and in a public forum was unusual. Second, to hold himself accountable for being late and not point a finger at someone or something else – like traffic – was unheard of. This was clearly a leader who fostered responsibility and accountability on his team. Instantly we forgave the captain, and our opinion of him, his crew, and the airline skyrocketed. Imagine how his crew felt about their leader. Imagine anyone on the team attempting to fling an excuse at the captain for something that went wrong, whether it was excusable or not. By modeling accountability, this captain set the standard for how he expects his team to operate.

Contrast this exemplary model to the finger-pointing leaders at General Motors. GM's bankruptcy blanketed the covers of the *New York Times* and the *Wall Street Journal* in 2009. The tone of the articles conjured images of high-level GM employees in Detroit standing around dumbfounded, wondering what could have happened to this iconic American company.

Contrary to what the GM executives wanted us to believe, their failure was not due to the economy, the credit crunch, the Japanese competition, or even global warming. It was an obsession with reacting instead of a commitment to responding that had pervaded the GM workforce, starting with the role models at the top. GM executives had become skilled at pointing fingers instead of taking responsibility. Over the nine years from 2000 to

2009, the blue chip stock price dropped from $93.62 per share to a paltry $0.75 per share. Notably, GM salaries and benefits never followed suit. In fact, the five key executives each paid themselves an average of $1 million every year over those nine years not including any stock, pension, bonuses, etc. (which for the CEO alone totaled over $14 million in 2009).

What does it do to people when they watch their leaders blame others and then get compensated nicely for doing so? They model it. The people at GM have spent decades observing their leaders shirk responsibility for pitiable results, while cashing five- and six-figure paychecks each month. The message is loud and clear: "Shun responsibility, protect your paycheck." That message quickly oozes down the chain of command.

In the words of recently retired Vice Chairman Robert A. Lutz, General Motors experienced a "world of hurt, much of it not our own doing." Late GM Chief Executive Roger Smith said in 1995 that he would have reorganized the company if there had been an easy way to do so. Interesting. He actually believed he was getting paid millions of dollars for easy solutions. Even the executives blamed Wall Street for demanding a profit and not respecting "this thing called image." Huh?

Soon the people at GM became so adept at eschewing any sort of accountability that there was no one that they did not blame for the train wreck. They blamed the government regulators for not giving them a break. They blamed the media for not appreciating their new cars. They blamed the dealers for not supporting them. They blamed the unions for being greedy (Really? Wonder where they got that from?). They even blamed consumers for not being loyal. Never mind that consumers were tired of driving subpar vehicles.

The bottom line is that the executives at General Motors did not execute. But worse than not executing, they failed to take any responsibility, leaving them to react instead of respond, to be stuck in blaming instead of discovering. Their failure trickled down and permeated people's mindsets, guaranteeing that the lack of responsibility, the failure to bounce, would destroy motivation at the company.

Fortunately for General Motors, leaders like Susan Docherty, the head of the U.S. Sales, Service, and Marketing team spotlighted in Chapter 4, and the leaders at the Lordstown factory spotlighted in Chapter 3, are changing the conversation.

Modeling behavior includes modeling the discovery mindset. As middle leaders, we cannot just talk about embracing failures (assuming we get past our Six Sigma rhetoric); we need to foster a *discovery environment*. One in which we share our own mistakes and lessons learned, make it safe to take calculated risks, and dedicate time to celebrate the failures and the successes. Even in the discovery mode, people fear the consequences – our reactions as leaders to their setbacks and failures – as much or more than they fear failure itself, because our reaction to their failure is where rejection proliferates. We can ease their anxiety by modeling what responding, not reacting, looks like on a regular basis.

### Giving People Permission to Respond

You cannot afford to let people get stuck under the boulder called "cognitive dissonance," especially when you have the power to influence them to bounce rather than deflate. Every person you meet has experienced their greatest success stories by bouncing in some way. Now they just require permission from you to respond instead of react, to discover instead of be proficient, to learn lessons instead of ignore mistakes, to be accountable for commitments instead of excuses, to bounce instead of diminish, to be remarkable instead of pedestrian.

## Putting It Into Action

- Notice when people on your team defend and react when they make a mistake or fail to follow through.

- Question excuses.

- Ask people: "What are you going to do in spite of your situation?"

- Observe when people claim responsibility for successes and when they create excuses for failures.

- Employ the five strategies to kick up the serotonin and the bounce in people:

    1. Advocate for discovery over proficiency

    2. Create an environment of accountability

    3. Look for the lessons learned

    4. Reframe the focus from feelings to commitments

    5. Model it for others

# Chapter 12

## Make Waves, Not Ripples

When I walked into his office the first time, PRIDE Industries CEO Mike Ziegler handed me a copy of this paragraph from the Jim Collins book *Good to Great:* "When all these pieces come together, not only does your work move toward greatness, but so does your life. For in the end, it is impossible to have a great life unless it is a meaningful life. And it is very difficult to have a meaningful life without meaningful work."

He said, "Ann, this is why I've been here since 1983."

In 1966 in the basement of a church in Auburn, California, a group of devoted parents gathered to find employment opportunities for their children, who each had some developmental disability. They knew that earning a paycheck would offer their children increased self-esteem and dignity. So the parents formed a charitable organization to help their children find work and ultimately to change the shocking statistic that 64 percent of people with disabilities are un- and under-employed.

After many years of fundraising, however, the Board of Directors discerned that the lack of a business model made the organization unsustainable. To impact the statistics, the organization needed to change its course. In 1983 they recruited Mike Ziegler to lead the company in this new business model. As CEO, Mike transformed the model from a scarcity-driven, charitable organization to a battle cry-driven, people-focused, money-generating company.

Today PRIDE Industries accomplishes its battle cry through its own service solution businesses: (1) manufacturing and logistics services, (2) integrated facilities services, and (3) secure document management. Today, PRIDE is the largest employer of people with disabilities, generating over $150 million in revenue and employing more than 4,300 people nationwide. Of those 4,300 people, over two-thirds (61 percent) have some disability.

All because Mike decided to think upside-down and sideways.

Why is Mike Ziegler the exception and not the rule? Why do most people barely ripple the water with their toe when battle cries are only accomplished by making waves? If they revere outside-the-norm thinkers, superheroes, action takers, doers, and wave-makers, what stops people from making their own waves?

To answer this, we need to understand the powerful influence of the herd, groupthink, the bandwagon, and the comfort zone.

## The Herd

People have a tendency to conform to their herd. The herd is everyone in their network — their friends, their family, their colleagues, their boss, their clients, and their community. They work hard not to stray too far from what their herd is doing.

When we deal with the influence of the herd, two underlying influences are competing for people's actions: fear of rejection and the desire to feel important.

First, recall that people are haunted by their deepest fear — being rejected. They fear that if they stray too far from what the herd deems acceptable, the herd will reject them. So they don't want to stand out too much, or they risk their herd rejecting them for being different. When people are unsure about whether something is "too different," they look to what their herd is doing. Consequently, people are endlessly editing themselves to assure their path is close to the herd's path. They edit their contributions in meetings, the ideas they present, their comments to their team, and their behavior at the office and in social settings.

Juxtapose that with the fears people harbor of being insignificant and unimportant, being forgotten, and not making a difference. We want our lives to have meaning and purpose and we want to make a difference, but those are difficult commitments to fulfill when we're busy blending in as a result of a fear of being rejected by the herd.

So how does this conflict get resolved? People make safe, predictable ripples instead of precarious, capricious waves. Ripples allow people to establish some significance, be somewhat important, and make a little difference – all without being rejected for it. In actuality people are literally testing the herd with their ripples. They downplay and qualify their ideas instead of owning them. "This may sound like a dumb idea, but ..." (If you don't like the idea, don't reject me – I told you it was probably a dumb idea.) "I'm not sure if this would work, but ..." (This is my caveat so that if it doesn't work I can say I warned you and then you can't reject me.) "I read about an idea at another company that maybe we could try ..." (Someone else tried it and succeeded so it won't get me rejected because it should work here too.) In Chapter 7 we saw that when people qualify their ideas, it signifies flimsy commitments. We now see that a flimsy commitment is actually grounded in a fear of rejection from the herd juxtaposed by the need for feeling significant and making a difference.

The sad irony that no one ever tells people is that while they are busy worrying about what the herd will think of them, the individuals in the herd are busy worrying what those people and others in the herd will think of *them*. The members of the herd are so concerned about being rejected by us and other members of their herd that they are vigilantly assessing whether we are about to reject them. If they sense it looming, they will kill us off first by preemptively rejecting us. In high school we call it "bullying"; at work we call it "office politics."

Leslie was obnoxious during the offsite training. Her hubris was off-putting and offensive to everyone. She must have sensed the community rejecting her, for upon returning to her office she immediately went to her boss to tattle on her colleague, Peter. Peter exhibited obnoxious behavior during the meeting and embarrassed the office, she reported. Leslie was determined to throw Peter under the bus before he had an opportunity to do it to her.

Let's see how these fears additionally operate to squelch ideas in the office. Suppose we generate a good idea and share it with someone else. That person instantly evaluates what our promising idea means about them. If it's a good idea, then they wonder why they hadn't thought of it first. They consider that perhaps something might be wrong with them; why are they not more innovative, savvy, and strategic? Then they fear that our success will indirectly cause others to reject them for not having been innovative, savvy, and strategic. And if they deem our idea to be a bad idea, they will still worry that someone might possibly think our idea is promising and they might credit us with being courageous enough to make waves. This other person suddenly realizes that our act of pluck will highlight their lack of courage. And the fact that they are only making ripples while we are making waves will mean something is wrong with them. So they destroy us and our idea first to justify their inaction and their harvesting of insipid ideas.

## The Bystander Effect

In April 2010, Hugo Alfredo Tale-Yax attempted to help a woman who was being attacked, and in the process, he was stabbed. As he lie dying on the sidewalk, 20 people walked by – but no one helped him. Hugo bled to death. This is the Bystander Effect in action, a social psychological phenomenon that occurs when people do not offer to help a victim when other people are present. At the crux of this is once again our fear of rejection.

According to social influence, suppose a woman named Betty was walking by Hugo as he was bleeding to death. Betty would literally scrutinize the reactions of the people in her immediate surroundings – her in-the-moment herd – to see if they are taking any action to help Hugo. If she observes that others are not doing anything, chances are that Betty won't either. She deems that there must be a reason that people are not helping Hugo. She doesn't want to do something that would cause people in her herd to reject her for taking action when they have, according to their inaction, decided not to take any action. Taking action would mean taking a risk that someone in the immediate herd would scold, criticize, laugh, or berate Betty – all forms of rejection. So Betty doesn't make a move toward Hugo. She stands back and waits to see what everyone else will do. If no one was in the area, Betty would not be socially influenced by the bystanders, and she would have taken action to help Hugo. In that case, there would be no one for her to check in with, and no threatening fear of rejection.

Now apply the Bystander Effect to a team meeting. People are so bullied by their own fear of rejection that they don't speak up when they notice ineffective policies, bad decisions, or illegal actions. They wait to see what "other people" will do first. If someone else raises their hand in a meeting to question a decision, they will feel safe to say something as well. If no one raises their hand, then they will feel awkward for being the only one to object. They will then muse that their objection or comment is probably not that valuable anyway. Instead of risking rejection, they just keep their mouths shut.

## Welcome to Groupthink

Because the herd mentality and the bystander effect are so pervasive and insidious, they generate "groupthink." When people are incessantly editing themselves out of fear of rejection, their ideas are stifled because they fear the herd will reject those ideas. So instead of considering new ideas, everyone begins to circle around the same idea until it is soon embraced unanimously. Any radically different ideas are internally squelched, not even voiced. Consequently, we have a group of people who think alike, hence the label.

Let's explore the danger of group polarization in the execution of a corporate battle cry. Imagine that a corporation has a commitment of being innovative in the way it brings solutions to customers. Leaders assemble a task force of 10 people to determine how to roll out a new product. Ideas and opinions start surfacing. A few voices are louder than others and soon a zealous belief in the value of television commercials emerges. A few participants are less passionate about television commercials, but they do believe in this method, so they nod, which fuels the zealots. The two people questioning the innovativeness of television advertising keep their mouths shut. Individually they each believe they must be the only one who doesn't agree with the group. And they may even hold some internal belief that their ideas are never that great anyway, so they don't offer any alternative ideas out of fear of being rejected.

Before long the group is influenced by confirmation bias. They start confirming their beliefs in TV advertising by sharing stories about past successful product launches through television commercial campaigns and filtering out any unsuccessful experiences. The lukewarm individuals are now on board with the idea, and the group has successfully talked itself into launching the product with a television commercial. And because the group's agreement soon becomes violent agreement, no one wants to discuss the drawbacks to television commercials or consider any other ideas. The two individuals who disagree with the group do not even think about contributing their alternative views for fear of putting their intelligence, taste, or competence into question. A decision was reached without 360-degree thinking. Group polarization has formally infected this team.

When people like the two individuals on this team relentlessly edit themselves due to a fear of what others think, they stagnate, and their stagnation causes the group to stagnate. Not caring what others think does not mean we treat others poorly, or disregard, disrespect, or offend them. It means that for teams and people to progress, you must promote a mindset in which people are not chastised for their ideas, individuality, and innovation.

## Jumping on the Bandwagon

Not surprisingly, the influence of the herd creates the "Bandwagon Effect." People have a tendency to follow the behaviors, actions, and beliefs of the people in their herd because individually, they prefer to conform over being rejected. Unfortunately, the comfort zone of the bandwagon suffocates new ideas and bolsters the status quo.

People love the comfort zone. We tend to like things to stay relatively the same because we know what the same is. We know exactly how to survive with our current circumstances. We know what is expected of us, and we are fairly certain we will not be rejected. In the comfort zone, we can make ripples without turning heads. The zone outside of the comfort zone is unpredictable – that is where the waves are, and waves have the potential to become tsunamis.

Because the bandwagon vilifies innovation-creating waves, people begin to engage in system justification. In system justification, people justify the current system and disparage alternatives, even if the alternatives might ultimately benefit the group. The shortsightedness that keeps us in the current system is in the long term detrimental to innovation and progress.

## Moving People Away from the Herd,
## Off the Wagon, and Out of the Zone

To make waves instead of safe, predictable ripples, we need to move people away from the herd, off the wagon, and out of the comfort zone. This does not mean that you need to fight the herd, puncture the tires of the wagon, or eradicate the zone. Instead, you are going to give people something juicier, something tantalizing, and something that will entice them into forgetting all about the herd, the wagon, and the zone. To make waves, you are going to appeal strictly to their hunger to feel significant and important, to have meaning and purpose in their work, and to make a difference. You are going to do this by promoting innovation.

## Innovation

At the height of the Great Depression, Chester Carlson graduated from the California Institute of Technology and was rejected by 82 companies before landing a job as a patent researcher. He found one part of his job utterly unbearable: reproducing the patent paperwork by hand. Fueled by a desire to end the pain and improve the process, he began to research ways to reproduce documents effortlessly. Eventually Chester created an image reproduction process he named "electrophotography." He quickly applied for and received a patent before determining what to do with it. Chester pitched the invention to at least 20 major companies prior to meeting Joe Wilson, the president of a photo paper company. Joe loved the wave that Chester made and the two teamed up. Together they renamed the company and the process "Xerox."

Innovation always results in waves. By definition, innovation requires improving and advancing with originality and imagination. With it comes waves of progress, instead of system-justifying, status-quo-clutching ripples. The entire concept flies in the face of the herd, the wagon, and the zone.

Innovation is deliberately attempting a new or different method to make a change in anything established. Albert Einstein once observed that "The problems that exist in the world today cannot be solved by the level of thinking that created them." We need a new level and a new direction of thinking in order to solve problems, and that is where we must encourage people to be innovative.

Innovation requires that people think upside-down and backward, that they see the world through a kaleidoscope, that they suspend judgment and editing, that they embrace fresh perspectives and new ideas, and that they not taint the process with their preconceived notions, fears, and beliefs. How do we do get people to do all of that? Intentionally.

Solving problems always causes waves because people's first instinct is to cling to the predictability of the status quo. What most people don't admit – but always discover – is that the status quo can be pretty boring. The reason they get stuck in boring is that they fear the unknown more than they fear dying of boredom. So, people numb themselves to the boredom and justify the status quo to avoid forcing themselves to make changes.

Here's the secret. People actually love change; they just hate *the process* of getting there. It's confrontational; it's unpredictable and unknown; it usually requires giving up some things for different things; and it is quite often uncomfortable. But people always adapt, adjust, and evolve. For example, when someone is fired after 25 years and is forced to leave a job they grew to dislike, they quickly discover that their fears of leaving were unfounded. They didn't melt, their friends and family didn't reject them, and they have the ability to seek out and find or create new opportunities. They are forced to start over, and in doing so they find a way to survive the change and usually discover something as a result. The reality is that people are far more adaptable than they think, or we give them credit for.

Here are six ways to lure people away from the herd and influence them to be innovative instead of fearful:

1. Embrace the word "Pilot"

2. Ask for forgiveness, not permission

3. Give the go-ahead

4. Encourage curiosity

5. Tickle the brain

6. Cheer for failure

*1. Embrace the word "Pilot."* "Pilot" is a magical word. Slap it on any idea or new project and you help people commit in the face of their fears. The word "pilot" communicates that you are experimenting with something new to evaluate it and that it may not be perfect, so please forgive the initial imperfections. This one word has the ability to reframe people's thinking from "Oh, I don't know what the herd would think about this and what if it doesn't work and maybe we need more approvals and research" to "OK. Let's try it as a test."

As we have explored in great depth, people fear change – but a pilot promises discovery of new information without a permanent change. It allows an innovative attempt but with a parachute. This magical word frees people from their fear of failing. If the project is unsuccessful, then everyone can say, "No worries! It was just a pilot. We tried, we didn't succeed, but we learned something. Let's move on."

Every time we design and develop a Smart Mentoring solution for a client, it triggers herd-like fears. For most organizations, a mentoring program is innovative, and as such, it is riddled with unknowns. We cannot eliminate the unknowns but we can shut down this sabotage before it shuts down our project. We do this by making the program tremendously attractive, exceptionally easy to implement, and enormously beneficial. And then we insist on using the word "pilot" before it's launched for the first time. In so doing, we set everyone up for success, including the program.

One of our client's employees brought us his inordinate amount of fear – a sky-might-fall kind of fear. Karl was on the verge of sabotaging the wave of excitement for a new program we were rolling out by focusing on all of the possible ways that the program could go wrong and ignoring the probability of those risks altogether. Karl expressed his concerns with a drama-saturated voice, stating bluntly "We need to be very careful about how this gets rolled out because if one person has a bad experience, then we are doomed." I had to mute my phone so they would not hear me laugh out loud at his performance. It is not atypical for employees to have an other-than-great experience with the rollout of a new program without warranting its death sentence. Before his fear-of-the-devil declaration doomed the roll-out, I shared with Karl the benefit of engaging in a pilot because of how forgiving people are with pilots, and that the pilot would give us the opportunity to learn and course-correct as we progressed. It was only the word "pilot" that got Karl to move past his fears of doom.

*2. Ask for Forgiveness, not Permission.* People want to stand out and be different. They are ripe with fresh ideas about how to do things differently. But the herds that dominate the corporate world and society have conditioned people to seek approval, literally and figuratively, before trying anything new. To break people from this thinking, we need to consent to ignoring the rules by using calculated risks. Calculated risks are those that are in furtherance of a battle cry but not at the expense of someone's life, someone's job, or a client. With a calculated risk, there is a sincere belief that the risk is in the best interest of the company.

Katherine Hepburn once said, "If you obey all the rules, you miss all the fun." Work should be fun, so let's be like Katherine and not obey all the rules. Instead, let's ask for forgiveness instead of permission. People ask for permission when they are unduly concerned about protecting themselves from the herd's potential rejection. When they ask for forgiveness, however, they are making a calculated move without garnering the herd's pre-approval. If the herd vociferously disapproves, then they invoke an apology. "Wow. I apologize. I didn't realize we had a corporate policy about that." Or "I didn't realize we don't do it that way. My apologies."

In April 2006, Coca-Cola's Chairman and CEO, E. Neville Isdell, exemplified this concept. He asked for preemptive forgiveness. He announced to his investors at the annual meeting, "You will see some failures. As we take more risks, this is something we must accept as part of the regeneration process." He was bypassing the permission and going straight to the forgiveness. Traditionally, Coke cultivates a risk-averse mindset, but in order to grow, the leaders became cognizant that they would need to take bigger risks. With bigger risks come inevitable flops. Instead of asking for permission to take some risks, Isdell took the initiative to change the mindset and was warning his investors by asking for forgiveness in advance.

Dennis is a role model for asking for forgiveness, not permission. Dennis works in the Transportation Services Group (TSG) of a utility company, and like managers at most utility companies, he was facing a talent pipeline challenge. He had a great pool of in-house talent without college degrees, but the company required a college degree to move into management. To address this requirement, the company created a tuition-reimbursement program to assist individuals in getting the requisite degree. But Dennis noticed that people in TSG were reluctant to go back to school at night due to family commitments. So he took an unconventional approach to the college degree requirement.

Welcome to Transportation Services University, Dennis's solution for providing people with a college-equivalent certification program that allows interested, capable individuals in the TSG to acquire the essential knowledge, learn on-the-job technical and professional skills, and gain the abilities that are critical for stepping into and succeeding in leadership positions in his department. He designed it, developed it, and piloted it. With his program, Dennis shifted the focus from having a college degree to obtaining the knowledge, skills, and abilities required by the roles that needed to be filled, while helping people simultaneously become job-ready in an accelerated way.

Dennis's solution made waves in many areas. Not only did it solve TSG's talent issue, it saved the company thousands of dollars in tuition reimbursement. In addition, his idea salvaged productivity and succession planning for TSG by ensuring that individuals continued to work full-time while becoming certified and job-ready. In addition, participants in his program felt important, felt the world revolved around them, and felt like they were making a difference in TSG. The program is brilliant.

What's even more brilliant is the way Dennis rolled it out. He knew that seeking permission would drive the idea into endless meetings, conference calls, approvals, and paperwork. Granted, he definitely ruffled some feathers, but he did so in furtherance of a battle cry and not at the expense of any lives, jobs, or clients. When the Leadership Development group at headquarters caught wind of his program, they were initially a bit miffed (likely because they did not feel important in the process and because Dennis didn't make the world revolve around them). But after hearing Dennis's passionate pitch and after he asked for forgiveness, they realized Dennis was actually doing them a favor without making them look bad. Soon they were offering support to Dennis to ensure he had the tools and resources needed for success. Today they point to Dennis as a model for other employee-development initiatives.

*3. Give the Go-Ahead.* Glen Rossman, my very first boss after law school, was notorious for thinking upside-down and looking through kaleidoscopes to view situations differently. He was the managing partner of Coopers & Lybrand in the San Jose, California, office in the early '90s, and responsible for the Dream Team described in Chapter 4. Granted the Dream Team was not a wild success, but it was innovative and enlightening. Glen definitely ruffled feathers with the Dream Team, but he did it in furtherance of a battle cry, and not at the expense of lives, jobs, or clients. While on the Dream Team, I regularly brought ideas to Glen to address the morale issue in the office. It was not my job to do so, nor was it even remotely related to my job. I was hired to research tax issues. But I was fascinated with what I deemed an unhappy group of people and felt I had a different perspective to offer the partners. Glen agreed and never even paused to consider how this project would fit with my job responsibilities. He was just delighted with the opportunity to work with someone who wanted to think upside-down to improve the office. With each idea I brought to him he gave me the go-ahead. Some worked, some didn't, but each one taught us something new.

*4. Encourage curiosity.* Curiosity is the key to innovation. With curiosity comes the magical questions: "Why?" and "Why not?" When people approach the world with curiosity, they inevitably generate new perspectives, ideas, and solutions.

Carson's middle name must be "curious." He studied agriculture for six years in central Illinois and knows more about the physical, mental, and emotional facets of cows than most farmers. In addition, he knows how to run a farm like an innovative business. It's his curiosity that has him constantly seeking ways to improve the operations. For example, noticing that the tractor's plow was doing only a mediocre job of cleaning manure from the barn, Carson used recycled tractor tires to greatly enhance the performance of the plow to clean the barn.

In another instance, Carson's curiosity caused him to find a way to improve how farmers groom and level cow beds. Cow beds are groomed and leveled daily to make the cows more comfortable, which increases their milk production. The task takes on average two people 40 minutes to complete. Carson saw the inefficiency and invented the "Freestyle Rake" to reduce the amount of time from 40 minutes to four minutes and from two farmhands to one, thus freeing up one person to assist in milking.

In addition to the element of curiosity, Carson uses the ask-for-forgiveness-not-permission strategy in implementing his improvements, inventions, and ideas. He is cognizant that asking for permission from farmers would surely be met with hesitancy, pushback, objections, and questions. Understandably, these farmers have been running their farms the same way for 30+ years and the cognitive dissonance would be too great to admit they were doing it wrong all those years. So Carson identifies an area to improve, nonchalantly and often covertly introduces an enhancement, and improves the operations before the farm owner ever notices.

Carson's battle cry to improve the operations of every farm he touches often ruffles feathers of farm owners, who are often set in their ways. But when their initial fears are allayed, they realize what a contribution Carson's curiosity to improve really is.

5. *Tickle the brain.* To leverage that curiosity, we need to help people generate fresh, gripping ideas. There are three activities that result in breakthrough ideas: brainstorming, brainwriting, and brainsteering. Brainstorming is the traditional method for generating ideas, usually in a group, with people bouncing ideas off each other. It's limiting, however, as a result of the influences of the herd and groupthink. Because people are influenced by what others think, they are constantly editing their contributions in a brainstorming session. And if they sense they will be personally rejected for suggesting any idea too far outside the

zone, they'll hold back an idea altogether, as we saw previously in this chapter.

Brainwriting is similar but set up in a way to address the drawbacks of brainstorming. With brainwriting, people consider a variety of problems and generate ideas individually before they ever share them with the group. Each person in a group is given a piece of paper. At the top they write a challenge with which they are struggling. For example, the problem statements are written as "How to increase participation in the quarterly sales webinar," "How to develop the team's talent," "How to decrease the company's costs," or "How to win Client X back from the competition." The paper then gets passed around the room until everyone has had a chance to weigh in on each problem and contribute their fresh ideas to the page. Everyone brainstorms independently without editing due to concern about *how* their ideas will be received. No names are attributed to the problem statements or to the ideas, thereby creating anonymity and eliminating the innovation-suffocating influences of groupthink. The brainwriting sheet demonstrates for the owner of the problem many different ways to look at potential solutions.

Lastly, brainsteering is a concept created by Kevin P. Coyne and Shawn T. Coyne, authors of *Brainsteering: A Better Approach to Breakthrough Ideas*. Brainsteering addresses the limitations of out-of-the-box free-for-alls that are at the crux of brainstorming and brainwriting. In brainsteering, ideas are generated using structured questions that force people to think upside-down and backward. As an example, instead of asking a broad question such as "How can we increase profits?" the authors recommend asking a more focused question such as "What's the biggest hassle customers face when using products/services in our category, and how could we eliminate that hassle (in ways that others haven't done already)?" Their book is a fabulous resource for generating the mind-bending questions that generate mind-bending solutions.

*6. Cheer for failure.* Stanford University psychologist Carol Dweck has spent a career studying the neural pathways in the brain and discovered that failure is a great brain expander. Each time we fail, we learn how *not* to do something, and that learning connects synapses in the brain. New synaptic connections link nerve cells, which become stronger the more learning is repeated. Consequently, failure is a great opportunity for improvement whereas, doing the same and constantly succeeding causes the brain to shrivel. People need brain-expanding experiences, not brain-shriveling ones. So get ready to cheer for people's failure as well as their successes. Of course, it's all how you frame the cheer. Cheer for the learning about how not to do something, and for the connected synapses in the brain. Don't just cheer because someone failed.

## Waves vs. Ripples

Want to see a wave in action? Check out the YouTube video of Fordham University baseball player Brian Kownacki. On April 21, 2010, he was on first base during a game when the batter hit a long drive into the outfield. Brian started running toward second. Seeing the ball still in the outfield, he ran for third base, then headed for home plate. The outfielder threw the ball to the catcher, who was crouched between third base and home plate, ready to tag Brian out as Brian ran for home. But Brian had his eye on home plate and the catcher was an obstacle to home plate, but not an insurmountable one. Brian didn't even hesitate. He ran full speed toward home plate, saw the ball hit the catcher's mitt, and literally dove into the air above the catcher in what could only be described as a soaring Superman. Stunned by the man diving through the air above him, the catcher raised his mitt in the air to tag him out, but Brian had taken such a huge leap that the mitt never touched him. His leap turned into a handspring as he hit home plate with his hands and then sprung to land solidly on his feet. He walked back to the dugout as if it were a regular part of his routine. He was so professional and respectful, that it would have made Vince Lombardi proud. The umpire called him safe at home plate and Fordham went on to win the game.

Brian Kownacki not only defied the laws of gravity, he defied the laws of mediocrity. He could have done what typical baseball players do in a similar situation. He could have played it safe by holding at third base. He could have headed for home plate, and upon seeing the catcher, run back to third. He could have run right into the catcher on his way to home plate, been tagged out, and just shrugged his shoulders communicating to his teammates, "You all saw that I tried, but the catcher got me." He could have yelled and screamed at the umpire in an attempt to save face in spite of knowing he was out. But Brian did not do any of those things. Instead he went above and beyond in his commitment to excellence and his pursuit of a battle cry. He is a wave-maker, not a toe-rippler.

Billionaire entrepreneur Richard Branson, founder of Virgin Enterprises, is a master of making waves. He admits to thriving on a cocktail of opportunism, adventure, innovation, and exploration. Stemming from this moxie, Branson regularly puts the "Virgin" name on a wide variety of companies and products. He cannot resist trying out interesting and emerging ideas, regardless of the outcome. He is committed to calculated risk over a clear vision of success. What makes Branson a wave-making leader is his advocacy of the same upside-down thinking in others. In 2007 he launched the "Virgin Earth Challenge," offering a $25 million prize for the inventor who develops a viable mechanism for scrubbing carbon gases from the atmosphere.

Branson wouldn't know a ripple if it lapped him on the ankles. But we can easily identify them because the people making the ripples wear expressions of exhaustion, annoyance, and despondency. They have been lulled into pursuing a harmless idea and taking the safe route of asking permission from everyone in the herd. This then lands them in endless, frustrating, eye-rolling meetings to explore nonexistent risks. Ripples are maddening.

Waves, on the other hand, are wonderful to witness. We can always spot a wave because the people causing the wave are smiling, enjoying their work, and relishing in the adventure. Paul Hawken, co-author of *Natural Capitalism: Creating the Next Industrial Revolution*, described this phenomenon when he said, "Good management is the art of making problems so interesting and their solutions so constructive that everyone wants to get to work and deal with them." So driven by their battle cry, they rarely care what others think, instead engaged in experimenting and busy asking for forgiveness instead of permission.

### Putting It Into Action

- Notice how the herd effect is creating groupthink in your team.
- Observe how people edit themselves when in a group.
- Cultivate innovation by employing the following six strategies:
    1. Embrace the word "Pilot"
    2. Ask for forgiveness, not permission
    3. Give the go-ahead
    4. Encourage curiosity
    5. Tickle the brain with brainstorming, brainwriting, and brainsteering
    6. Cheer for failure
- Notice if people are making ripples or making waves.

# Chapter 13

## From Manager to Superhero

. . . . . . . . . . . . . . . . .

The 1994 Northridge earthquake rocked Los Angeles before dawn on a Monday morning. The earthquake triggered the sprinklers and threatened to destroy the office and the computers of a publishing company. Within 10 minutes of the city's largest earthquake, Roger, an associate in the IT department who worked at the publishing house and lived nearby, rushed over to the office to check for damage. He immediately shut off the sprinklers, saving the computers. This was not Roger's responsibility, nor did anyone call him to ask him to do this. He could have rolled over at 4:00 am thinking, "Not *my* problem. It's my day off. Someone else will deal with it today." But not Roger.

Why did Roger go out of his way to save his company thousands of dollars and its people days of work? Because he could make a difference. Influencing Tenet #3 states that we each are dying to make a difference.

So what can we assume about Roger's managers? We can assume that they help Roger to make a difference, that they acknowledge the difference Roger makes to others and to the company, that they appreciate and value the difference Roger makes, and they make Roger feel important as a result. In addition, they likely advocate his discovering and learning on the job, while encouraging his innovative side to solve problems by thinking upside-down and inside-out.

When we work for people who encourage our need to make a difference, then we continue to find ways to make that difference. And when that happens, we don't hesitate to wake up at 4:00 am to make that difference – earthquake or not.

The way to help people make a difference is to employ the strategies we have covered throughout this book. First, we need to understand why people show up – what is their battle cry? What difference do they *want* to make? Second, we need to show them how they could be significant to the success of the company. Next, we need to show them how to win, which includes fog-less communications and clear expectations. Then we need to give them some control in making that difference. Finally, we must be constantly cognizant of the fear of rejection that is competing with their desire to make a difference. That's the formula. And when you help people fulfill their need to make a difference, you become more than a boss or a manager. You become a leader.

People are dying to make a difference and you have the opportunity to lead them in a way that allows them to do just that. In addition to the above formula, you must operate mindful of the pressure of the 10 principles that are influencing people every day – sometimes positively, sometimes negatively.

1. We all think the world revolves around us.

2. We each desperately need meaning in our lives and our work.

3. We each are dying to make a difference.

4. We all just want to be winners, not losers.

5. We each crave control.

6. We each urgently want to feel as though we are important.

7. We each have an insatiable appetite to be respected, appreciated, valued, and heard.

8.  We all are at risk of succumbing to the herd.

9.  We each allow our beliefs and thoughts to dictate our ambitions and perseverance.

10. We each dreadfully fear rejection.

### You the Superhero

At the beginning of this book, we determined that you may have a title that connotes middle manager, but at the core you are a walking opportunity to make huge impact above and below you. You are a clandestine superhero with the power to influence people's behaviors and actions. Your power only works, however, if you operate with the knowledge of the 10 Influencing Tenets. Ignore these and you are no different than every other person who calls themselves a "manager" – ineffective, unproductive, unremarkable, and unexceptional. Apply the moxie strategies outlined in each of the chapters to fuel those 10 Influencing Tenets and you have the power to impact change in people regardless of your position in the organization.

You are becoming a leader who leads differently – not just better, but differently. In that journey, never forget that the 10 Influencing Tenets apply to you as well. If you want to influence your own intrinsic motivation, acknowledge the influence that the 10 tenets have on you in your personal and professional life. Then apply the moxie strategies to yourself and discover how your own effectiveness will skyrocket.

- What is your battle cry? What meaning are you creating in your work? What is the vision for your career and is it aligned with the company's vision? What is your vision for your role as a middle leader?

- How do you want to make a difference at work, with people, and in the world?

- How do you make sure the world revolves around you?

- How do you fuel your own self-delusion so it doesn't become self-deflation?

- Are you receiving recognition, applause, and appreciation for your efforts? Do you feel valued? If not, how are you going to feed your own need to be respected, appreciated, valued, and heard?

- Do you know how to win at your job? Do you feel set up for success? If not, what can you do to lift the fog and understand expectations?

- What victim beliefs are dictating your ambitions and perseverance? What action can you take to crush patterns that are not serving your extraordinary success?

- What labels have others placed on you in the past or present that you are confirming daily? Are these empowering labels or disempowering ones? How have you allowed them to box you in?

- What fears are causing you to procrastinate or make other excuses instead of fulfilling your commitments?

- Are you stuck in a proficiency mindset, or thriving in a discovery mindset? Do you hesitate to start projects or activities until you are guaranteed to succeed? What would it look like to advocate for more discovery in your own work?

- What do you do when you fail or make a mistake? Do you own it or make excuses to alleviate the cognitive dissonance? What lessons have you learned lately, or are you too busy justifying to look for lessons learned?

- What waves have you made lately? Do you embrace innovation or shun it for the safe, predictable, herd-approving moves? What would it take for you to take some calculated risks even in how you execute in your own work?

As a leader, you have three main responsibilities: (1) declaring the battle cry, (2) providing iconoclastic service to your people's success, and (3) relentlessly holding those people accountable for their success. As we have seen throughout this book, everyone needs a reason to show up. Declare the battle cry and you can rally people around a purpose and give them a forum in which to make a difference. You then serve those people who are serving that battle cry, and you serve them like no one has ever served their success before. You make the world revolve around them, you make them feel important, you appreciate, you communicate, you label them powerfully, you spoil their sabotage, you crush their patterns, you advocate for their discovery, and you help them bounce. Through it all, you will be competing with people's fears, which will be fighting you like Lex Luthor fought Superman. With ruthless compassion, you must relentlessly hold people accountable to their commitment to the battle cry.

It is irrelevant where you sit in any organization. It is irrelevant if you work for people who have ignored these responsibilities to *you* your entire career. It is irrelevant the size of your team, the politics in your department, or the broken culture of your organization. You have the power and the obligation to fulfill these responsibilities with every person who works with you. Ignore them and you are nothing more than a middle manager. Embrace them and you will be a superhero.

## Fire Spreads but Only with a Constant Flow of Oxygen

Once you ignite your own leader moxie, it will spread. Regardless of where you are in an organization, you have the power to influence the mindset of others. Whether you are responsible for a team, a department, the entire company, or one other person, never underestimate your power to influence change in others.

Before long people will talk about the battle cry as if it's their own. They will consider themselves servants of that battle cry, holding themselves and each other accountable to commitments that drive the battle cry to victory. That's the power of a moxie mindset – it spreads.

Unmistakably, however, creating this self-generating moxie mindset requires discipline. The discipline to operate cognizant of the influence that the Tenets have on people. The discipline to incorporate the moxie strategies consistently into your day-to-day interactions. The discipline to do all of this on a daily basis, not once a month or whenever you happen to think about it. And the discipline to apply all of this to the core responsibilities of your role as the leader: (1) declaring the battle cry, (2) providing iconoclastic service to your people's success, and (3) relentlessly holding those people accountable to their success. These must be cornerstones of every conversation, not a once-a-year bullet on a performance review.

All of this takes discipline. This is why leaders who operate differently are so rare. This is why superheroes seem to exist only in the pages of Marvel Comics. It takes work to train people to have different conversations than the ones they've been having for 25 years. It takes work to train *yourself* to have different conversations than the ones you've been having your whole career.

I met Eugene at the Hudson Newsstand at Chicago O'Hare Airport. As the cashier, his job is to collect money from people who purchase gum and magazines. But clearly it is so much more than that. Eugene has made it his job to connect with busy travelers and help them create an enjoyable traveling experience amid the chaos and agitation that swirls throughout the airport.

Walk into Eugene's corner of the terminal and he welcomes people with a huge smile, an inquiring face, and curiosity enough for two. Eugene asks about the cities people are headed to and what they might need in order to enjoy the plane ride. He then makes suggestions based on whether people look stressed, tired, fretful, or excited, whether they're traveling for business or pleasure, whether they are alone or with children. A magazine, a book, a bottle of water, or some gum? Have you read this new book? How about this interesting magazine? Seems right up your alley. Eugene compels people to stop by and connect so he can contribute to them before they rejoin the frenzy of the plane-chasing crowd.

Arguably we could say it's all about Eugene's personality that makes him stand out from the disgruntled, rude, detached, indifferent, blasé newsstand workers at this and every other airport in the world. But there are certainly plenty of people with personalities who relate to their job as just that, a job. They don't see their work as anything other than an obligation and a paycheck. Not Eugene. He clearly sees his job as making a difference to travelers. And nowhere in his job description or training did anyone instruct Eugene to operate this way or even to have fun at work. His boss didn't demand that Eugene act gleefully and do anything other than collect money from people.

Here's what we can surmise about Eugene's boss. He lets the world revolve around Eugene – Eugene is in charge of his own universe. He allows Eugene to create meaning in his work and to make a difference. He showed Eugene how to win at work using clear communications about how to do his job, so that missed expectations and frustrations do not sabotage Eugene's results or suffocate his personality. He allows Eugene to feel significant. He recognizes and applauds Eugene's efforts and his success regularly. He doesn't remind Eugene that there is a herd that doesn't operate its newsstands like Eugene does. He labels Eugene as energetic and a people-person. He likely granted Eugene the opportunity to run that newsstand before protocol said Eugene should. He doesn't reject Eugene for standing out from the crowd and doing it differently. And he gets out of Eugene's way and allows Eugene to make a difference for the customers, for himself and, as a result, for Hudson Newsstand.

## Using Your Superhero Powers

You now know the magic of the 10 Influencing Tenets that can cause people to sabotage themselves and each other or that can cause people to succeed. In your treasure chest, you now possess powerful strategies that will allow you to leverage these Tenets to influence people's intrinsic motivation in order to impact change at individual and organizational levels.

- People crave a purpose for their work. Help them identify one.

- People get trapped by their own fears. Help them see past those.

- People operate best when they think it's all about them. Let them.

- People want some control over their work and their lives. Give it to them.

- People yearn for recognition and applause. Recognize and applaud.

- People need communication like they need water. So, communicate.

- People listen to their naysayers, including the ones in their head. Help to mute them.

- People require practice to rebound after a setback and role models to show them the way. Help them bounce. Be their role model.

- People seek continuous improvement. Teach and mentor them.

- People want to make a difference. Let them.

Our time on the planet is limited. If we are going to spend so much of it working with others, why wouldn't we want the experience to be as productive, valuable, satisfying, and amusing as possible? Why would we want to show up to work insignificant and inferior when we have the opportunity at every moment to play big and be brilliant? If we don't operate with a moxie mindset determined to serve others in doing the same, then what's the point of showing up every day? (And if you are ever hesitant to have your people play big and be brilliant along with you, then revisit the 10 Influencing Tenets to see which ones are influencing you negatively and causing you to sabotage their success.)

Our boss, our colleagues, our team members, our company politics, even our clients, can never control how we experience work, in spite of how difficult they may make it sometimes. If your own managers are ignoring their core responsibilities to you, remember that they are also being influenced by the 10 Influencing Tenets. Acknowledge that their limitations are not yours. Their limitations are generated out of their own human motivations, influences, and fears, usually masked as policies, procedures, bravado, and even hubris. Your best response is compassion and empathy toward them, while maintaining perseverance and determination toward your own battle cry.

Paige left the corporate world as an executive coach to join a local school district with the intention of making systematic changes to the way the district promotes science, technology, engineering, and math throughout its schools. A year in she was ready to quit, frustrated by what she perceives is a dearth of innovative willingness. She wasn't making a difference, she didn't feel important, and she was missing the meaning of her job. One day Paige noticed that she was coaching people on her team – one of her strengths – to be more innovative, and they were. She realized that while she was busy focusing on systemic changes, the real change was happening one person at a time. She is now in love with her job again, having shifted her focus from influencing a change in the system to influencing a change in the people who operate that system.

An educator commented once that we could alter education in this country if we could remember what teachers teach. They don't teach fifth grade or even science or math. They teach people. Without people, there is nothing to teach. Similarly, we could change corporate America if we could remember that leaders lead *people*. We don't lead information technology groups or marketing plans or finance reports or even entire companies. We don't even lead employees. We lead people. Without people – human beings – like you, who show up every day wanting it to mean something, we would have nothing to lead.

A woman was overheard at the park exasperatingly telling her daughter, "I don't know why you keep trying things you can't do." It's always easy for us to see what is wrong with that statement; it's not so easy for that mom, who was likely raised by parents who regularly put the lid on the mason jar to stop her from jumping too high and getting hurt. It starts somewhere else and it gets passed on from parent to child, from leader to follower.

You have the power to break that pattern.

Victor Frankel was a psychotherapist who survived the Auschwitz concentration camp both physically and emotionally. Following World War II, Frankel documented his experiences in his renowned book, *Man's Search for Meaning*. In it he shares his observations about the impact the horrific experience had on people. During his days in captivity, he watched as apathy set in and people lost sight of their purpose and meaning in life. He concluded that when people gave up, they died.

So too do leaders.

Before you is an opportunity. Every day you are either growing a little or dying a little, and the people you work with are doing the same. There is no in between. Standing still is never an option. Physically it is impossible to stand still, as cells stop moving only when they die. So it is that if you aren't growing, you are dying. But therein lies your choice: you can choose to grow a little or you can choose to die a little. It is always up to you. What are you going to do differently today, this week, this month, and this year to grow yourself and other people? How are you going to lead differently? How are you going to unleash that superhero and evolve from manager to leader? How are you going to help others do the same?

# Acknowledgements

· · · · · · · · · · · · · · · · · ·

It never ceases to amaze me what it takes to create a book. And it never ceases to amaze me how much I discover about myself and about the people in my life each time I do. In everything I write, I rely heavily on my observations and perspectives. As a result, I pay attention to the people and situations around me. However, because creating a book requires me to be so selfish with my time and energy, it appears as if I am actually not paying attention to these people at all.

So, allow me to gush about the people in my world who have welcomed my observations and perspectives, who have supported me in creating this book, and who continue to teach me about people, relationships, and life.

1. Without Rob I would not know what moxie even looks like. A true partner and best friend, his patience and cheerleading throughout this process are unmatched. His ideas, perspectives, and experiences continue to confirm all of my ideas throughout this book. If anyone asks who is on the cover of this book, I'm going to say, "Rob." He models everything I espouse, and the people who work with him are fortunate to have a leader like Rob paving the way to their greatness.

2. Without my mom I would not have grown up using my moxie. She was the first person in my life to help me create a battle cry, fight off the naysayers, and pull away from the herd. It is because of her that I have approached my life and my work with inspiration and passion.

3. The LifeMoxie team is amazing. If you ever use your moxie to start a business, you want to surround yourself with champions like Cindy, Sue, Trish, Joe, and Kim. They make changing the

world so much more fulfilling. I could not have completed this book and continued to grow LifeMoxie without them.

4. Because writing a book is a work of art, I have intentionally surrounded myself with wicked smart people, each of them willing to read my manuscript and offer feedback. I am grateful for the generosity of their time, energy, and eyeballs: Rob, my mom, Ann Smith, Wendy Willow Wark, Jeff Lown, Gail Webber, Laurie Gibson, Erika Kosina, and Mary Anne Walsh.

5. This book would not be possible had I not learned from some amazing mentors and bosses over the course of my careers. Thank you for being committed to my success and for showing me what it means to be a moxie leader: Glen Rossman, Jorge del Calro, Allison Tilley, Stan Wong, Robert Siegel, Piyush Patel, and Mr. Rogina.

# Ann Tardy

## Founder, Chief Catalyst of LifeMoxie

From Silicon Valley corporate attorney to mentoring expert and advocate for business as unusual, Ann Tardy has never met a dull moment. Sally Jesse Raphael called her "energetic!"

As the Founder and Chief Catalyst of The LifeMoxie Consulting Group, Ann combines the art of management with the science of behavioral economics. By providing the emotional context to create behavioral change and real-world solutions, she prepares middle leaders to implement high-stakes initiatives in complex, bureaucratic environments.

Ann first experienced the power of moxie while closing over $2 billion of venture-backed financings at two of Silicon Valley's largest law firms. While leading her entrepreneurial clients, Ann was surprised to discover that it's not willpower that separates the magnificently successful from the mediocre. It's moxie. Ann went on to lead the legal departments of two high-tech start-ups, taking one company public and the other to acquisition. Following her in-house tenure, Ann launched her own law firm, growing it to 75 loyal clients before merging it with a larger firm.

She now helps visionary companies unleash moxie where they need it most – in the middle. Ann and the LifeMoxie team are changing mediocrity and complacency into moxie in companies such as Pacific Gas & Electric, Kaiser Permanente, Southern California Edison, and Metro-North Railroad.

Ann is also the founder of the JEWELS Forum Mentoring Community, connecting corporate employee networks for mentoring relationships. In addition she served for five years as the volunteer Director of the Entrepreneurial Education program at a middle school, training twelve-year-olds how to start and run businesses through a community-based mentoring program.

Ann passed the CPA exam before graduating with an accounting degree from the University of Illinois, Champaign-Urbana. She then graduated with honors from Chicago-Kent College of Law and passed the Bar exams in Illinois and California.

Ann was honored as an Outstanding Business Woman of the Year by the American Business Women's Association and honored with the Vanguard Award from The McGraw-Hill Companies for her contributions to their employees.

In 2011, Ann rode her bike over 3,700 miles from San Francisco to the New Jersey Shore to discover what people across the country love about their jobs. Read more about The Moxie Ride at: www.moxieride.com.

Ann is the author of:

- LifeMoxie – 9 Strategies for Taking Life by the Horns

- Moxie for Managers – The Secret to Evolving from Manager to Leader

- Moxie for Mentoring – The Secret to Make Mentoring Matter

Ann Tardy • The LifeMoxie Consulting Group
ann@lifemoxie.com • www.lifemoxie.com
1.888.Ms.Moxie (1.888.676.6943)
27 Madison Avenue • Red Bank, NJ 07701

# About LifeMoxie

### What does LifeMoxie do?

We prepare middle leaders to make a difference with people.

### How?

We are influence experts, people strategists, and work enthusiasts. In concert, this creates a fresh approach to leading people.

We help middle leaders discover how to:

- influence people to become more work-effective, job-ready, and leader-ready

- ....which increases effectiveness, enthusiasm, and moxie

### What's really happening?

We leverage behavioral economics to provide middle leaders with the emotional context they need to affect the behavioral change they want.

### What's the goal?

Middle leaders are prepared to implement high-stakes initiatives in complex, bureaucratic environments. (A snazzy way of saying, middle leaders make a difference in spite of office politics and red tape.)

### What kinds of solutions?

- **Smart Mentoring** – our proprietary approach to creating effective mentoring

- **Moxie for Managers** – our unique approach to the

evolution from floundering manager to effective leader

- **People-to-People Skills Development** – our programs that develop people to own their own success, essentially getting the followers on the same page as the middle leaders

### What's LifeMoxie's battle cry?

In the beginning, in the middle, and in the end, we are committed to *business-as-unusual* for leaders-as-influencers, for work-as-fulfilling, for *life-as-extraordinary.*

The LifeMoxie Consulting Group
www.lifemoxie.com
1.888.Ms.Moxie (1.888.676.6943)
27 Madison Avenue • Red Bank, NJ 07701

# Index

* * * * * * * * * * * * * * * * *